Advance Praise

Minority rights are a hotly debated issue. Dutta's book enriches this discussion from a decolonial perspective, exploring Muslim minority rights in India. Their nuanced ethnography of women's activism on family law issues leads to a number of extremely interesting arguments about how minority rights function in everyday life. Dutta explores these rights' relation to religion and spatiality, but also to the state that acts as a 'shadow', enabling actors on the ground to negotiate fairer solutions. I highly recommend this book to everyone interested in ethnographically informed political theory, in decolonial theorising or in understanding how minorities can really be protected – a topic that could hardly be more timely!

Lisa Herzog, University of Groningen

In this highly readable book, Dutta highlights with immense sensitivity the role of women-led *sharia* courts, used primarily by working-class Indian Muslim women, in pushing against both a hostile majoritarian state and entrenched patriarchal social norms. In the process, readers gain an invaluable insight into ethically and spatially grounded activism that challenges the binaries which continue to dominate political theory debates about secularism and religious politics, minority rights and gendered empowerment, as well as the agency of the oppressed.

Humeira Iqtidar, King's College London

Dutta's book is both valuable and timely. In an era where discussions of processes of 'decolonisation' are becoming widespread, they provide a valuable corrective: by deploying ethnographic methods, they demonstrate the ways in which such processes are lived and practised rather than engaging with them in purely theoretical terms. Indeed, by examining the practical ways in which minority rights and gender are experienced and negotiated in localised settings, Dutta presents a cogent argument that abstract conceptions of rights are insufficient in making sense of complex social and cultural dynamics. The book is a wonderful entrée into a practical and experiential form of comparative political theory that presents a substantive challenge for contemporary political theory – namely, how do theorists comprehend the differences between the *practice* of political theory and the *practices* of its individual and collective subjects?

Adrian Little, University of Melbourne

Dutta's book focuses on an aspect that the feminist movement in India has taken seriously since the 1990s in the debate over a Uniform Civil Code, what has come to be called 'reforms from within'. Rather than uniformity, the feminist movement has taken gender justice to be the goal of legal reforms of personal laws, thus accepting legal pluralism as a positive value. In this emerging field, Dutta's study is an invaluable contribution, drawing attention to religiously observant Muslim women who attempt to make space for equality and justice within scriptural provisions, the Constitution remaining as an ethical horizon. Dutta's study of everyday activism of Muslim women demonstrates in a granular manner how they shape an ethical practice of justice by negotiating both formal laws and the everyday violence of patriarchy and majoritarianism.

Nivedita Menon, Jawaharlal Nehru University, Delhi

In the Shadow of Minority Rights provides an innovative and necessary approach to minority rights that moves beyond the language of liberalism and liberal nationalism. Drawing upon ethnographic research in Mumbai, this feminist and postcolonial analysis challenges some of the core methodological presumptions of political theory as it offers a novel and important analysis of the gendered, institutional politics of minority rights in India.

Jeanne Morefield, University of Oxford

In the Shadow of Minority Rights

How and where do religious minorities claim their rights?

This book challenges abstract liberal approaches to minority rights and colonial constructions of the minority. It charts a new way of understanding minority rights based on an exploration of the everyday life of Muslim women's activism in Mumbai and its intersection with transnational feminist networks and a global politics of Islamic reform. It shows how women deploy everyday ideas of ethics and bodily practices to challenge inequality in Muslim family law. They construct a just community based upon the ethical ideals of the Quran and rights guaranteed by the Indian Constitution and negotiate for rights within homes, police stations and neighbourhoods in ghettoes. Everyday familiarity is interlaced with violence in interactions with state and non-state actors as women claim their rights, and practices of ethics and intimate negotiations with processes of ghettoisation and violence shape the everyday life of rights.

Sagnik Dutta is a researcher in the Department of Cultural Studies, Tilburg University, and Associate Professor at Jindal Global Law School, O.P. Jindal Global University, Sonipat. They were awarded the Gates Cambridge Scholarship for their doctoral studies. They work on decolonial and postcolonial theory, minority citizenship, securitisation and data justice. Their scholarship has appeared in several prominent peer-reviewed journals.

In the Shadow of Minority Rights

Decolonising Gender, Liberalism and the Politics of Difference

Sagnik Dutta

Shaftesbury Road, Cambridge CB2 8EA, United Kingdom

One Liberty Plaza, 20th Floor, New York, NY 10006, USA

477 Williamstown Road, Port Melbourne, VIC 3207, Australia

314–321, 3rd Floor, Plot 3, Splendor Forum, Jasola District Centre, New Delhi – 110025, India

103 Penang Road, #05–06/07, Visioncrest Commercial, Singapore 238467

Cambridge University Press is part of Cambridge University Press & Assessment, a department of the University of Cambridge.

We share the University's mission to contribute to society through the pursuit of education, learning and research at the highest international levels of excellence.

www.cambridge.org
Information on this title: www.cambridge.org/9781009582032

© Sagnik Dutta 2025

This publication is in copyright. Subject to statutory exception and to the provisions of relevant collective licensing agreements, no reproduction of any part may take place without the written permission of Cambridge University Press & Assessment.

First published 2025

Printed in India by Avantika Printers Pvt. Ltd.

A catalogue record for this publication is available from the British Library

ISBN 978-1-009-58203-2 Hardback
ISBN 978-1-009-58200-1 Paperback

Cambridge University Press & Assessment has no responsibility for the persistence or accuracy of URLs for external or third-party internet websites referred to in this publication, and does not guarantee that any content on such websites is, or will remain, accurate or appropriate.

For EU product safety concerns, contact us at Calle de José Abascal, 56, 1°, 28003 Madrid, Spain, or email eugpsr@cambridge.org.

*For my mother, Urmila Dutta, to whom
I owe my love for the written word*

Contents

Acknowledgements   xi

Introduction   1

Part I | Ethics

1. Right to be righteous: constituting rights, travelling constitutions   49
2. Becoming equals: gender equality as an ethical commitment   67

Part II | Spaces

3. Remaking the ghetto: sites of resistance   91
4. Estranged attachments: the carceral state and the everyday life of Muslim law   113
5. Between the home and the world: the many publics of Muslim law   131

Conclusion   160

Bibliography   167
Index   180

Acknowledgements

Nine years ago, I took a leap of faith to leave a full-time job in journalism to return to university for my doctoral studies. I am grateful to all my friends, family and mentors over the years who have shaped the writing of this book in various ways.

This book is an outcome of my doctoral research at the University of Cambridge. My doctoral studies at the University of Cambridge were supported by the Gates Cambridge Scholarship. I am very grateful to the Gates Cambridge Trust for their generous support. I would like to thank my dissertation supervisor, Dr Iza Hussin, for her generous support and careful guidance and her tireless effort towards perfecting my writing and scholarship. I have benefitted from her erudition and her investment in constantly expanding my intellectual horizons. I would also like to thank my advisor, Dr Leigh Denault, for her careful insights. My thesis examiners, Anne Phillips and Manali Desai, were particularly generous and insightful in their engagement with the work. I am grateful for the many interactions and conversations I have had with faculty members at the University of Cambridge. I would like to thank Duncan Kelly, Waseem Yaqoob, Annabel Brett, Ayse Zarakol, Duncan Bell, Shruti Kapila, Saumya Saxena, Luna Sabastian, Lauren Wilcox, Samuel Zeitlin, Joya Chatterjee and the late David Washbrook. The Global Intellectual History seminars convened by Dr Shruti Kapila helped me think deeply about several key debates in political theory. I am grateful for insights and comments of many other academics I must thank. I am particularly grateful to Faisal Devji, Justin Jones, Julia Stephens, Katherine Lemons, Nandini Chatterjee, Humeira Iqtidar, Rochana Bajpai, Matthew J. Nelson, Lisa Wedeen, Sharon Krause, Ali Altaf Mian, Leigh Jenco and Udit Bhatia. Humeira Iqtidar has been a constant source of support and encouragement. Her astute comments as well as incisive criticism of some of my work has been particularly helpful in sharpening my insights and engagement with key debates in political theory. Udit Bhatia has been extremely supportive as both a friend and a critical interlocutor and scholar of political theory. Rochana Bajpai's work has been particularly influential in shaping my engagement with liberalism and secularism in India. Matthew Nelson's deep and critical engagement with some of the insights generated by my fieldwork played an important role in shaping the manuscript. Saumya Saxena's work on personal laws and our long conversations on the topic have had a profound influence on the book. I would like to thank the librarians of the Centre for South Asian Studies at the University of Cambridge: Barbara Roe, Rachel M. Rowe and Kevin Greenbank.

Sections of the manuscript were presented at the European Consortium for Political Research Conference and at the book manuscript workshop of the British and Ireland Association for Political Thought in Oxford. I am grateful for generous comments, engagements and provocations by several scholars at these conferences, particularly Patti Lenard, Lisa Herzog, Udit Bhatia and Jonathan Floyd. Sections of the book were also presented at the Law and Society Association of South Asia workshop in Lahore. I am grateful for the generous engagement by Jeff Redding, Maryam S. Khan, Yasser Kureshi and several other participants in this workshop.

In academia, we often forget how much work is dependent on the unrecognised labour of administrators. I would like to thank Tessa Milne, the graduate administrator of Corpus Christi College, and Hayley Askew, the PhD administrator of the Department of Politics and International Studies, University of Cambridge, for their generosity and efficiency.

What was originally a thesis evolved into a book manuscript during my time at O.P. Jindal Global University, Sonipat. I am very grateful to colleagues, friends and, above all, to all my wonderful students for their enthusiasm and engagement with my work. Colleagues have engaged my published work at several forums, and I would like to thank them for their comments, provocations and insights. I am particularly grateful for the generous engagement of Dipika Jain, Saumya Uma, Jhuma Sen, Albeena Shakil and Karanraj Singh Bhatia. My long interactions with students at O.P. Jindal Global University, especially those studying for the Postcolonial Democracy and the Law elective course, on religion, secularism and the law, have always been a great source of inspiration. I would like to thank Qudsiya Ahmed, Anwesha Rana and Anandadeep Roy, editors at Cambridge University Press, for their support, guidance and patience throughout the process of the publication. It was a pleasure to work with their team. Chapter 2 of the book is a reworked version of an article that appeared in the journal *Feminist Theory*, published by Sage Publications.

I am grateful to the activists of the Bharatiya Muslim Mahila Andolan and the Mohalla Committee Movement Trust who were generous with their time. I am grateful to them for allowing me to closely observe and participate in their everyday activist interventions. I am indebted to the women who frequented these spaces, who shall remain anonymous. One hopes that this scholarship does justice to their rich inner lives and their struggles for justice. I shall remain indebted to the kindness of numerous strangers in Mumbai, a city whose everyday congeniality I appreciated very much.

I am grateful for the affection and companionship of my friends in Cambridge, Mumbai, Sonipat and Delhi who have always been there for me during the rigorous and emotionally taxing process of dissertation writing as well as during the equally onerous process of converting the thesis into a book while handling teaching and administrative responsibilities. Romit Chowdhury's friendship and affection have always been a source of strength in difficult times. My deep gratitude to Saumya Saxena for always finding time for chats about everything academic and non-academic despite her extremely busy schedule and the difficulties of navigating multiple time zones. My enormous gratitude to Jhuma Sen for being a wonderful friend, mentor and a voice of reason in my life.

My time in Cambridge and the UK was enriched by the friendship and affection of Tanvi Bhatkal, Saumya Saxena, Callie Vandewiele, Alice Musabende, Bhasi Nair, Martina Kuvalja, Garima Sahai, Ananya Mishra, Vincent Kim, Farhana Rahman, Arif Naveed, Amrita Dasgupta, Suha Priyarashini Chakravorty and Madlen Maehlis. I have formed many valuable friendships in Delhi and Sonipat for which I am grateful. I must acknowledge Avantik Tamta, Shaurya Upadhyay, Avirup Bose, Suruchi Mazumdar and Sambuddha Chaudhuri who have enriched my life in Sonipat and Delhi. Avantik Tamta's humour, care and affection cheered me up during stressful times. Shaurya Upadhyay's calmness and sagacity have helped me navigate many a crisis in my personal and professional life. My old friends in Delhi are always a source of enormous strength and comfort. I am particularly grateful to Divya Trivedi, Georgina Maddox, Rahul Dutta, Ajoy Ashirwad Mahaprashasta and Manjusha Madhu.

Finally, I would like to thank my parents, Urmila Dutta and Tapan Kumar Dutta, and my brother, Saptarshi Dutta. I am grateful to them for believing in me and appreciating the worth of higher education, learning and scholarship.

Introduction

In a small, rectangular dimly lit room, Khatun Shaikh, a female *qazi* (Islamic judge) in a women's *sharia* court, lent a patient ear to women who approached her with complaints of marital discord and violence. The *sharia* court is an alternative dispute resolution forum run by members of the Bharatiya Muslim Mahila Andolan (Indian Muslim Women's Movement, henceforth BMMA), a social movement led by Muslim women aimed at achieving equality and justice in the adjudication of Muslim family law in India.[1] These alternative forums were frequented by women from poor neighbourhoods in Mumbai who did not have the wherewithal to access the formal justice system. As cases of marriage, divorce, maintenance and domestic violence were discussed and debated in these forums, quarrels broke out between the spouses and their relatives. Allegations of abuse and counter-allegations flew thick and fast. In the midst of these heated exchanges between spouses, Shaikh often emphasised the importance of *raham* (compassion) as an everyday, lived ethical ideal that both the spouses ought to practice. While the disputes revolved around women claiming specific rights during and after the breakdown of their marriage, Shaikh insisted on how both men and women needed to be compassionate. According to Shaikh, one could display compassion in moments of crisis in the marriage by avoiding the use of harsh words, refraining from overt displays of anger and addressing each other respectfully. This practice of compassion thus entailed using the body in specific ways while claiming one's rights. Shaikh construed compassion as a lived ideal that resonated with the teachings of the Quran and the life of the Prophet. The pursuit of this ideal was closely tethered to the realisation of equality (*barabari*) and justice (*insaf*) in the domain of the family.

The *sharia* court emerged as a space of self-making for both the activists of the BMMA and the women visiting the court. Women spoke their mind. They spoke about the violence and injustice in the family. Interactions between activists, lawyers and the women who visited these forums helped in creating a supportive community space for women who faced injustice in their marital homes. On some days, the court room also doubled as a space where activists of the BMMA conducted training sessions on Muslim family law, the Quran and the Constitution for women of the neighbourhood. Activists conceptualised the right to freedom of religion guaranteed under the Indian Constitution as the right to collectively fight for a just community space for Muslim women. This space nurtured an ethical life according to the tenets of the Quran. These interactions in alternative dispute resolution forums and activist spaces played out against the backdrop of shrill debates on the criminalisation of some aspects of Muslim family law and the codification of Muslim law in the public forum in India. Drawing out these myriad moments helps us understand how the body, everyday lived ethical commitments and particular ways of inhabiting space shaped the everyday life of Muslim family law and minority rights in India.

This book is based upon ethnographic research in Mumbai on the activism, pedagogy and alternative dispute resolution activities of the BMMA, a social movement that works for justice and equality in the adjudication of Muslim family law in India. It also explores the legal aid work carried out by members of the Mohalla Committee Movement Trust (MCMT), a citizenship initiative in Mumbai, in Muslim neighbourhoods in the city. The BMMA is a movement inspired by transnational Islamic feminist networks and activists in the Middle East, Southeast Asia and the United States that challenges gender inequality in the practice of Muslim family law on marriage, divorce and maintenance in both state and non-state forums in India.[2] The MCMT is a citizen's initiative aimed at enhancing access to public services for citizens, especially those belonging to minority religious groups, following the communal riots in Mumbai in 1992–1993.[3]

My analytical labour in this book is to draw out myriad moments of gendered ethical self-fashioning that take place in alternative dispute resolution forums and activist spaces of Muslim family law. These embodied, everyday engagements with the law and the notions of rights are left out in the public discourse on family law, gender and minority rights in India. The framework of Muslim family law that regulates marriage, divorce and maintenance of Muslim minorities in India has often been analysed by scholars vis-à-vis the relationship between minority rights and the liberal, secular state. In public debates on minority rights, the adjudication of Muslim family law in India is taken to represent the guarantee of minority rights by the Indian state, even though religious family laws are not formally recognised as laws by the Constitution.[4]

Public debates are fixated on putative conflicts between the individual and community, constitutionalism and religion, uniformity and minority accommodation to the neglect of the rich, sophisticated ways in which Muslim minorities inhabit the domain of minority rights and religion. Building upon participant observation in multiple spaces of the BMMA and the MCMT, this book makes some key arguments that help us reconceptualise the study of minority rights, liberalism and gender in political theory. First, I show how the practice of minority rights and related liberal guarantees such as the right to religious freedom and gender equality are constituted by conceptions of duty and compassion in Islamic feminist ethics. These registers and conceptions of ethics are not merely a means to a liberal end. They entail particular embodied and everyday practices of ethics that mediate the construction of minority rights and associated liberal categories by Muslim minorities. These ethical commitments shape and come into conversation with local struggles for gender equality within the framework of Muslim law and minority rights. Second, spatial and material ways of engaging the city and everyday interactions with the state constitute the practice and meaning of minority rights. Hence, we can understand the politics of minority rights as conceptually linked to processes of ghettoisation and communalisation of minorities in the city as well as a range of affective registers that constitute everyday negotiations with the state.

Drawing upon this ethnographic material, I make a larger contribution to debates on minority rights, gender and liberalism in political theory. The two key contributions of this book are (*a*) to show how non-textual sources and grounded methods such as ethnography can reconstitute existing conceptualisations and questions in political theory, in this case debates on minority rights, and (*b*) contribute to a project of decolonising political theory by exploring minority rights, liberalism and gender in ways that challenge colonial epistemologies and reified categories of minority rights, gender, liberalism and religion. The ethnographic approach of this book contributes to its decolonial aims. The use of ethnographic methods expands our understanding of minority rights, the law, community and religion beyond the reified, textual ways of understanding these categories. Reified categories of religion and community only concretise neo-colonial and neo-imperialist conceptions of minorities as a religious 'other' different than the ethnic majority of a nation state. This book aims to critique and thereby decolonise this politics of 'difference'. The title of the book *In the Shadow of Minority Rights* underscores this project of understanding how the everyday life of minority rights plays out in the shadow of dominant public discourses of minority rights and liberalism that privilege presumed tensions between individual and community and reified conceptions of religion, liberalism and the state.

A critical, decolonial theory of minority rights

My aim in this book is to chart new ways of theorising minority rights that move beyond the preoccupation with normative liberal goods. I aim to decolonise predominant ways of conceptualising minority rights and religious difference by drawing attention to the everyday, lived life of minority rights conceptualised by religious minorities. In doing so, we can transcend neo-colonial, reified ways of conceptualising minority rights and a static minority community. It is possible to present a very different narrative and conception of minority rights and liberalism if we move beyond our preoccupation with standard, normative liberal arguments for justification. This can be achieved by paying attention to non-textual, everyday ways in which religious minorities engage the framework of liberalism and minority rights as well as by being alive to the particularities of minority rights and liberalism in a non-Western context that decentres a Western European conception of the liberal state.

Political theorists have predominantly conceptualised the relationship between minority rights and gender using the framework of liberal multiculturalism. The key question that animates liberal approaches to minority rights and gender is how a balance might be achieved between women's individual rights and autonomy and the rights of minority cultural and ethnic groups, especially in the domain of the family.[5] In these theories, the liberal state is often the arbiter of the project of 'accommodation' of minority rights. Since the publication of Susan Moller Okin's provocatively titled essay 'Is Multiculturalism Bad for Women?' approaches to minority rights and gender have been informed by the theme of accommodation of minority rights by the liberal state.

The secular, liberal state's normative aims are to apportion rights to communities as well as to protect the individual rights and liberties of their members, especially women. Ayelet Shachar notes that the basic dilemma that the 'mulitcultural' state needs to resolve is the tension between the rights of individual citizens and the 'accommodation' of minority group traditions. While multicultural policies might ensure the decentralisation of power and promote diversity in the public sphere, they do not benefit all group members equally. In fact, they might work to the detriment of certain group members.[6] Therefore, she proposes a concept of citizenship that enhances justice between groups as well as within members of a group.[7] She advocates for state multicultural policies based upon a joint governance model that balances minority group traditions and individuals' citizenship rights.[8]

Benhabib proposes a model of accommodation of cultures based on democratic deliberation. This model ultimately privileges an individual's right to voluntary self-ascription into cultures, freedom of exit and association, and egalitarian reciprocity between members of cultures.[9] Benhabib's model is based upon a dynamic conception of group identity premised upon an understanding of cultures as 'internally riven and contested'.[10] Her conception of voluntary self-ascription and the freedom of exit and association is premised upon a particular understanding of individuals and individual autonomy putatively in conflict with group identity. Hence, she argues that the state should ensure an individual's freedom to self-ascription and self-identification in a group and not allow the group the right to 'define and control membership at the expense of the individual'.[11] Individuals should have unrestricted freedom to exit a group.[12]

These approaches draw from and build on Okin's work on gender equality and cultural accommodation, where she argued that some non-negotiable rights of individuals must be respected even within a paradigm of multiculturalism.[13] The tensions that animate these approaches reflect the wider discussions in scholarship on multiculturalism regarding minority group rights within a liberal framework. Kymlicka argued that minority rights were compatible with liberal concerns of individual autonomy as cultural practices shaped individual capacities and thereby enhanced individual autonomy.[14] But minority cultures had to be amenable to the liberal value of individual autonomy for a liberal justification of minority rights to work.[15] Theorists have defended group rights on the grounds of individual autonomy,[16] limitations on state power,[17] recognition of difference[18] and regard for various cultures.[19]

An important body of scholarship foregrounds a contested, anti-essentialist view of cultures and analyses the politics of multicultural accommodation in a more nuanced way. This includes the work of Anne Phillips, Uma Narayan and Chandra Talpade Mohanty.[20] Narayan critiques the neo-imperial framing of certain cultures that leads to an exaggerated emphasis on saving women belonging to minority cultural groups from their cultures.[21] Similarly, Mohanty critiques the image of the impoverished and exploited Third World woman in feminist literature.[22]

Yet this body of scholarship glosses the liberal state's historical complicity in consolidating a minority identity. Much of this scholarship also fails to take into account the specificities of the liberal state and minority rights in a postcolonial context. The liberal state, far from being a neutral arbiter of minority rights, has been actively involved in processes of minoritisation. Existing liberal ways of conceptualising the relationship between minority rights, the liberal state and gender fall short of analysing the notion of the liberal state itself and its historical entanglements with colonialism and empire.[23] As a result, the liberal state's historical complicity in forging the category of the minority remains undertheorised.

This is especially true when we conceptualise the relationship between minority rights and gender. Debates on minority rights and gender are often premised on reified conceptions of culture, religion and religious law. This is an outcome of a presumption that the liberal state is the neutral arbiter of rights that regulates the rights of individuals and balances sets of rights between individuals and communities. When it comes to questions of regulation of religion, the liberal state is construed as defining the limits of religion, especially religion-based personal laws and their potential impact on gender equality. In working with a reified category of the minority and legal, juridical concepts of minority rights, liberal theory reproduces colonial conceptions of religion.

My ethnographic and theoretical exploration of minority rights in this book is inspired by a rich body of scholarship on the anthropology of secularism and religion. Inspired by the pioneering work of Talal Asad, this body of scholarship has been particularly attentive to the generative and disciplinary powers of political secularism and its ability to define and reconstitute religion.[24] In Mahmood's work on minority rights, secularism and Islamic reformists, she explores how the disciplinary power of political secularism constitutes minority rights. Minority rights, especially in their iteration as religion-based personal laws, are framed as a function of the sovereign power of the secular state and understood within a framework of secular governmentality.[25] In her ethnographic study of secularism and religious minorities in nineteenth-century and contemporary Egypt, Mahmood argues that political secularism is entangled with the modern state's sovereign power to 'reorganise substantial features of religious life' as it regulates religion and stipulates what religion ought to be.[26] This is symptomatic of what Mahmood calls the 'double movement' of political secularism, as it relegates religion to the private domain while amplifying religious difference.[27]

Minority rights are instruments of secular governance aimed at managing religious, racial, ethnic and cultural differences. The category of the minority comes into being when the 'transformation of the state from an instrument of the law to an instrument of the nation had been completed'.[28] To that extent, the framework of minority rights connotes 'hierarchised difference' even as the state claims to stand for equality of all citizens.[29] Family law that relates to the governance of minority communities is one iteration of this politics of difference. Family law based on religion becomes a technique of modern governance and sexual regulation of the family.[30] Family law amplifies jurisprudential dimensions of religion while marginalising its 'moral and ethical concerns'.[31]

Mahmood's critical exploration of minority rights provides useful insights for new ways of conceptualising minority rights in political theory. Her approach throws light on the constructed category of the religious minority. It expands our domain of theorising beyond standard liberal normative approaches that justify the rights of minorities and purported special legal protections for minorities.

We can develop Mahmood's insights on minority rights in novel directions through explorations of minority rights and liberalism in India. In narrating an account of minority rights in India, it is indeed helpful to bear in mind the constructed character of minority rights as emphasised by Mahmood. Minority rights are tethered to the liberal state's project of imagining the Muslim citizen in legal, juridical terms. Yet the story of minority rights and liberalism in India also provides a fertile ground for exploring the creative ways in which the legal domain of minority rights or group-differentiated rights might be engaged by a range of social movements, subaltern groups and everyday political protests. To that extent, this book will argue that minority rights are constituted in the everyday life of Muslim communities in India through a range of discursive, ethical, embodied and spatial ways. These engagements with the legal domain of minority rights are reducible neither to abstract, liberal normative goods nor to the sovereign power of the secular state. And this, I argue, is the complex story of minority rights in India, which enhances our existing theorisations of minority rights and gender in political theory.

I embark upon a project of decolonising minority rights by focusing on ethics, embodiment, lived everyday experiences and spaces where minority rights are reconstituted in creative ways by religious minorities. This book is not fixated merely on adjudication of family law but on questions of how minority rights are claimed and reconstituted. To that extent, the analytical labour and theoretical contribution of this book are significantly different from empirical and conceptual analyses of the adjudication of family law in India.[32] In fact, the book aims to move beyond the question of 'adjudication' of minority rights and regulation of religious difference, which are moored in neo-colonial ways of understanding religion, minority rights and nationalism. It presents thick descriptions of interactions between transnational Islamic feminist ethics and ethical moorings of everyday local activisms. The book also draws out how the process of claiming rights is tethered to particular ways of inhabiting and embodying ethical ways of being and the politics of occupying and renegotiating spaces in gendered ways. The empirical moments in the book recreate a universe where religious minorities are creating consciousness about rights and activism. The book's contribution, hence, is to think about the politics and ethics of engaging family law over and beyond mere questions of 'adjudication' of family law disputes.

Recent work on liberalism in India shows how the story of liberalism in India is one of creative interpretations rather than merely one of appropriation of a Western discourse.[33] The recognition of group-differentiated rights is at the heart of this story. Rochana Bajpai emphasises a long tradition of liberalism in late nineteenth- and early twentieth-century India, focusing specifically on strong state intervention to address social inequality and a recognition of group-differentiated rights.[34] Anupama Rao traces Ambedkar's engagement with 'liberal thought and democratic discourse' to position the Dalit 'as a unique cultural and political subject of historic suffering'.[35] Chetan notes how women members of the Constituent Assembly introduced a 'feminist authorial voice' and gendered debates that helped in shaping the Constitution of India. Women made important contributions to debates on rights, state, federalism, secularism and education and heralded the emergence of 'the new woman' as a 'rights-bearing citizen in the Constituent Assembly'.[36]

This scholarship on India gestures towards the creative reconstitution of liberal categories in postcolonial contexts. My book echoes Menon's recent important intervention on secularism, where she argues for thinking from the Global South. The Global South, however, is not imagined as a monolithic geographical region but rather in terms of 'a space of thought' which offers the possibility of learning from 'speech that exists in the margin' and of freeing ourselves from both the hegemony of Eurocentric universalising narratives and the 'East–West' distinction that shaped discussions in political theory and social sciences at large.[37]

We can expand this domain of enquiry considerably by looking beyond abstract liberal ideas, texts and institutions. In understanding this story of minority rights, we cannot merely reduce it to abstract, liberal goods. Hence, I focus on the entanglement of ethics, ethical self-fashioning and everyday gendered spatial negotiations with rights in moments when Muslim women engage the legal framework of minority rights in India.

Recent approaches in feminist political theory and anthropology have paid particular attention to the vernacularisation of rights.[38] Abu-Lughod, for instance, explores the active social life of Muslim women's rights in Egypt as a counter to neo-colonial, Eurocentric discourses of saving Muslim women. The discourse of saving Muslim women has gained ground globally since 9/11. Sumi Madhok's recent work makes an important contribution to our understanding of vernacularisation of human rights. Madhok traces subaltern negotiations with rights discourses and entitlements in rural Rajasthan to enhance our knowledge of 'political imaginaries, gendered subjectivities and critical vocabularies of rights and political agency' that inform these struggles.[39] Inspired by these recent approaches, my book theorises minority rights, gender and liberalism in India beyond institutional and textual approaches. In focusing excessively on institutions and texts, we risk merely replicating canonical approaches to political theory in a non-Western context. This will only impoverish our imagination of what political theory can do or what forms it can take beyond the bounds of the text.

Decolonising political theory

At this stage, a few comments are in order about how my project is tied to an epistemological commitment to decolonising political theory. To my mind, the project of decolonisation needs to be carefully distinguished from mere nativism or a critique of the 'West'. This is particularly significant in the context of the appropriation of the decolonial paradigm by authoritarian states and right-wing ethnonationalist leaders in many postcolonial contexts.[40] Decolonisation is different from a temporal project of anticolonial nationalism as it entails a more thoroughgoing critique of Western modes of knowledge production and Eurocentric knowledge itself. My book is an attempt to contribute to a project of decolonising political theory. I do so by challenging the standard ways of theorising minority rights in liberal political theory, which I discussed earlier. These methods of understanding minority rights within a framework of liberal multiculturalism and liberal nationalism, despite their universal pretentions, draw upon a long tradition in European political thought of viewing religious difference as a 'problem' to be solved, tolerated or accommodated by the liberal state.[41] Liberalism and nationalism had a co-constitutive relationship in nineteenth-century Europe as romantic ideas of 'national identity and solidarity' developed along with ideas of political liberty, individual freedom and constitutional government.[42] This narrative of liberal nationalism was also tethered to notions of racial, religious and cultural others.[43] In fact, Mamdani casts a critical glance at the notion of tolerance that shaped the relationship between national majorities and national minorities during the consolidation of nation states in Western Europe. He observes that the relationship between the national majority and minority was consolidated based on the regime of tolerance.[44] Minorities were tolerated to the extent that they were perceived to be non-threatening by the national majority.[45]

In the colonies, the creation of minorities under colonial rule preserved the power of the native elite. Though the native elite's power was said to be derived from custom, the support of the coloniser consolidated their authority. The emergence of violent nationalisms in postcolonial contexts was a function of the creation of minorities under indirect rule.[46] According to Mamdani, postcolonial nationalists struggled to consolidate their power in the face of the upsurge of minorities claiming multiple homogeneous nationality status.

In non-Western contexts such as South Asia, societies were explicitly multi-ethnic and multi-religious.[47] We risk losing sight of the rich discursive, ideational, life and practices of minority rights and minority communities in these contexts if we merely import the standard theoretical frameworks of liberal multiculturalism. By paying attention to the everyday life of minority rights in an Indian context, we can move beyond some of the standard theoretical premises and assumptions of liberal multiculturalism – such as the tension between individual and community rights and the need for liberal 'accommodation' of minority rights – that animate academic scholarship as well as public debates and discourses on minority rights. These frameworks have inadvertently, and sometimes explicitly, endorsed the idea that religious and cultural difference is a problem that needs to be resolved by a purportedly neutral, secular, liberal state. Moving away from this framework as also from the language of accommodation can be an important step towards decolonising knowledge on minority rights.[48] My focus on the lived life of minority rights advances our imaginaries of theorising in novel directions that challenge the Eurocentric, hegemonic language and frameworks of liberalism.

It is particularly productive here to explore the conceptual architecture of the practice of minority rights in India with regard to religion-based personal laws. The long history of codification and standardisation of religion-based family laws through the colonial period is an example of minoritisation and the gradual consolidation of national majorities and minorities. The study of family laws in India inevitably ends up being mired in standard liberal, normative enquiries of how they ought to be regulated, whether they should be uniform marriage laws for all communities and how they come into conflict with individual rights. Minority rights linked to religion-based personal laws are nested within colonial epistemologies of religion and the law and the long process of minoritisation of Muslims by both the colonial and the postcolonial states in India.

Standard liberal approaches to minority rights replicate to some extent the colonial logics of understanding religion and religion-based personal laws. Within the liberal paradigm, religion is reduced to a set of prescriptions that can be written into the law. The question then comes down to whether these practices or sets of rights of religions can be balanced with standard liberal guarantees. This approach can be challenged by exploring what ethical commitments and spatial practices minority communities bring to bear upon their engagement with rights. Ethnographic approaches can thus unsettle a fixation with religion and the law, understood in strictly codified, textual forms. Using an ethnographic approach, we explore the myriad, non-textual ways in which the practice and meaning of minority rights are constituted.

This book aims to unsettle a universalist, hegemonic language of liberalism using which debates on minority rights and gender are framed in political theory. In addition to presenting a grounded approach to minority rights, my book delineates how transnational feminist praxis and deterritorialised registers of belonging shape the everyday politics of negotiations with minority rights. The BMMA was inspired by transnational Islamic feminist activists and networks in the Middle East and Southeast Asia. Recent efforts in decolonial feminist theory are aimed at developing non-ideal and decolonial ways of conceptualising purportedly universal categories such as gender equality and rights.[49] Khader emphasises the need to explore transnational feminist praxis as a way of enhancing justice. A grounded and everyday understanding of transnational feminist praxis helps in unmooring universal categories such as rights and gender equality from the 'moral grandstanding' of Western, liberal feminism and its stereotypes concerning 'oppressed women'. Mohanty has argued for exploring the 'limits and possibilities of feminist critique across borders'.[50] Transnational feminist analyses can unravel neoliberalism, militarism and heterosexism as nation-state building projects.[51] Exploring the everyday life of transnational feminist ethics, networks and ideas and the ways in which they shape liberal legalism is a novel contribution to the study of liberalism and minority rights. It helps us unmoor discourses of minority rights from the hegemonic frameworks of liberal nationalism.

Situating the movements

The BMMA movement emerged at the intersection of a transnational narrative of Islamic feminism and piety in the late twentieth and early twenty-first century across the Middle East and Southeast Asia, an awareness of a Muslim minority identity and a tradition of women's rights activism in India that aims at resolving problems of marriage and divorce through alternative dispute resolution forums involving both state and non-state actors. The MCMT is a citizen's initiative based in Mumbai aimed at enhancing access to public services for citizens, especially those from minority religious groups, following the communal riots in Mumbai in 1992–1993. I conducted fieldwork in Mumbai, the epicentre of both these movements. Several Muslim women's social movements, non-governmental organisations and voluntary groups emerged from the late twentieth to the twenty-first century in India demanding gender justice while affirming their Muslim identity. These movements reclaimed the legal discourse and space of Muslim personal law and their identity as rights-bearing citizens.[52] The BMMA, along with several of these groups, demand a more gender-just framework for religion-based personal laws which govern the Muslim family in contemporary India. In contrast to the reactionary right-wing demands for a uniform civil code by the Hindu right, these groups ask for changes to the law without eschewing their identity as members of a minority religious group.[53] Their assertion of rights is shaped by an awareness of the minority status of Muslims in a country that is home to the second-largest Muslim population in the world and has seen continuous violence against Muslim minorities over the past few decades.[54] These organisations advocate the reform of personal laws that govern marriage, divorce and maintenance for Muslim women and the enhanced involvement of Muslim women in the governance of Muslim law in community sites of adjudication.[55] In their publications, members of the BMMA emphasise the marginalised social location of Muslim women in India and therefore the need for a Muslim women's organisation.[56]

A report by the Sachar Committee, a committee appointed in 2005 by the former Prime Minister Manmohan Singh to study the socio-economic status of Muslims in India, showed how Muslims fared far worse than other minorities in terms of social indicators such as access to health, education, credit and employment.[57] The Sachar Committee report noted that the state and civil society often blame a putative 'unified religious-community space' for Muslim women's deprivation, which allows the state to absolve itself of the neglect of Muslim minorities.[58] The Committee also noted that women had become the 'torchbearers of community identity' as their 'lives, morality and movement in public spaces' were under constant scrutiny and control.[59] The report argued that as the Muslim minority identity came under siege, women withdrew into the boundaries of the home and the ghetto.[60]

A survey carried out by the BMMA in 2015 across 10 states in India – Bihar, Gujarat, Jharkhand, Karnataka, Maharashtra, Madhya Pradesh, Odisha, Rajasthan, Tamil Nadu and West Bengal – showed that 78.7 per cent of Muslim women were homemakers and 12.4 per cent worked in the unorganised sector.[61] This survey also emphasised the unequal bargaining power of women in the practice of Muslim personal law. Niaz and Soman note that 47 per cent women did not have a *nikanama*, a kind of prenuptial agreement which ensures some security for women in the event of a divorce.[62] Many of the women had settled with a very low amount of *mehr*, a dower amount promised to the woman at the time of marriage.[63]

The BMMA's demands include that the state stipulate a standard *nikah nama* to enshrine women's marital rights, ban polygamy, restrict men's rights to arbitrary divorce, enshrine a proper procedure for divorce in accordance with the principles of compassion in the Quran, ban oral, unilateral divorce and compulsorily register all marriages.[64] In addition to these official demands for changes in the law, organisations such as the BMMA are actively involved in challenging the gendered inequality in the everyday practice of Muslim personal law in community sites of adjudication.[65] To this end, the BMMA runs a network of *shariat adalat* across the country where female *qazis* adjudicate marriage, divorce and maintenance. As part of its aim to address gender inequality in the everyday adjudication of Muslim personal law on marriage, divorce and maintenance, the BMMA has trained female activists as *qazi*. These women adjudicate marital disputes in women's *shariat adalat* or alternative dispute resolution forums run by activists of the BMMA. They aim to challenge the predominance of male adjudicators in the traditional alternative dispute resolution forums that administer Muslim family law on marriage and divorce in India. These institutions exist at the intersection of state and civil society and function within the legal pluralist domain that regulates Muslim family law in India.

The other bodies involved in activism concerning Muslim family law include the All India Women's Personal Law Board, founded in Lucknow in 2005; Bazme Khawateen based in Lucknow; Awaaz-e-Niswaan (Women's Voice [AeN]), a Muslim women's NGO based in Mumbai which was founded in Mumbai in 1987; and Muslim women's rights networks such as the All India Muslim Women's Rights (MWRN), which was founded in 1999.[66] They are also engaged in addressing livelihood issues, self-employment generation and enhancing access to public resources for Muslim women.[67] Anthropologist Sylvia Vatuk has read this development as the emergence of a nascent 'Islamic feminist' movement in India.[68] Other anthropologists remain more cautious of the title 'Islamic feminist' but recognise these movements as Muslim women's movements.[69] This development has amplified the voices of Muslim women in public debates about gender justice and the family, a domain hitherto confined to the voices of self-proclaimed male representatives of the community and the state.[70]

History of personal laws and minority rights in India

At this stage, it will be helpful to unpack the colonial genealogy of religion-based personal laws, especially Muslim family law, in India and reflect on how this genealogy is mirrored in current debates on the relationship between minority rights, liberalism and gender in postcolonial India. It is important for us to revisit some key moments in the history of personal laws on the sub-continent. In this section, I trace how religion-based personal laws are gradually rendered into written and standardised forms through the eighteenth and nineteenth centuries in colonial India and how they come to be closely tethered to a legal, juridical and political conception of a Muslim community in twentieth-century India. The entanglement between a Muslim minority identity and religion-based Muslim personal law in contemporary India is a function of this complex history of both the minoritisation of Muslims and the standardisation and textualisation of Muslim personal laws in colonial India.

The adjudication of marriage, divorce, maintenance and inheritance according to religious laws was a creation of the colonial state in India.[71] The prevalent narrative in legal history traces the genealogy of personal laws to a declaration in the judicial plan of Warren Hastings, the governor-general of Bengal in 1772.[72] The plan sought to centralise the adjudication of the decentralised Mughal legal system.[73] A section of the plan stated that the 'inheritance, marriage, cast [sic] and other religious usages, or institutions, the laws of the Koran with respect to the Mussalmans, and those of the Shasters with respect to the Hindoos, shall be invariably adhered to'.[74] More recent scholarship takes issue with this genealogy. Stephens shows that colonial officials referenced religious laws in a wide range of areas, from criminal law to contract law in the eighteenth century. It was only during the middle decades of the nineteenth century that legal reform efforts by the colonial state transformed Muslim law into a 'personal law' applicable only to Muslims in matters of marriage, divorce and inheritance.[75]

The emergence of personal law as a legal category in South Asia in the nineteenth century was part of a wider narrative of a legal order based on territorial sovereignty, legal historicism and the application of laws to particular religious communities in familial and ritual matters.[76] The Indian Law Commission, appointed in 1833, carried out the task of formulating new legal codes, including codes that applied only to members of a particular religious community in matters of marriage, divorce and maintenance.[77] In 1864, the Law Commission consolidated this realm of the law as it declared that Hindu and Muslim law could only be applied to matters of marriage, divorce, maintenance and inheritance.[78]

While the Law Commission confined Muslim law to the domain of the family in the late nineteenth century, the early twentieth century witnessed the emergence of a distinct Muslim minority community, produced by a range of bureaucratic apparatuses and colonial forms of knowledge.[79] The colonial state's understanding of cultural and religious difference informed its legislative and constitutional moves to bestow rights on communities.[80] The conception of subject populations as 'different' and made up of distinct communities began as part of a late imperial ideological project in late nineteenth-century India.[81] The logic of representation and enumeration of communities according to religion consolidated categories of majority and minority religious communities.[82]

Following the Morley Minto reforms in 1909, the increased representation of Indians in the provincial and central legislative councils bolstered the logic of a distinct Muslim minority identity. Yet this logic existed in tension with a deterritorialised conception of Muslimness. Mohammad Ali Jinnah, a constitutional liberal who had been trained as a lawyer, was initially a member of the Indian National Congress and joined the All India Muslim League in 1913.[83] The All India Muslim League sought to represent the interests of Muslims as a unified community in colonial representative bodies as well as in negotiations about future constitutional arrangements in an independent, unified India.[84] In Jinnah's speeches as a member of the All India Muslim League, Jinnah linked communal solidarity with minority rights and liberal nationalism. Jinnah deemed communal solidarity a precondition for freedom, a necessary step in the project of nationalism and national reconstruction. He deemed freedom a possibility for Muslims only if they united under the banner of the League.

Shaping a Muslim family

The political representation of a unified Muslim community by the Muslim League coincided with the shaping of the Muslim family as a juridical and legal entity. Stephens observes that in the early twentieth century, direct government intervention became more 'palatable as more Indians were elected to the provincial and national legislative assemblies'.[85] The rhetoric of political representation of a Muslim community and a Muslim minority went hand in hand with a narrative of legal liberalism and legislation to ostensibly improve the social and economic lot of the people. [86] This was evident in the debates around the Mussalman Wakf Validating Act in the earlier part of the decade and the Muslim Personal Law Shariat Application Act and the Dissolution of Muslim Marriages Act in the 1930s. The shaping of the Muslim family as a juridical and legal entity was tied to this tradition of legal liberalism. Debates around these legislations in the colonial legislative assembly revolved around legal interventions to address social concerns. But at the same time, these debates framed gendered roles in the family as a constitutive unit of a Muslim minority community.

In 1911, the Muslim League passed a resolution making demands on the government to pass the Mussalman Wakf Validating Act.[87] The Mussalman Wakf Validating Bill was introduced as a 'codified form' of the Muslim law of *wakf-alal-aulad*, which allowed Muslims to make trusts for their family, children and descendants.[88] The law was necessitated by a judgment of the Privy Council in 1894, which placed limits on the ability of Muslims to create trusts in perpetuity for family, children and descendants.[89] The debates on the Mussalman Wakf Validating Act further consolidated the notion of a Muslim community premised on a family with gendered roles as a primary unit of this community. In rooting for this legislation, Jinnah and his followers reinforced the colonial construction of Muslim law as a unified code.[90] Similarly, the enactment of the Muslim Personal Law Shariat Application Act (1937) provided Jinnah with an opportunity to create a pan-Indian, unified Muslim community. Contrary to the intentions of some of its framers, the Bill did little to alleviate economic inequalities among Muslims.[91] The debates around the Bill, while emphasising the economic rights of women, were grounded in a gendered division of labour between men and women in the family. While there was an emphasis on the absolute property rights of women, her rights were envisaged in relation to a 'genuine desire' to be ruled by Islamic law, her role in the family and her desire to share the life of a man.[92]

The interlocutors in the debates in the Central Legislative Assembly acknowledged and wrestled with the difficulty of translating the *sharia* into a legal code. In these debates we see the difficulty of translating what was essentially a moral, ethical ideal into codified law. This further bears out the tensions between a Muslim minority identity as a juridical unit and non-territorial, moral and ethical notions of Muslimness, exemplified in this instance by the *sharia*. Muhammad Yamin Khan, a member of the Assembly, conceived of the word *sharia* as including a realm of interpretive possibilities and hence opposed the inclusion of the word in the statute to avoid 'arguing what the *sharia* law is and what it is not'.[93] Muhammad Anwar-ul-Azim, a member of the Chittagong division, emphasised the 'expressive' aspect of the *sharia* as something that would be 'understood' by the community.[94] Khan Bahadur Shaikh Fazl-i-Haq Piracha pointed to the 'present degradation of the Indian Muslims in social and spiritual sphere' due to the 'progressive abandonment of the social code of Islam'. The Bill, he argued, offered Muslims an opportunity to base their conduct in 'social, religious, and spiritual spheres on the basis of equality and humanity'.[95]

Subsequently, the Dissolution of Muslim Marriages Act enacted in 1939 not only expanded the divorce rights of Muslim women but also consolidated the notion of a homogeneous Muslim community governed by Muslim family law. In the wide-ranging consultations and public debates that preceded the enactment of this legislation, the conception of a Muslim community that needed to be defined as a legal entity was at stake. Muhammad Ahmad Kazmi, a member of the Central Legislative Assembly, stated in the objects and reasons of the Bill that the purpose of the Bill was to 'consolidate' the 'whole Law relating to the dissolution of Muslim marriages' to be brought in one place to satisfy a 'long-felt want' of the Muslim community.[96] The Bill was occasioned by rising instances of apostasy by Muslim women to escape unhappy marriages. The colonial courts were granting suits for divorce based on the argument that apostasy automatically dissolved their marriage.[97] While the law did provide divorce rights to Muslim women, it further consolidated the notion of Muslim law as personal law governing a Muslim community.

Kazmi cited the support of *fatwa*s issued by a number of *ulema*s to this effect, such as Maulana Ashraf Ali Thanawi's *Heelat ul Najeeza*, an exhaustive study in Urdu of the provisions of Maliki law, which can be said to be applied in cases where Hanafi law does not provide for divorce. Thanawi was a theologian who had trained in Dar-ul-uloom Deoband. He was trained in a theological tradition that had emerged in the late nineteenth century as a result of the loss of Muslim political sovereignty.[98] The Deoband seminary was one of the many centres of reformist movements in the late nineteenth century that emphasised the cultivation of a 'particular form of religious subjectivity and sociality centered on the *sharia*'.[99] Thanawi articulated a system of 'rights' for Muslims. However, these rights were inextricably linked to a social ideal of proper Muslim conduct.[100] In his well-known treatise for young married Muslim women titled *Bihisht Zewar*, Thanawi emphasised the need to educate women, award property inheritance rights to women and allow remarriage of widows.[101] The impulse to educate women was clearly linked to an Islamic ideal of a transformed moral self. The text stressed how educated women prayed correctly, managed their homes properly and raised their children well.[102] In *Hilyah-yi Najizah*, a treatise on the rights of married women, Thanawi elucidated the right of women to initiate divorce according to the Maliki tradition.[103] He wrote that women were given the privilege of a certain kind of divorce in Islam. However, the context of this discussion was a number of women becoming *murtad*, or turning apostate.[104]

The history of Muslim personal laws in nineteenth- and twentieth-century India can be a useful entry point into exploring how the idea of the Muslim minority was tied to liberal nationalism. As Muslim law came to be textualised and standardised, a Muslim communal identity was constructed on the edifice of the family, with clearly defined gendered roles for men and women. The construction of Muslims as a political community within a framework of liberal nationalism went hand in hand with a legal liberalism concretised in the standardisation and textualisation of *a* Muslim personal law.

As Muslim politics engaged in the colonial logics of majorities and minorities, other ways of conceptualising a Muslim community were gradually sidelined. Alternative structures of conceptualising a Muslim community included the idea of Muslims within a South Asiatic federation which defied the concept of majority and minority. This manner of conceptualising Muslimness was proposed by Aga Khan, the founder of the Muslim League, in his book *India in Transition*.[105] Prominent poet and philosopher Muhammad Iqbal, who later became sympathetic to a territorial project of Muslim nationalism, had also developed a non-territorial, non-teleological notion of ethical community. This vision was articulated in a series of lectures titled *Reconstruction of Religious Thought in Islam*. In these lectures, he repudiated a teleological view of politics as evolving towards a preconceived temporal end. He argued that the Quran proposes an alternative notion of human agency which is not premised on a 'far-off distant goal' but on 'progressive formation of fresh ends, purposes, and ideal scales of value as the process of life grows and expands'.[106] Hence, time and temporality, he argued, is not a 'line already drawn' but rather a line 'in the drawing'.[107] Even in his renowned presidential address delivered at the All India Muslim League session in 1930, Iqbal posited a critique of territorial nationalism. Iqbal understood the Protestant reformation of Europe as a point of displacement of the 'universal ethics of Jesus' by the growth of a 'plurality of national and hence narrower system of ethics'.[108] He contended that the 'intellectual movement' led by Rousseau and Luther had resulted in the breakup of 'one (humanity) into many, the transformation of a human into a national outlook, requiring a more realistic foundation, such as the notion of the country', and this resulted in the organisation of polity along national lines.[109] Islam, as a 'living force', he felt, had the ability to decouple the 'outlook of man from its geographical limitations'.[110]

In twentieth-century India, the politics of minority representation was also organised around debates on 'franchise and procedures of representative government'.[111] During the inter-war years, as ideologies of anticolonial thought were transformed into nationalist claims to state power, marked particularly by the Congress laying claim to state power, the rhetoric of minority rights deepened.[112] Trained in political science at Columbia University and the London School of Economics and later at the bar in England, Ambedkar played an important role in shaping the notion of minority rights and representative democracy in India in the early decades of the twentieth century.[113] Ambedkar worked within liberal thought to articulate a conception of minority by defining untouchables as a political minority whose rights were threatened by the Hindu majority.[114] Rao argues that in the changing narrative of Dalit minority identity in the first three decades of the twentieth century, there was a shift in emphasis from a category of enumeration of communities to questions of social segregation and access to public amenities.[115] In 1918 and 1928, Ambedkar, in his testimony to the Southborough and Simon commissions respectively, constructed the Depressed Classes as a political constituency united by material deprivation.[116] Ambedkar distinguished the political conception of minority from the territorial and numerical conception of minority.[117] He distinguished the logic of minority representation of Dalits from that of Muslims. In his testimony to the Simon Commission in 1928, Ambedkar argued for the representation of the Depressed Classes as a distinct and independent minority.[118] He argued that the Depressed Classes needed separate representation as they were 'educationally very backward, economically poor, socially enslaved, and suffer from grave political disabilities' from which no community suffers.[119] In the same speech, he carefully qualified the minority as an oppressed group whose 'rights are denied' by the majority and would therefore be fit for consideration for political purposes.[120] This was clearly differentiated from a principle of representation of minorities according to the population, which Ambedkar felt would only make the Legislative Council a 'museum' with many specimens.[121]

In a statement relating to the protection of the interests of the Depressed Classes as a minority, Ambedkar argued for political equality in the treatment of all communities. He therefore argued for an extension of the principles of separate representation to the Depressed Classes that had been granted to Muslims.[122] Franchise, he argued, meant the right to 'determine the terms of associated life'.[123] It followed that franchise 'should be given to those who by reason of their weak power of bargaining are exposed to the risk of having the terms of associated life fixed by superior forces in a manner unfavourable to them'.[124]

Ambedkar's conception of the minority's antagonistic relationship with the majority is evinced in his important work 'Pakistan or the Partition of India', where he expressed principled support for the project of a territorial Muslim nation state. In this text, Ambedkar traced the genesis of Muslim nationalism to the Muslim minorities' desire for political power.[125] He envisaged the Muslim minority as a distinct identity closely tethered to the nation state. The Muslim minority was construed as being in an antagonistic relationship with the Hindu majority. Responding to Congress criticisms of the demand for Pakistan, he argued that demands by a nationality for a national state need to be understood vis-à-vis the sovereignty of the will of the people. Citing Mill and Lord Acton, Ambedkar argued that freedom meant the freedom to 'determine with which of the various collective bodies of human beings' people choose to associate themselves.[126] He located Muslim demands for sovereignty within a narrative of a long history of Muslim loss of sovereignty in India since the fall of the Mughal empire. This was marked in the colonial period, in Ambedkar's narrative, by a replacement of Muslim criminal law by the colonial penal code, the 'abridgement' in the field of 'application of the Shariat or Muslim Civil Law' by restricting it to matters of marriage and inheritance, the abolition of the position of the Qazis who administered the *shariat* and the replacement of Persian with English as the official language of the Court.[127] He was also deeply aware of the antagonism that informed the relationship between the majorities and the minorities:

> Both (Hindus and Muslims) forget that the communal problem exists not because the Muslims are extravagant and insolent in their demands and the Hindus are mean and grudging in their concessions. It exists and will exist wherever a hostile majority is brought face to face against a hostile minority. Controversies relating to separate versus joint electorates, controversies relating to population versus weightage are all inherent in a situation where a minority is pitted against a majority. The best solution of the communal problem is not to have two communities

facing each other, one a majority and the other a minority, welded in a steel frame of a single government.[128]

Ambedkar remained acutely aware of the difficulty of attaining political unity without a social union. The danger of a mixed and composite state, he felt, lay in the 'internal resurgence of nationalities which are fragmented, entrapped, suppressed, and held against their will'.[129] The minority, in other words, remained a distinct entity different from the majority. In a multi-ethnic state, there was always a risk of insurgent nationalities.

Muslim law in postcolonial India

The 1940s saw a retrenchment of minority rights, understood as political representation for religious minorities. It was also a period where the Muslim minority identity came to be associated with Muslim family law. The existing scholarship on the Constituent Assembly debates has noted how the period of Constitution-making in the shadow of the Partition of the sub-continent led to the curtailment of minority rights. Separate electorates for religious minorities were abolished, and a clear distinction between religious and caste minorities was carved out in the deliberations in the Constituent Assembly.[130] In the aftermath of the Partition, minority rights were weighed against concerns of political integrity of the nation and the common sense of nationhood by Congress nationalists in the Constituent Assembly.[131] After the Partition of the sub-continent, the remaining representatives of the religious minority communities themselves deployed a language of preservation of a cultural identity instantiated in the demands for the preservation of Muslim family law. In the Constituent Assembly debates, the women framers of the Constitution were in favour of a uniform civil code to be made justiciable. Hansa Mehta, in her final speech in the Constituent Assembly, argued for a common, national civil code that would encapsulate the most progressive aspects of all personal laws.[132] Meanwhile, in the debates on Hindu law reform in the public sphere, women members strongly advocated for the reform of personal laws. Mehta's vision of codification of Hindu law entailed the use of the law to address existing inequalities in the practice of religion-based laws and not mere codification of existing customs.[133]

By 1949, Muslim family law, a creation of the regulatory apparatus of the colonial state, became a marker of Muslim identity. The conception of minority politics as a form of political representation and a notion of Muslimness that was not tied to the space and time of the nation were largely absent in the debates on minority rights in the Constituent Assembly. Mahboob Ali Baig Sahib Bahadur, a Muslim representative in the Constituent Assembly, argued that people of several communities were governed by their personal laws and a secular government should not interfere with the 'religious rights of the people'.[134] He argued that the majority did not need this safeguard as they were a majority, but the minority did not enjoy this privilege. Hence, he argued that 'the personal law of the Muslims and other minorities who so desire should be preserved from interference by the legislature without the concurrence of a vast majority of the members thereof'.[135] The emphasis on Muslim family law as a marker of Muslim minority identity coincided with the gradual socio-economic disenfranchisement of the Muslim minority in postcolonial India.[136]

Legal scholars have traced the history of Muslim family law in postcolonial India in terms of the state regulation of the Muslim family and the Muslim minority.[137] This history is framed around judgments and case law pertaining to maintenance claims of Muslim women and questions of the state regulation of the Muslim family.[138] An important moment in this legal history is the Shah Bano case, in which a divorced Muslim woman appealed to the Supreme Court of India demanding maintenance be granted under the secular Criminal Procedure Code.[139] In this case, the Supreme Court was called upon to adjudicate two central questions: (*a*) if s.125 of the Criminal Procedure Code (CrPC) was applicable to a divorced Muslim wife and (*b*) if s.127(3)(b) insulates a Muslim husband from the liability to pay maintenance for his wife once the dower has been paid within the period of *iddat*.[140] The appellants had argued that the Muslim husband had no obligation to pay maintenance to a divorced wife beyond three months of the *iddat* period and that s.127(3)(b) of the CrPC provided them with this protection. The Supreme Court held that s.125 of CrPC applied to all women irrespective of religion and was meant to prevent vagrancy of women.

The gains of Shah Bano were diluted by the enactment of the Muslim Women's Right to Protection of Divorce Act 1986 by the then Congress government, which limited the maintenance claims available to Muslim women under secular law.[141] However, in the decades following Shah Bano, the Indian courts evolved a framework for rewarding enhanced maintenance claims to divorced Muslim women.[142] This legal development itself has been read in different ways by commentators. Some legal scholars understand this as enhancing a vision of social justice as the state creates obligations for the 'economically stronger members' of the family to take care of women and children.[143] However, more recently, scholars have construed this as part of the state's 'paternalistic logic', which formalises women's 'reliance on kin and community, in contrast to a masculinised sphere of remunerated labour'.[144] My own exploration of this archive of case law leads me to concur with the latter view. While judges do try to reward maintenance claims for Muslim women, their enunciations are usually couched within a paternalist logic of women's dependence on the institution of the family.[145]

In the subsequent decades in postcolonial India, the Muslim identity and a minority cultural identity based on Muslim family law were conflated in official debates on minority rights. In the 1960s, family laws became a pan-Indian issue. During this period, several Muslim organisations constituted a united coalition against interference in Muslim law.[146] Organisations such as the Majlis-e-Mushawarat joined ranks with the Jamat-e-Ulema-e-Hind and the Indian Union Muslim League (IUML) to resist any 'interference' in Muslim law, the range of Anglo-Mohammedan statutes which were codified to create a Muslim personal law in the 1930s.[147] Ironically, this only reified the category of Muslim law and further concretised a Muslim identity in legal, juridical terms. The process of colonial codification and colonial production of a legal, juridical Muslim identity was reproduced in the politics around Muslim law in the first few decades after independence.

In the 1970s, intra-Muslim differences about personal law shaped the debates around Muslim personal law reform.[148] During this period, attempts to 'reform' Muslim law, led predominantly by activists based in Maharashtra, were based on the language of constitutional rights. These initiatives sought to create a binary between religion and liberal constitutional rights. On the other hand, the All India Muslim Personal Law Board (AIMPLB) was formed in 1973 as an attempt to consolidate Muslim personal law and prevent any further state interference in Muslim personal laws.[149] The adjudication of Muslim family law involves multiple state and non-state actors and a range of authorities. Solanki classifies the actors involved in the adjudication of Muslim personal law into three categories: (*a*) individual actors such as lawyers, clergy and family members; (*b*) organisations such as religious organisations, women's organisations and sect-councils; and (*c*) doorstep courts, including residential committees and women's ad-hoc groups.[150] Muslim family law is also made up of a variety of local customs, Islamic laws and precepts, customary laws made by sect-based organisations, state law enactments and judicial precedents.[151] The rhetoric of law reform occasionally obscures this diverse and complex landscape of Muslim family law.

Prominent pro-reform activists in this period felt that religion was an object of reform that ought to be contained in the private realm; this necessitated the intervention of the state in religion.[152] A prominent voice in this movement was the Muslim Satyasodhak Samaj, which organised against unjust practices of Muslim family law. This organisation led a concerted protest against iniquitous practices of Muslim law such as the oral, unilateral divorce, or triple *talaq* (oral, unilateral divorce).[153] The 1970s in India were also a period of the upsurge of several autonomous women's movements that recognised the reformative potential of the law as an instrument of social justice.[154] However, secular women's movements of the 1970s were not particularly attentive to the concerns of Muslim or lower-caste women.[155]

The secular women's movement in India had steered clear of concerns related to religion and had even rejected religious practices outright as inimical to gender justice. The few projects of 'indigenising' feminism in the 1980s broadly drew upon Hindu cultural idioms, thereby alienating non-Hindu women from the women's movement.[156] In 1985, the Shah Bano verdict of the Supreme Court of India marked an important moment in the discourse on Muslim women's rights and the rights of religious minorities.[157] On the one hand, this moment saw the misogynist and patriarchal leadership of the AIMPLB resisting any changes to Muslim personal law.[158] On the other hand, the Hindu right, which had been steadily gaining popularity, exploited this moment as a political opportunity; the aggrieved Muslim woman became a bearer of a community identity, and the Muslim community was imagined by the Hindu right as urgently in need of 'reform'.[159] Hindu majoritarian engagements with family law also build upon the trope of the 'inequitable' and 'insufficient' control of Muslim men's sexuality and the unfair state control exercised by the state over Hindu men because of state-regulated monogamy in the Hindu Marriage Act, 1955.[160] Against the backdrop of these multiple patriarchal appropriations of the Muslim woman by the Hindu right and the AIMPLB, Muslim women organised to articulate their own identity vis-a-vis a community and the state.[161]

Through the 1970s–1980s, the Supreme Court and the High Courts adopted a more interventionist approach to personal laws and customary practices as it weighed them against the fundamental rights provisions of the Indian Constitution.[162] For example, in *Shamim Ara*, the Supreme Court ruled against the arbitrary issuance of triple *talaq* by invoking multiple Islamic legal sources.[163] Justice R. C. Lahoti upheld the eligibility of the divorced wife's claims for maintenance under s. 125 of CrPC. It thereby used multiple Islamic sources to construct an argument for ensuring the welfare of women under a secular statute. The judgments of various High Courts also emphasised how the tenets of the Quran restricted the right to oral, unilateral divorce. For example, in *A. Yousuf Rawther Sowramma*, Justice Krishna Iyer observed that the arbitrary, unilateral power of the Muslim husband to pronounce a divorce is not in accordance with the teachings of the Quran.[164] The Gauhati High Court, while ruling on the validity of triple *talaq*, interpreted the 'correct law of talaq as ordained by the Holy Quran'. The judgment stated that the 'correct law' entails a reasonable cause for divorce and must be preceded by an attempt at reconciliation by the husband and the wife with the help of two arbiters, one each from the family of the husband and the wife respectively.[165]

Muslim women's mobilisations against unjust gendered domination from the 1980s drew upon iterations of rights discourses to challenge everyday sexist and gendered oppression in interactions with the state, the family and community adjudication forums. An array of social movements, non-governmental organisations and voluntary groups led by Muslim women emerged in India in the 1980s. These groups asserted their Muslim identity as well as their identity as rights-bearing citizens. The members of these groups include women from various socio-economic backgrounds and sects who primarily emphasise their Muslim identity in their fight for gender justice with respect to the family. These bodies include the All India Women's Personal Law Board; *Bazme Khawateen* based in Lucknow; Awaaz-e-Niswaan (Women's Voice [AeN]), a Muslim women's NGO based in Mumbai; and Muslim women's rights networks such as the All India Muslim Women's Rights Network (MWRN).[166] These organisations came into prominence in the public sphere in the 1990s in the backdrop of heightened communal violence against Muslim minorities and a crisis in the self-understanding of the Muslim community.[167] These organisations and movements demand reform of personal laws that govern marriage, divorce and maintenance for Muslim women and enhancement of the bargaining power of Muslim women in the governance of Muslim law in community sites of adjudication.[168] Some of the demands of these organisations include the outlawing of the discriminatory cultural practice of oral, unilateral divorce which gives Muslim men arbitrary power over women; a more comprehensive codification of Muslim personal law to lay down a proper procedure for divorce; enhancing the divorce rights of Muslim women; and drafting model *nikahnama*s (marriage contracts), which can give women greater bargaining power in marriages.[169] They also address livelihood issues, self-employment generation and enhancing access to public resources for Muslim women.[170] This development has brought to the fore the voices of Muslim women in conversations on gender justice and the family, a domain hitherto confined to the voices of self-proclaimed male representatives of the community and the state.[171]

This assertion of Muslim women in the legal domain of minority rights in the 1980s–1990s coincides with the emergence of a transnational narrative of Islamic feminism premised on piety. In the formation of the BMMA in the early twenty-first century, these two narratives come together. The tensions between space and time, and the different modalities of regulation of the Muslim minority identity, that predominated the twentieth century continue to animate this movement.

In 2007, the BMMA emerged as a movement for addressing gender inequality within the Muslim community and the socio-economic inequality of Muslims in India.[172] Activists of the movement build upon a transnational activist network of Islamic feminism and piety panning the Middle East, South Asia and Southeast Asia, a Muslim minority identity in contemporary India and an awareness of the marginalised social location of Muslim women.[173] The embrace of the ideals of Islamic feminism has often led the BMMA to be at loggerheads with some other Muslim women's and secular, feminist women's groups.[174]

Dr Noorjehan Safia Niaz and Zakia Soman, the founder members, along with several other activists of the BMMA, were affected by the communal riots in Mumbai in 1992 and the pogrom against Muslims in Gujarat in 2002 respectively.[175] They were also involved in the relief and rehabilitation work following the riots. Activists of the BMMA distinguish themselves from other NGOs and Muslim women's rights groups. They emphasise their allegiance to Islamic feminism and an ethical commitment to the principles and teaching of the Quran that distinguishes them from secular women's groups, which are wary of any engagement with religion. They constitute a movement which enrols Muslim women across the country.[176] As of 2019, the BMMA had about 110,000 members spread across Maharashtra, Gujarat, Madhya Pradesh, Rajasthan, Tamil Nadu, Karnataka, Telangana, West Bengal, Odisha and Delhi.[177] In addition to their fight against gender inequality in the practice of Muslim personal law, leaders of the BMMA address the socio-economic status of Muslims in India and aim to cultivate leaders within the Muslim community.[178]

A note on methodology and method

In terms of both epistemology and methodology, this book draws upon the emerging tradition in comparative political theory that envisages the task of political theory as one of 'conceptual reconstruction of real-world political processes' as well as critical theory approaches that use grounded theory to speak to normative political theory debates.[179] The sub-field of comparative political theory has been defined by the twin aims of fostering 'greater engagement with non-Western thought within mainstream political theory' and initiating conversations between political theory and empirically grounded political science, as well as anthropology to 'enhance the lived world relevance of political theory'.[180]

An interpretive comparative political theory approach extends the domain of comparative political theory beyond traditions in the non-West to the mediated lives of ideas in political processes.[181] In contrast to historians of political thought and comparative political theory approaches that work with particular intellectual traditions in the non-West, this book is more attendant to the performative aspects of 'meaning-making, practices of agents, and their interaction with symbolic systems that they are located in'.[182] An interpretive comparative political theory approach can be especially productive in parochialising debates on religion, liberalism, minority rights and gender in normative political theory and unsettling the normative assumptions and categories that underlie normative political theory. An important recent contribution in this vein is Humeira Iqtidar's contribution that presents a political ethnography of the Jamat-e-Islami in Pakistan. Iqtidar redefines secularisation by delineating the limits of current debates on secularism and secularisation in political theory.[183] Anthropologists of secularism and religion have also initiated conversations between political theory and anthropology and brought to the fore the ways in which immersion in particular contexts reveals the parochialism of categories in political theory.[184]

Political ethnography is a particularly productive way of tracing the imbrication of discourses, ideas and performances in the everyday to advance abstract debates on minority rights, liberalism and gender in normative political theory. Wedeen argues that ethnographic work is especially useful in theorising the dualism of practices as the ethnographer is positioned to register both the 'categories a community uses and to enjoy the distance necessary to develop relevant analytical categories'.[185] Practices, she argues, are dual as they consist of both what is observable to the outside world and 'the actors' understanding of what they are doing'.[186]

I carried out participant observation, non-participant observation and semi-structured interviews in multiple spaces of the BMMA and the women's legal aid cells of the MCMT in Mumbai. I spent 11 months from October 2017 to September 2018 working as an intern in BMMA's office in Mumbai. During this time, I carried out participant observation in the workshops and training sessions on the Quran and the Constitution conducted by activists in neighbourhoods and the *sharia adalat* (shariah court) run by the BMMA in Mumbai. In the *sharia* court, I helped litigants with filing cases and electronic data entry of cases. I followed litigants and members of the *sharia* court to local police stations, the state women's commission and other *qadi* courts in the neighbourhood. The *sharia* court is part of a network of *sharia* courts run entirely by women started by the BMMA in 2013. This initiative was called Dar-ul-uloom-e-Niswan.

In the training sessions conducted in neighbourhoods in and around Bandra East in Mumbai, I participated in reading pamphlets and verses on the Quranic text and sections of the Indian Constitution with other female participants. Conversations on the Quran and the Constitution were always interspersed with discussions on ongoing debates in the Parliament and the courts on Muslim personal law, everyday instances of patriarchy, and sexism in the neighbourhood, and collective organisation to counter the same. The workshops were conducted by a founder member in the office of the BMMA in Bandra East and other locations in Mumbai, mostly with women who were already active members of the BMMA. These members would then conduct workshops in other neighbourhoods in Mumbai to recruit women of various age groups between 18 and 50 to the movement. The workshops were mostly conducted in Bharatnagar, Golibar, Behrampada and Navpada. All of these neighbourhoods have a sizeable Muslim population and were badly affected during the communal riots in Mumbai in 1992–1993. A Muslim identity has subsequently been quite pronounced in the self-understanding of community in these spaces.

In the process of my enmeshment with the lives of litigants and activists, I also interacted with other state and non-state actors, human rights organisations, *qadi* courts and social movements that are inextricably linked to the functioning of the *sharia* court in Mumbai. This led me to conducting observation and interviews in women's legal aid cells in neighbourhoods with a sizeable Muslim population in Mumbai that are part of the MCMT. Written consent was obtained from the members of the BMMA. For women who frequented these spaces, oral consent was obtained. All the women interviewed and observed were apprised of the aims of the project. Most of the members of the BMMA, lawyers and activists consented to their names being used. Activists of the MCMT preferred to remain anonymous, and accordingly pseudonyms have been used for them. Pseudonyms have been used for all other informants.

Given my positionality as a gender non-binary, queer person (biologically assigned male at birth), I was able to cultivate a relationship of empathy and trust with my informants. I was appreciative of their struggles. As a sexual minority who has been at the receiving end of patriarchal policing, abuse, bullying, physical violence and harassment by men, I felt a deep sense of empathy with their everyday struggles against patriarchy. The *sharia* courts, though largely predominated by women who act as judges and activists, are not closed to men. The spaces and networks of the shariah court were frequented by men who were themselves litigants and relatives of women who would visit these courts. In fact, distressed women and their relatives visiting the court often expected the gathered audience, including the men, to be sympathetic to their woes.

Female litigants and their relatives would always express gratitude for the help that I offered them with filling up forms, accompanying them to other *qadi* courts, the police station, and so on. The men in these neighbourhoods were far less welcoming. While accompanying members of the *sharia* courts as well as activists who were conducting workshops, I often met with cold icy stares from elderly men in the neighbourhood. I understand that my identity as an English-speaking, upper-caste Hindu male who clearly looked and sounded different than men who 'belonged' to the neighbourhood and who was spending quite a lot of time with women of the neighbourhood occasioned these glances. I was deeply aware throughout the fieldwork of my position of privilege as an upper-caste Hindu ostensibly cis-representing male and the consequent power differential between my informants and me. Hence, I approached the field with humility and took utmost care to cultivate solidarity and a sense of community with my informants. I cultivated friendships with many of my informants through close enmeshment with their everyday lives. I was actively involved with the day-to-day running of the court, which further helped in cultivating an ethic of solidarity and shared struggles with the women I was working with.

While conducting my fieldwork and writing this manuscript, I was keenly aware of my position of privilege. Therefore, I approached the field and the lives of my informants with an attempt to carefully reconstruct their ideas about rights, activism, ethics and their spatial practices. My analytical labour in this book is primarily to make these moments in my fieldwork speak back to dominant debates on political theory and thereby contribute to decolonising political theory. I carefully avoided imposition of any judgement or external conceptual categories on their political praxis. I allowed my theoretical universe to be shaped by their political praxis.

Plan of the book

In the first half of the book, I explore how minority rights interact with other liberal freedoms such as the right to religious freedom and gender equality and delineate what ethical commitments mediate engagements with these sets of rights. I draw out how religious minorities make sense of a set of rights using a range of ethical commitments and delineate the precise nature and conceptual architecture of these commitments.

In the second half of the book, I explore how the legal domain of minority rights is experienced and constituted in spatial and material ways. I do so through close enmeshment with the everyday life of activists and through closely observing the spatial politics of alternative dispute resolution forums. My spatial exploration illuminates conceptual engagements with minority rights that cannot be captured by abstract liberal, normative accounts. My claim is that these thick descriptions of the spatial negotiations with the legal domain of minority rights enrich our conceptual and theoretical understanding of minority rights. These are not merely empirical descriptions. In the chapters in this section of the book, I trace how gendered negotiations with minority rights are entangled with and shaped by the politics of ghettoisation and an everyday relationship of estranged intimacy with the state. The politics and practice of minority rights is embedded in a relationship of intimacy, familiarity and violence between the state and religious minorities. This relationship is constituted in the everyday life of quasi-legal, alternative dispute resolution forums, ghettoes and sites of activism for gender equality where the state is constituted in materials, moments and interactions. At the same time, the legal apparatus of alternative dispute resolution is tethered to a politics of reconfiguration of the public–private divide. These spatial dimensions are often left out in conversations on minority rights and gender, which are premised on rigid distinctions between the state and the non-state as well as abstract liberal values and communal, religious norms.

The first chapter titled 'Right to be righteous: Constituting Rights, travelling constitutions' builds on participant observation in the workshops on the Quran and the Constitution conducted by members of the BMMA. It traces how discourses on marriage and divorce rights within the framework of Muslim personal law interact with the fundamental rights of the Indian Constitution and how transnational ideas of Islamic feminist ethics mediate these interactions. This chapter shows how the conception of marriage and divorce rights in these spaces is tied to an ethic of piety and a notion of a duty and responsibility towards creating a compassionate and just world as God's agents inspired by an Islamic feminist ethical framework. This articulation remains circumscribed within a discourse of marriage and divorce rights as part of a framework of minority rights. Similarly, fundamental rights in the Indian Constitution, especially the right to freedom of religion, is understood as the right to reconstitute epistemic and legal authority within the community. This right is also conceptualised as a duty towards the ideals of the Quran.

In the second chapter titled 'Becoming Equals: Gender Equality as an Ethical Commitment', I trace how gender equality is constituted as an everyday ethical commitment by invoking Quranic ideals of compassion. Through close enmeshment with the everyday life and adjudication of a female *qazi* and an activist, I show how notions of everyday ethical conduct are constituted in bodily ways and build upon a moral imperative to emulate the qualities of the Prophet. These ethical commitments come together with an ethic of concerted struggle against social and legal inequality led by working-class Muslim women in Mumbai.

The third chapter of the book titled 'Remaking the Ghetto: Sites of Resistance' traces how the spatial marginalisation and ghettoisation of Muslims in the city- and state-directed violence against Muslim minorities are negotiated by women to articulate novel forms of community solidarity. This chapter shows how gendered negotiations with minority rights are constituted by a negotiation with the politics of ghettoisation. These negotiations resonate with a global politics of Islamophobia and Islamic reform. The practice of minority rights is made in moments of gendered reconceptualisation of the Muslim ghetto. I trace how alternative dispute resolution forums come into being in moments of Hindu right-wing violence against Muslim minorities. In these very moments, Muslim women activists reconceptualised their relationship with the spaces of Muslim neighbourhoods. They reconfigured the home, the police station and the neighbourhood as sites of resistance against the patriarchy of both the state and non-state actors. Alternative dispute resolution forums functioned within this altered geography of new relationships of women to space.

The fourth chapter titled 'Estranged Attachments: The Carceral State and the Everyday Life of Muslim Law' shows how the coercive, carceral state looms as a shadow and an imminent threat in these alternative spaces of adjudication. This chapter traces the relationship of estranged intimacy of Muslim women activists and adjudicators of alternative dispute resolution forums with the state, manifested in everyday interactions with the police and everyday engagement with materials such as leaflets, booklets and manuals outlining legal remedies and police action in domestic violence cases. This chapter draws upon the adjudication and public debates concerning a proposed legislation by the Hindu right-wing government in India that criminalises the practice of oral, unilateral divorce in Muslim law and explicitly targets Muslim religious minorities, as well as everyday negotiations with secular, criminal laws that regulate gendered violence in India. This chapter gives us a sense of the pervasive presence of the state in alternative dispute resolution forums that cater to religious minorities, not just as discourse and ideology but also in shadowy, insidious and material forms.

The final chapter shows how the public–private divide is negotiated by women in the shadow of the rhetoric of Muslim law reform by the Hindu right-wing state. This chapter traces the many publics of Muslim law where the gendered logics of public–private divide vis-à-vis the state and the family are renegotiated in multiple ways. The practice of minority rights is tethered to the particular gendered logics of public and semi-public spaces. These multiple gendered logics are often in tension with each other. Drawing upon newspaper reportage, posters, slogans, press conferences and public rallies pertaining to Muslim law reform, this chapter shows how the public sphere of debate on Muslim law stands in tension with a range of gendered performances and semi-public spheres where Muslim law is constituted. This chapter traces the tension between the institutional and the everyday life of minority rights by highlighting how multiple spaces reside in particular gendered logics that constitute the Muslim family.

Notes

1. These *sharia* courts are alternative dispute resolution forums where marital disputes of Muslim women in India are adjudicated. I use the word 'court' here as a shorthand for alternative dispute resolution forums. It is important to note here that these forums were described as *adalat* by the locals, roughly translating to court. The sharia constitutes the moral, ethical ideal that constitutes the domain of Islamic law. Wael Hallaq defines the sharia as the 'hermeneutical, conceptual, theoretical, practical, educational, institutional system' that defines attempts to discover God's moral will. Only women adjudicated marital disputes in the women's sharia court of the BMMA. They were referred to as *qazi*. The female *qazi* had been trained by activists of the BMMA to carry out this role. The training sessions for *qazi* included lessons on the Quran, the Constitution, and other secular legislations, such as the Protection of Women from Domestic Violence Act 2005.
2. Mengia Hong Tschalaer, *Muslim Women's Quest for Justice: Gender, Law and Activism in India* (New Delhi: Cambridge University Press, 2017).
3. Thomas Blom Hansen, *Wages of Violence: Naming and Identity in Postcolonial Bombay* (Princeton, NJ: Princeton University Press, 2001).
4. A plural legal system governs the adjudication of marriage, divorce and maintenance by the Indian state. This system includes both state and non-state law. The statutes that govern Muslim family law are the Muslim Personal Law (Shariat Application) Act 1937, Dissolution of Muslim Marriages Act 1938, Muslim Women's (Protection of Rights on Divorce) Act 1986, Muslim Women's (Protection of Rights on Marriage) Act 2019. At the same time, a range of alternative dispute resolution forums, including *dar-ul-qaza*s (alternative dispute resolution forums run by male *qazi*), women's panchayats (community forums) and newly founded women's sharia courts, also play an important role in the adjudication of marriage, divorce and maintenance claims. Their authority is recognised by men and women in predominantly Muslim neighbourhoods. Even though the state does not officially recognise these forums, state courts often rely on their decisions when adjudicating marital disputes. They provide an affordable means for settling marital disputes. Given that access to state law

is often determined by gender, religion and caste, these forums constitute an important part of the informal justice delivery system.
5. Ayelet Shachar, *Multicultural Jurisdictions Cultural Differences and Women's Rights* (Cambridge: Cambridge University Press, 2001); Cécile Laborde, *Critical Republicanism: The Hijab Controversy and Political Philosophy* (Oxford: Oxford University Press, 2008); Seyla Benhabib, *The Claims of Culture: Equality and Diversity in the Global Era* (Princeton, NJ: Princeton University Press, 2002).
6. Shachar, *Multicultural Jurisdictions*, 2.
7. Ibid., 4.
8. Shachar, *Multicultural Jurisdictions*, 19.
9. Benhabib, *Claims of Culture*, 19.
10. Ibid., 16.
11. Ibid., 19.
12. Ibid., 19.
13. Susan Moller Okin, 'Is Multiculturalism Bad for Women?' in *Is Multiculturalism Bad for Women?* ed. Joshua Cohen, Howard Matthew and Martha Nussbaum, 7–24 (Princeton, NJ: Princeton University Press, 1999).
14. Will Kymlicka, *Liberalism, Community, and Culture* (Oxford: Oxford University Press, 1989).
15. Ibid.
16. Joseph Raz, *Ethics in the Public Domain: Essays in the Morality of Law and Politics* (Oxford: Oxford University Press, 1994).
17. Chandran Kukathas, 'Are There Any Cultural Rights?' *Political Theory* 20, no. 1 (1992): 107–139.
18. Charles Taylor, 'The Politics of Recognition', in Multiculturalism and the Politics of Recognition, ed. Arny Gutmann, 25–73 (Princeton, NJ: Princeton University Press).
19. Bhikhu Parekh, *Rethinking Multiculturalism: Cultural Diversity and Political Theory* (Basingstoke: Macmillan, 2000).
20. Uma Narayan, 'Essence of Culture and a Sense of History: A Feminist Critique of Cultural Essentialism'. Hypatia 13, no. 2 (1998): 86–106; Chandra Talpade Mohanty, Russo Ann, and Torres Lourdes (eds.), *Third World Women and the Politics of Feminism*, vol. 632 (Bloomington, IN: Indiana University Press, 1991); Anne Phillips, *Multiculturalism without Culture*, vol. 8 (Princeton, NJ: Princeton University Press, 2007).
21. Narayan, 'Essence of Culture and a Sense of History'.
22. Mohanty et al., *Third World Women and the Politics of Feminism*.

23. For a detailed discussion, see Mahmood Mamdani, *Neither Settler Nor Native: The Making and Unmaking of Permanent Minorities* (Cambridge, MA: Harvard University Press, 2020).
24. Talal Asad, *Formations of the Secular: Christianity, Islam, Modernity* (Redwood City, CA: Stanford University Press, 2003); Saba Mahmood, *Religious Difference in a Secular Age: A Minority Report* (Princeton: Princeton University Press, 2015); Hussein Ali Agrama, *Questioning Secularism: Islam, Sovereignty, and the Rule of Law in Modern Egypt* (Chicago: University of Chicago Press, 2012).
25. Mahmood, *Religious Difference in a Secular Age*, 3; Saba Mahmood, 'Secularism, Hermeneutics, and Empire: The Politics of Islamic Reformation', *Public Culture* 18, no. 2 (2006): 323–347.
26. Mahmood, *Religious Difference in a Secular Age*, 3.
27. Ibid., 63.
28. Ibid., 53.
29. Ibid., 54.
30. Ibid., 117.
31. Ibid., 128.
32. Gopika Solanki's wok is the most important contribution in this vein. Solanki conceptualises an Indian model of legal pluralism. In this model, the regulation of marriage and divorce is shared by the state, internally heterogeneous religio-cultural communities, and civil society, especially women's groups. These forums provide avenues for intra and inter-cultural accommodation and they can contribute to gender equality in the law. Gopika Solanki, *Adjudication in Religious Family Laws: Cultural Accommodation, Legal Pluralism, and Gender Equality in India* (New York: Cambridge University Press, 2011).
33. Rohit De, *A People's Constitution: The Everyday Life of Law in the Indian Republic* (Princeton, NJ: Princeton University Press, 2018); Gautam Bhatia, *The Transformative Constitution: A Radical Biography in Nine Acts* (Harper Collins, 2019); Rochana Bajpai, 'Liberalisms in India: A Sketch', in *Liberalism as Ideology: Essays in Honour of Michael Freeden*, ed. Jackson, Ben and Stears, 53–76 (Oxford: Oxford University Press, 2012); Anupama Rao, *The Caste Question: Dalits and the Politics of Modern India* (London: University of California Press, 2009).
34. Bajpai, 'Liberalisms in India'.
35. Rao, *The Caste Question*, 17.

36. Achyut Chetan, *Founding Mothers of the Indian Republic: Gender Politics of the Framing of the Constitution* (New Delhi: Cambridge University Press, 2021), 11.
37. Nivedita Menon, *Secularism as Misdirection: Critical Thought from the Global South*. (Durham: Duke University Press, 2024), 2–3.
38. Sumi Madhok, *Vernacular Rights Cultures: The Politics of Origins, Human Rights, and Gendered Struggles for Justice* (New York: Cambridge University Press, 2022).
39. Madhok, *Vernacular Rights Cultures*, 2.
40. Alexandra Lewis and Marie Lall, 'From Decolonisation to Authoritarianism: The Co-option of the Decolonial Agenda in Higher Education by Right-Wing Nationalist Elites in Russia and India', *Higher Education* (2023): 1–18, https://doi.org/10.1007/s10734-023-01074-0; Banu Subramaniam, 'Recolonizing India: Troubling the Anticolonial, Decolonial, Postcolonial', *Catalyst: Feminism, Theory, Technoscience* 3, no. 1 (2017): 1–47.
41. Jeremy Waldron, 'Locke: Toleration and the Rationality of Persecution', in *Justifying Toleration: Conceptual and Historical Perspectives*, ed. Susan Mendus, 61–86 (Cambridge: Cambridge University Press, 1988).
42. Paul Kelly, 'Liberalism and Nationalism', in *The Cambridge Companion to Liberalism*, ed. Steven Wall, 329–352 (Cambridge: Cambridge University Press, 2015).
43. Linda Colley, 'Britishness and Otherness: An Argument', *Journal of British Studies* 31, no. 4 (1992): 309–329; P. T. van der Veer, *Imperial Encounters: Religion, Nation, and Empire* (Princeton, NJ: Princeton University Press, 2001).
44. Mahmood Mamdani, *Neither Settler Nor Native: The Making and Unmaking of Permanent Minorities* (Cambridge, MA: Harvard University Press, 2020).
45. Ibid., 3.
46. Ibid., 3.
47. Humeira Iqtidar, 'Jizya against Nationalism: Abul A'la Maududi's Attempt at Decolonizing Political Theory', *Journal of Politics* 83, no. 3 (2021): 1145–1157.
48. Some recent approaches in political theory that seem to demonstrate a similar epistemological commitment are Iqtidar (2020) and Iqtidar (2021). Iqtidar reconstructs Maududi as a decolonial political theorist.

She shows how Maududi could not altogether escape the categories of liberal imperialism even though he was aware of their limitations. Hence, he drew upon his wide knowledge of Islamic history and philosophy to rework European ideas. He asserted the moral dignity of the minority without referring to liberal discourses of individual rights or legal equality and was inspired by his understanding of justice in Islamic thought. See Humeira Iqtidar, 'Theorizing Popular Sovereignty in the Colony: Abul A'la Maududi's 'Theodemocracy', *Review of Politics* 82, no. 4 (2020): 595–617; Iqtidar, 'Jizya against Nationalism'.
49. Chandra Talpade Mohanty, 'Transnational Feminist Crossings: On Neoliberalism and Radical Critique', *Signs* 38, no. 4 (2013): 967–991; Serene J. Khader, *Decolonizing Universalism: A Transnational Feminist Ethic* (Oxford: Oxford University Press, 2019).
50. Mohanty, *Transnational Feminist Crossings*, 968.
51. Ibid.
52. For a detailed discussion of the emergence of these groups, see Sylvia Vatuk and Mengia Tschalaer. Vatuk groups them as constituting a nascent Islamic feminist movement in India. Tschalaer is reluctant to use the term 'Islamic feminism', but she does recognise the commonalities in the strategies and rhetoric of these groups in their use of various configurations of Islamic law and a constitutional framework to talk about gender justice. Tschalaer, *Muslim Women's Quest for Justice*; Sylvia Vatuk, 'Islamic Feminism in India: Indian Muslim Women Activists and the Reform of Muslim Personal Law', in *Islamic Reform in South Asia,* ed. F. Osella and C. Osella, 346–382 (Cambridge: Cambridge University Press, 2013).
53. Vatuk, 'Islamic Feminism in India'.
54. Tschalaer, *Muslim Women's Quest for Justice*, 21.
55. Ibid., 359.
56. Noorjehan Safia Niaz and Zakia Soman, *Seeking Justice within Family: A National Study on Muslim Women's Views on Reforms in Muslim Personal Law* (Belgaum: Omega Publications, March 2015), 8.
57. Sachar Committee, *Social, Economic and Educational Status of the Muslim Community of India: A Report* (2006), http://www.minorityaffairs.gov.in/sites/default/files/sachar_comm.pdf (accessed 20 December 2024).
58. Sachar Committee, *Social, Economic and Educational Status of the Muslim Community of India*, 19.
59. Ibid., 19.
60. Ibid., 19.

61. Niaz and Soman, *Seeking Justice within the Family*, 28.
62. Ibid., 36.
63. Ibid., 36.
64. BMMA (Bharatiya Muslim Mahila Andolan). *Muslim Family Law, 2017: Draft for the Bill* (Belgaum: Omega Publications, 2017).
65. Vatuk, 'Islamic Feminism in India', 349.
66. Vatuk, 'Islamic feminism in India', 358
67. Ibid., 359.
68. Ibid., 358.
69. Tschalaer, *Muslim Women's Quest for Justice*, 4.
70. Vatuk, 'Islamic Feminism in India'.
71. Robert Travers, *Ideology and Empire in Eighteenth-Century India: The British in Bengal*, vol. 14 (Cambridge: Cambridge University Press, 2007), 117.
72. Ibid., 118–119; Scott Alan Kugle, 'Framed, Blamed and Renamed: The Recasting of Islamic Jurisprudence in Colonial South Asia', *Modern Asian Studies* 35, no. 2 (2001): 257–313.
73. Travers, *Ideology and Empire in Eighteenth-century India*, 118.
74. Ibid., 118.
75. Julia Stephens, *Governing Islam: Law, Empire, and Secularism in Modern South Asia* (Cambridge: Cambridge University Press, 2018), 7.
76. Ibid., 7.
77. Ibid., 9.
78. Ibid., 10.
79. Joya Chatterji, 'South Asian Histories of Citizenship, 1946–1970', *Historical Journal 55*, no. 4 (2012): 1051; Vazira Fazila-Yacoobali Zamindar, *The Long Partition and the Making of Modern South Asia: Refugees, Boundaries, Histories* (New York: Columbia University Press, 2007), 146; Shabnum Tejani, *Indian Secularism: An Intellectual History 1890–1950* (Bloomington: Chesham: Indiana University Press, 2008), 142.
80. Tejani, *Indian Secularism*, 142.
81. Karuna Mantena, *Alibis of Empire: Henry Maine and the Ends of Liberal Imperialism* (Princeton, NJ; Oxford: Princeton University Press, 2010) 6.
82. Tejani, *Indian Secularism*, 142.
83. Saleem M. M. Qureshi, 'Iqbal and Jinnah: Personalities, Perceptions and Politics', in *Iqbal, Jinnah, and Pakistan: The Vision and the Reality*, ed. C.M. Naim, 23 (Syracuse: Maxwell School of Citizenship and Public Affairs, 1979).

84. Jalal, *The Sole Spokesman*, 4.
85. Stephens, *Governing Islam*, 168.
86. Christopher Bayly, *Recovering Liberties: Indian Thought in the Age of Liberalism and Empire* (Cambridge: Cambridge University Press, 2011).
87. IOR/ L/PJ /6/1079 Statement of Objects and Reasons 1911, 6.
88. Ibid., 6.
89. *Abul Fatha v. Russomoy Dhar Chaudhuri* (1891) ILR 18 Cal 399.
90. Stephens, *Governing Islam*, 169.
91. Ibid., 170.
92. Legislative Assembly Debates (LAD) 1937, vol. 5, no. 6, p. 1445.
93. LAD 1937, vol. 5, p. 1436; LAD 1937, vol. 5, p. 1434.
94. LAD 1937, vol. 3, p. 2537.
95. Ibid.
96. Statement of Objects and Reasons, 27 December 1935, Muslim Dissolution of Marriages Act 1939, File No. IOR/ L/ PJ/ 1065: 23 April 1936–9 Jun 1939, India Office Records, British Library.
97. Muhammad Khalid Masud. 'Apostasy and Judicial Separation in British India', in *Islamic Legal Interpretation: Muftis and Their Fatwás*, ed. Muhammad Khalid Masud, Brinkley Messicak, and David S. Powers, 193–203 (Cambridge: Harvard University Press, 1996).
98. Ali Altaf Mian, 'Invoking Islamic Rights in British India: Mawlana Ashraf 'Ali Thanawi's *Ḥuqūq Al-Islam*', *Muslim World* 99, no. 2 (2009): 312–334, 313.
99. Ibid., 312.
100. Ibid., 313.
101. *Bihisht Zewar*, trans. Barbara D Metcalf, 74, 102.
102. Ibid., 59.
103. *Hilyah-yi Najizah, ya ni Auraton ka Haq-I Tansikh e nikah* (Daruishaat: Karachi, 1987), 242.
104. Ibid., 13 (translation mine).
105. Aga Khan, *India in Transition: A Study in Political Evolution* (London: The Medici Society, 1918).
106. Muhammad Iqbal, *The Reconstruction of Religious Thought in Islam* (Lahore: Ashraf Press, [1934] 1960), 54.
107. Ibid., 55.
108. Iqbal, 'Presidential Address Delivered at the Annual Session of the All-India Muslim League at Allahabad on 29 December 1930', 163.
109. Ibid., 163.

110. Ibid., 164.
111. Anupama Rao, *The Caste Question: Dalits and the Politics of Modern India* (University of California Press, 2009), 21.
112. Ibid.,124.
113. Ibid., 122.
114. Ibid., 124.
115. Rao, *The Caste Question*, 131.
116. Evidence of Dr. Ambedkar before the Indian Statutory Commission on 23 October 1928, in BAWS, vol. 2, 465.
117. Ibid., 465.
118. Evidence before the Simon Commission, in BAWS, vol. 2, 465.
119. Ibid., 465.
120. Ibid., 478.
121. Ibid., 471.
122. Statement concerning safeguards for the protection of interests of the Depressed Classes as a minority in the Bombay Presidency and the changes in the composition of and the guarantees from the Bombay Legislative Council necessary to ensure the same under Provincial Autonomy, submitted by B. R. Ambedkar on behalf of the Bahishkrit Hitakarini Sabha (Depressed Classes Institute) to the Indian Statutory Commission, 29 May 1928, in BAWS, vol. 2, 438–439.
123. Ibid., 441.
124. Ibid., 441.
125. B. R. Ambedkar *Pakistan or Partition of India*, 2nd ed. (Bombay: Thacker and Company, 1945), 41.
126. Ibid., 41.
127. Ibid., 65.
128. Ibid., 111.
129. Ibid., 188.
130. Bajpai, *Debating Difference*, 6; Tejani, *Indian Secularism*, 201.
131. Bajpai, *Debating Difference*, 6.
132. Chetan, *Founding Mothers of the Indian Republic*, 215.
133. Ibid., 219.
134. Constituent Assembly Debates, vol. 8, 8 November 1948, 323.
135. Ibid., 323.
136. Joya Chatterji, 'South Asian Histories of Citizenship, 1946–1970', *The Historical Journal* 55, no. 4 (2012): 1049–1071; Zamindar, *The Long Partition and the Making of Modern South Asia*.

137. Werner Menski, 'The Uniform Civil Code Debate in Indian Law: New Developments and Changing Agenda', in *The Many Faces of India: Law and Politics of the Subcontinent*, ed. M. McLauren, 136–182 (New Delhi: Samskriti, 2012); Flavia Agnes, *Family Laws and Constitutional Claims* (New Delhi: Oxford University Press, 2011).
138. Agnes, *Family Laws and Constitutional Claims*.
139. Zakia Pathak and Rajeswari Sunder Rajan, 'Shahbano', *Signs: Journal of Women in Culture and Society* 14, no. 3 (1989): 558–582; Menski, 'The Uniform Civil Code Debate in Indian Law'.
140. As per s. 125(1)(a) of the CrPC 1973 a wife who is 'unable to maintain herself' has the right to approach a first-class magistrate to claim a monthly maintenance of INR 500 from her husband. The definition of the wife includes a divorced wife, 'a woman who has been divorced by or obtained divorce from her husband and has not remarried'. S. 127(3)(b) states that in case a woman has received before the date of an order under s. 125 the whole of the sum under any customary or personal law applicable to such parties payable on such divorce, the magistrate shall cancel such an order.
141. Pathak and Sunder Rajan, 'Shahbano', 560.
142. Solanki, *Adjudication in Religious Family Laws*.
143. Agnes, *Family Laws and Constitutional Claims*; Maitrayee Mukhopadhyay, *Legally Dispossessed: Gender, Identity, and the Process of Law* (Calcutta: Stree, 1998).
144. Katherine Lemons, 'Paying for Kinship: Muslim Divorce and the Privatization of Insecurity', *History of the Present* 7, no. 2 (2017): 197–218.
145. Sagnik Dutta, 'From Accommodation to Substantive Equality: Muslim Personal Law, Secular Law, and the Indian Constitution 1985–2015', *Asian Journal of Law and Society* 4, no. 1 (2017): 191–227.
146. Saumya Saxena, *Divorce and Democracy: A History of Personal Law in Post-Independence India* (New Delhi: Cambridge University Press, 2022, 145).
147. Ibid., 148.
148. Ibid., 151.
149. Ibid., 144.
150. Solanki, *Adjudication in Religious Family Laws*, 268.
151. Ibid.
152. Ibid., 151
153. Saxena, *Divorce and Democracy*, 152.
154. Ibid.

155. Nida Kirmani, 'Beyond the Impasse: "Muslim Feminism(s)" and the Indian Women's Movement', *Contributions to Indian Sociology* 45, no. 1 (2011): 1–26; Vatuk, 'Islamic Feminism in India'; Flavia Agnes, 'Redefining the Agenda of the Women's Movement within a Secular Framework', in *Women and Right-Wing Movement: Indian Experiences*, ed. Tanika Sarkar and Urvashi Butalia, 136–157 (New Delhi: Kali for Women, 1995).
156. Agnes, 'Redefining the Agenda of the Women's Movement within a Secular Framework'; Kirmani, 'Beyond the Impasse'.
157. In *Mohammed Ahmed Khan v. Shah Bano*, a 62-year-old divorced Muslim wife had been awarded maintenance by the Supreme Court of India, which held that there was no conflict between s. 125 of the Criminal Procedure Code and the Quranic text as far as obligation of the husband towards the divorced wife was concerned. This judgment caused a furore, as some conservative sections of Muslim society saw it as interfering with Muslim personal law. Following protests by sections of the Muslim community, the Congress government headed by Prime Minister Rajiv Gandhi enacted the Muslim Women's (Protection of Rights to Divorce) Act 1986, which mandated that maintenance and a 'reasonable provision' be made and paid to the woman during the *iddat* period.
158. Agnes, 'Redefining the Agenda of the Women's Movement within a Secular Framework'.
159. Zoya Hasan, 'Gender Politics, Legal Reform, and the Muslim Community', in *Appropriating Gender: Women's Activism and Politicized Religion in South Asia*, ed. P. Jeffery and A. Basu, 71–88 (New York: Routledge), 1998; Zoya Hasan, *Forging Identities: Gender, Communities and the State in India*. Boulder: Westview, 1994.
160. Srimati Basu, *The Trouble with Marriage: Feminists Confront Law and Violence in India*, vol. 1 (Oakland, CA: University of California Press, 2015), 302.
161. Niaz and Soman, *Seeking Justice within the Family*.
162. Sagnik Dutta, 'From Accommodation to Substantive Equality: Muslim Personal Law, Secular Law, and the Indian Constitution 1985–2015', *Asian Journal of Law and Society* 4, no. 1 (2017): 191–227.
163. *Shamim Ara v. State of UP and Anr* (2002) 7 SCC 518.
164. *A Yousuf Rawether v. Sowramma* AIR 1971 Ker 261.
165. *Jaiuddin Ahmed v. Anwara Begum* (1981) 1 Gau LR 358; *Rukia Khatun v. Abdul Khalique Laskar* (1981) 1 Gau LR 375.

166. Vatuk, 'Islamic Feminism in India'; Niaz and Soman, *Seeking Justice within the Family*, 71.
167. Tschalaer, *Muslim Women's Quest for Justice*, 359.
168. Ibid., 359.
169. Ibid.
170. Vatuk, 'Islamic Feminism in India', 359.
171. Vatuk, 'Islamic Feminism in India', 359; Tschalaer, *Muslim Women's Quest for Justice*, 14.
172. Kirmani, 'Beyond the Impasse'; Vatuk, 'Islamic Feminism in India'; Justin Jones, '"Where Only Women May Judge": Developing Gender-Just Islamic Laws in India's All-Female 'Sharī 'ah Courts', *Islamic Law and Society* 26, no. 4 (2019): 437–466.
173. Tschalaer, *Muslim Women's Quest for Justice*; Sagnik Dutta, 'Divorce, Kinship, and Errant Wives: Islamic Feminism in India, and the Everyday Life of Divorce and Maintenance', *Ethnicities* 21, no. 3 (2021): 454–476.
174. The tension between secular and Islamic feminism plays out in some Muslim majority contexts such as Pakistan as well. For example, Afiya Zia, writing on Islamic feminism and the women's movement in Pakistan, notes that Islamic feminists working within the paradigm of religion in Pakistan have 'subsumed' other forms of feminist expression. See Afiya Shehrbano Zia, 'The Reinvention of Feminism in Pakistan', *Feminist Review* 91, no. 1 (2009): 29–46. However, the relationship between Islamic feminism, the state and religion plays out differently in a context like India where Muslims are a religious minority and Islam is not the state religion.
175. Kirmani, 'Beyond the Impasse'.
176. Jones, 'Where only Women May Judge', 439.
177. Interview, Noorjehan Safia Niaz, 15 April 2021.
178. Kirmani, 'Beyond the Impasse'.
179. Brooke Ackerly and Rochana Bajpai, 'Comparative Political Thought', in *Methods in Analytical Political Theory*, ed. Adrian Blau, 270–296 (New York, NY: Cambridge University Press); Banu Bargu, *Starve and Immolate: The Politics of Human Weapons* (New York: Columbia University Press, 2014); Lisa Herzog and Bernardo Zacka, 'Fieldwork in Political Theory: Five Arguments for an Ethnographic Sensibility', *British Journal of Political Science* 49, no. 2 (2019): 763–784.
180. Bajpai and Ackerley, 'Comparative Political Thought', 290.
181. Ibid., 284.

182. Lisa Wedeen, 'Conceptualizing Culture: Possibilities for Political Science', *American Political Science Review* 96, no. 4 (2002): 713–728.
183. Humeira Iqtidar, *Secularizing Islamists? Jama'at-e-Islami and Jama'at-ud-Da'wa in Urban Pakistan* (Chicago: University of Chicago Press, 2011).
184. Asad, *Formations of the Secular*; Mahmood, *Politics of Piety*; Agrama, *Questioning Secularism*.
185. Lisa Wedeen, 'Ethnography as Interpretive Enterprise', in *Political Ethnography: What Immersion Contributes to the Study of Power*, ed. Edward Schatz, 75–94 (Chicago, IL: University of Chicago Press, 2009), 87.
186. Ibid.

Part I
Ethics

1
Right to be righteous
Constituting rights, travelling constitutions

> Say if you go to the police *chowki* and speak to them and it appears that our rights are of no consequence. This attitude will not do. They [the police] must register a complaint. You must confront them and tell them that these are our rights (*humara huq*) and you [the police] must take action.
>
> —Mumtaz Shaikh, BMMA activist

Mumtaz Shaikh, an activist of the BMMA, conducted a range of workshops and training sessions with other working-class Muslim women in her neighbourhood. In these sessions, she spoke about the difficulties that Muslim women faced when they approached the police for redressal of grievances such as domestic violence. In her discussion of these difficulties, she invoked the rights (*huq*) of Muslim women in terms of the rights of a collective, communal entity. For Shaikh, rights became meaningful in these moments of collective communal mobilisation for rights.

In a similar training session, Noorjehan Safia Niaz, a founder member of the BMMA, spoke of the right to religious freedom for Muslim women. She construed the right as the freedom that allowed women to carry out the duty towards individual and collective self-improvement. The right to religious freedom was exercised through political action. Activists understood the right as the right to collectively challenge and reconstitute religious authority in spaces of adjudication of Muslim law on marriage, divorce and maintenance. This was not merely a form of individual freedom that enabled women's autonomy. Collective organising to challenge religious authority in communities was considered a pious obligation and a duty for women who wanted to construct a more just world in accordance with the principles of the Quran. In the activism of the BMMA, an ethic of duty reconstituted liberal freedoms such as the right to religious freedoms in moments of negotiation with Muslim family law and minority rights.

This chapter builds on participant observation in the workshops on the Quran and the Constitution conducted by members of the BMMA. It traces how discourses on marriage and divorce rights within the framework of Muslim Personal Law interact with the fundamental rights guaranteed by the Indian Constitution, especially the right to religious freedom and how transnational ideas of Islamic feminist ethics shape these interactions. I show how the conception of marriage and divorce rights in these spaces is mediated by an ethic of piety and a notion of a duty and responsibility towards creating a compassionate and just world as God's agents inspired by an Islamic feminist ethical framework. This articulation remains circumscribed within a discourse of marriage and divorce rights conceptualised as part of a framework of minority rights. Similarly, the right to freedom of religion is understood as the right to reconstitute epistemic and legal authority within the community. This right is also conceptualised as a duty towards the ideals of the Quran. The central aim of this chapter is to show how notions of rights are constituted by the idea of duty in the everyday life of the legal framework of minority rights in India. This notion of duty shapes the practice of minority rights and its interactions with standard liberal guarantees such as the right to religious freedom.

This chapter is divided into four sections. The first section discusses the textual and the discursive universe of the workshop. These workshops and training sessions were conducted by members of the BMMA in neighbourhoods in Mumbai once a month. The second section explores the everyday construction of the right to freedom of religion guaranteed under the Indian Constitution. The third section explores the articulation of marriage and divorce rights in these workshops. The fourth section builds on the interpretive claims of my ethnographic work to outline my contribution to reconceptualising debates on minority rights and gender in political theory as well as decolonising the study of minority rights in political theory.

Workshops of the BMMA

In the workshops of the BMMA, conversations on Muslim women's rights were mediated by a range of texts, including a pamphlet with Quranic verses relating to marriage, divorce and maintenance; a draft Muslim Personal Law Bill popularised by the BMMA; and a booklet that highlighted fundamental duties, fundamental rights and directive principles of State Policy of the Indian Constitution. The founders of the BMMA were inspired by a wave of transnational Islamic feminist scholarship and activism in the 1990s. They drew upon the work of Quranic scholar Amina Wadud and Islamic feminist Ziba Mir-Hosseini to foreground Muslim personal law reform as a part of a transnational narrative of piety (*taqwa*) and a vision of harmonious existence with a unified God (*tawheed*). Interpreting the Quranic text from a woman's perspective to cull out principles of compassion (*raham*), equality (*barabari*), reason (*aql*) and justice (*insaf*) is at the heart of this project.[1] The movement advocates for laws on Muslim women's marriage and divorce rights to be based on the ideals of the Quran. In the workshops and written publications of the movement, the principles of the Quranic text itself are considered infallible. This is a major bone of contention between the BMMA and other liberal feminist and secular women's organisations such as the Bebak Collective. Members of the BMMA consider owing allegiance to the text and collectively fighting for the moral, ethical ideal that it stands for as their responsibility and duty (*zimmedari*) as God's agents (*khalifa*s) on earth. This line of thought is inspired by Amina Wadud's writings.

The workshops and training sessions were carried out by founder members of the BMMA as well as women who had trained as *qazi*s (roughly translated as Islamic judges) under an initiative begun by the BMMA in 2013. The training modules of the *qazi* involved lessons on Islamic schools of jurisprudence and knowledge of fundamental rights, fundamental duties and directive principles of state policy of the Indian Constitution, as well as other laws related to violence against women, such as the Domestic Violence Act 2005, the Dowry Prohibition Act 1961, and so on.

Religious freedom and being righteous

In this section, I will pay particular attention to the concept of duty and how it is entangled with the act of claiming a set of rights, especially the right to religious freedom. The Constitution was envisaged by Niaz and other members as a document which outlined the rights and duties of all members of the nation. In Niaz's workshops, she emphasised the constitutive moment as a moment when we have given ourselves the Constitution. Niaz conceptualised the Constitution as an instrument of self-rule, where the self meant the community and the nation that constituted the imaginary 'people'. In all the workshops, the Constitution was introduced by members of the BMMA using the fundamental duties chapter, which was then used as an entry point into fundamental rights. In her workshops, Niaz defined rights as freedoms required for individual and collective self-improvement.

The right to freedom of religion was defined in one of Niaz's workshops as the 'freedom to *struggle* for the right to practice and obey one's religion' (*Mazhab ko man ney ki larai*) (emphasis mine). In one of the workshops, Niaz asked her participants to discuss the rights (*huq*) that the BMMA had fought for. Responding to her question, several participants pointed out that the BMMA had fought for challenging the authority of male *qazi*s in community spaces. To this, Niaz further added that the BMMA had trained 30 women *qazi*s all over India as part of its initiative called the Dar-ul-uloom e Niswan. Again, Niaz highlighted that the women *qazi*s would allow women to get easy access to divorce in respectful ways in community spaces. In the training sessions, one *qazi* said that women *qazi*s were able to reconfigure and challenge the gender hierarchies in neighbourhoods (*disha badalne ka kaam*). Earlier, a male *qazi* would pronounce a divorce without consulting the woman, whereas now there is greater awareness of the importance of listening to women.

In one of the workshops a young girl complained that the local *maulana* (male religious scholar) who owns a bookstore refused to give her a copy of an annotated version of the Quran. This moment was analysed by Niaz and the participants in terms of the right to freedom of religion. This girl recreated the moment where she was denied an annotated copy of the Quranic text by the local *maulvi*. When she was insistent, she was initially told by the religious scholar that she would not have the time to read the Quran. He later snubbed her for talking too much. Responding to this situation, the participants in the workshop resolved to collectively fight for her rights (*huq*). Niaz, who was conducting the workshop, stressed that it was their duty as a community to collectively fight for this girl's right to read the Quran.

She further emphasised:

> Our Mullahs and Maulvis say don't go here, don't go there. Don't read the Quran with translations. They always say that they are the scholars (*alim*). They say that we wrack our brains (*magaz maari*) and how come you women have become scholars (*alim*)? They fear the prospect of this young girl reading Surah Nisah, Surah Baqr, Surah Talaq and her

getting to know about her (*huq*) rights. Then she will become aware of the fact that she has as much right (*huq*) as men to read the Quran.

In a similar construction of religious freedom, Mumtaz Shaikh, another member of the BMMA, spoke of the right to religious freedom in terms of the freedom to recruit women to the movement. In her workshops, she encouraged more and more women to join the movement and fight for their rights (*huq*). She said that her vision for conducting these workshops was to get the participants themselves to conduct more workshops in other neighbourhoods and thereby spread awareness about the ideas that they had picked up. This trope of collective agency tied to rights circulated in the spaces of the movement. A woman in the workshop said that she had been able to claim her rights with the help of a women's organisation (*mahila mandal*), and she therefore wanted to organise and fight for the rights of others.

In workshops conducted by Mumtaz Shaikh, rights claims are invoked in relation to the communal personhood of Muslim women (*humara huq*). Shaikh invoked the right to access public services such as the police in instances of domestic violence. She invoked these moments quite dramatically in one of her workshops. An incident was described by one of her participants where the police would refuse to register a complaint in cases of domestic violence and come up with the usual refrain of how this was a 'domestic matter' (*gharelu mamla*) to be settled amicably by the spouses. She said that in such cases it was our responsibility (*zimmedari*) to invoke our rights (*huq*). The register of rights is invoked as something which we must collectively fight for. This is most succinctly expressed in her assertion:

> Say if you go to the police *chowki* and speak to them and it appears that our rights are of no consequence. This attitude will not do. They [the police] must register a complaint. You must confront them and tell them that these are our rights (*humara huq*) and you [the police] must take action.

She further added that because the public was scared, no one spoke about their rights. In fact, she spoke of her own rights as the right that allowed her to do something for others. She said that she joined a *mandal* (women's organisation) that allowed her to fight for the rights of other women.

The mandate of reconstituting religious authority in community spaces is an important aim of the BMMA. In both the ethnographic vignettes presented earlier, there is an attempt to challenge gendered hierarchies in the everyday practice of minority rights. The appointment and adjudication of female *qazi*s is a contentious debate in the realm of alternative dispute resolution forums in India. The BMMA has been at the forefront of a struggle for the training and appointment of female *qazi*s. The AIMPLB, a body that administers Muslim Personal Law in India, has refused to recognise the authority of female *qazi*s. Similarly, in the ethnographic vignette of the woman who was denied a copy of the Quran as well as the instance where women were denied access to the police station, there was an emphasis on collective agency and mobilisation to claim a right to religious freedom as a community of pious Muslim women. Both these attempts can be read as efforts to negotiate and reconstitute power in the domain of Muslim law, which consists of alternative dispute resolution forums. In negotiating this domain, women collectively organise to question gendered inequality as practised by both state and non-state actors – for example, the local *maulana* and *qazi* and the police who refuse to file women's complaints. Hence, these interventions are gendered engagements with minority rights. The right to freedom of religion is invoked to negotiate gendered hierarchies within the legal domain of minority rights. These negotiations with the right to religious freedom are mediated by a conception of both a pious, ethical duty as God's agents and an ethic of collective association and rights activism that draws upon the constitutional framework of rights. These negotiations are also informed by notions of self-constitution through commitment to a pious and ethical duty (*zimmedari*) towards one's community. The notion of duty is embedded in an Islamic feminist ethic of piety (*taqwa*) and a belief in the oneness of God (*tawhid*). Niaz and Soman, the founder members of the BMMA, write that Muslim women are embracing 'Islamic and universal ideas of *tawhid* [unicity of God] and *taqwa* [piety] which encourages us to love all as creations of God' and 'are seeking justice within families and reclaiming their right to read the Holy Quran and arrive at meanings based on their lived realities'. In a personal communication, Niaz drew extensively on the concept of unity of God (*tawheed*) in the works of African American scholar Amina Wadud. Drawing on Wadud's work, Niaz wrote that *tawheed* is a fundamental principle of Islam which she associated with good conduct (*akhlaqiyat*). She noted that Allah is one, and even contradictory attributes of nature are part of this one entity. She further added that Allah does not have a gender. She argued that since Islam is a complete way of life, allegiance to *tawheed* must be articulated in the everyday. As agents (*khalifa*s) of Allah on earth, humans had the responsibility (*zimmedari*) to maintain a relationship of reconciliation (*talmel*), unity (*ekta*) and equality (*barabari*) in their lives. It is important to note that the site of reconciliation and unity is not the family here. She went on to say that reconciliation and unity are part of a larger project of being, of harmonious existence not only with humans but with all of creation. Yet in the domain of political action of the movement, the desired ideal of *tawhid* often came into conflict with contingent human realities of domination, inequality and lack of respect towards fellow human beings.[2] In these instances, it was imperative for pious women to challenge inequality. This mode of challenging inequality was not merely an exercise of individual freedom or autonomy but part of a larger project of constituting oneself as God's agents within a *tawhidic* paradigm.

At the same time, these invocations of the right to religious freedom are embedded in an ethic of inhabiting constitutional guarantees of equality and non-discrimination in the everyday. In their writings, the founder members of the BMMA talk about Muslim personal law in terms of preserving and reclaiming the democratic space guaranteed by the Constitution for the 'development' of minority communities, building on provisions such as non-discrimination and equality before the law. Rights-bearing citizenship is constituted in the active role taken by Muslim women in 'organising and mobilising themselves across the country' in the political space guaranteed by the Constitution to fight for a 'just and Quran-compliant family law'.

While the Constitution did not explicitly recognise the protection of minority rights and religion-based personal law, a legal pluralist regime constituted by religion-based personal laws, criminal laws that provide protection against domestic violence and destitution to women and case laws on maintenance have made it possible for women to reclaim a space of rights activism while inhabiting the category of minority rights. In postcolonial India, minority rights claims for the Muslim minority could only be made vis-à-vis Muslim personal law as the political possibilities of Muslim political representation gradually diminished.

The right to religious freedom is not merely an abstract right, but it is also claimed in embodied ways through collective mobilisation against inequality. This is instantiated in the discussions on collective protests against the practice of triple *talaq*.[3] The activists and the participants of the workshop discussed particular kinds of collective mobilisation against triple *talaq* as an example of the exercise of the right to freedom of religion. The exercise of claiming the right to freedom of religion entailed an embodied experience of self-making.

In conversations in the workshop, women said that they organised a public campaign against the practice of triple *talaq*, obtained signatures of women in neighbourhoods in Mumbai and organised press conferences against this cultural practice. Participants in the workshops said that triple *talaq* was a human practice and not something mandated by the Quran. The movement had carried out the important task of disseminating this message about the rights (*huq*) in the Quran to women. In almost every workshop, Niaz would urge members who participated in the movement to reflect on how they had mobilised against the cultural practice of triple *talaq*. In response to these questions, women would come up with a detailed list of activities that they had carried out to mobilise others for the fight against triple *talaq*. In one of these workshops that was organised a few weeks after the Supreme Court judgment on triple *talaq*, there was a detailed conversation on the number of activities that eventually led to filing a petition in the Supreme Court demanding that the practice be declared unconstitutional. On this occasion, women especially emphasised the importance of public rallies that inspired them to assert their rights in the apex Court. I provide an exchange here between three members which demonstrates this assertion of collective agency:

> Lia: In 2012, we organised a big press conference. Women had come. They narrated their hardships, their stories. They narrated what all they have had to endure because of triple *talaq*. A lot of women were in tears. We carried out two–three sit-in demonstrations in Victoria Terminus. We carried out continuous advocacy.
>
> Noorjehan: How many public meetings did we carry out? How many times have we organised big meetings where we have provided space for women to talk?
>
> Mumtaz: We carried out many press conferences, *dharnas* [sit-in demonstrations].
>
> Suraiya: We organised many meetings and press conferences so that women knew that they could fight for their rights (*huq*) and they went up to the Supreme Court.

In these ethnographic vignettes, the right to freedom of religion as a conceptual category is conceptualised in embodied ways. The domain of protests against triple *talaq* is a way of claiming the right to freedom of religion. But the exercise of this right needs to be understood through the particular ways in which women use their bodies to claim it. In the discussions on triple *talaq*, right to religious freedom is claimed in public rallies, demonstrations, protests, meetings and press conferences. It is an assertion of collective agency that is prompted by the embodied performance of women suffering because of this cultural practice staged in demonstrations and public rallies.

These protests hinge on the perception that triple *talaq* is a human practice and not something mandated by the Quran. On one occasion, one of the participants in the workshop said:

> The BMMA has carried out the task of spreading the message of the Quran among women (*Quran ki baat auraton tak pahuchane ka kaam*). Women were not aware of what is written in the Quran. The BMMA carried out this useful job of disseminating the message of the Quran among the people. We impressed upon the people that triple *talaq* is a human 'practice' (*insano ki practice*) and not divinely mandated or condoned by the Quran. This is the most important point.

The centrality of the Quran and the dissemination of the message of the Quran are apparent in the conversation on triple *talaq*. The Quranic text is never challenged. Instead, the role of the BMMA in spreading the correct message of the Quran is emphasised. My aim in discussing the example of the triple *talaq* was to illustrate how the practice of minority rights and other liberal freedoms, in this instance the right to religious freedom, is shaped by particular uses of the body as well a range of ethical commitments. Tracing these embodiments and ethical commitments advances our understanding of novel ways in which we might conceptualise minority rights. Abstract discussions of liberal goods cannot shed light on these aspects of the practice of minority rights and liberal freedoms.

Divorce rights: Quranic *huq*, minority rights and obligation to God

In the workshops conducted by members of the BMMA, Muslim women's rights were derived from values in the Quran such as compassion (*raham*) and justice (*insaf*). Marriage and divorce rights went hand in hand, with an emphasis on women memorising relevant verses of the Quran and committing themselves to a life of faith and piety. At the same time, marriage and divorce rights were part of a conversation on addressing the gender inequality of the legal framework of Muslim personal law and were thus tied to a conception of a Muslim minority community governed by Muslim personal law.

In the workshops conducted by Noorjehan Safia Niaz, she emphasised the principle of *raham* as informing the conduct of the spouses at the point of breakdown of marriage and hence the need for spouses to be dignified and respectful were they to divorce each other. The divorce rights of Muslim women were derived from this principle of *raham*, which was conceptualised as a principle of the Quran. In the elaboration of the passages of the Quran, Muslim women's rights were envisaged within a framework of equal moral membership in a just, pious community guided by principles of the Quran. In all sessions, members emphasised the story of cosmic creation in the Quran, which highlighted how men and women were created by God out of the same *nafs* (substance). This was contrasted with the biblical story of creation, which emphasised how a woman was created from a man's ribs. Niaz stressed the importance of memorising the verses of the Quran that were relevant to women's rights (*huq*).

In workshops run by Niaz as well as other members, the Ayats of Surah Baqr and Surah Talaq of the Quran were used to frame an argument for restraint and compassion in the act of divorce. In framing a discourse of Muslim women's rights, the principle of compassion was privileged over the need to preserve the heterosexual family. This is amply borne out by the way in which members of the movement read the following verse from Surah Baqr to talk about divorce rights:

> If you have divorced the women, and they have reached their required interim period, then either remain together or part ways in a just fashion (*insaf se rahiye ya insaf se alag rasta apnaiye*). Do not reconcile with them so you can harm them out of animosity. Whoever does so is doing wickedness to his person [*sic*]. Do not take God's signs lightly; remember God's blessings towards you, and what was sent down to you of the book and the wisdom, He warns you with it. Be conscientious of God and know that God is Knowledgeable in all things.[4]

Verses from Surah Talaq (65: 1 and 65: 2) would usually be cited to argue for a just, compassionate method of divorce.

> O you prophet, if any of you have divorced the women, then they should be divorced while ensuring that their required interim is fulfilled and

keep count of the interim. You shall reverence God your Lord, and do not evict the women from their homes, nor should they leave, unless they have committed a proven adultery. These are God's limits. Anyone who transgresses God's limits has wronged his person. You never know; perhaps God will make something come out of this.[5]

Then, once the interim is fulfilled, either you remain together equitably, or part ways in a just manner and have it witnessed by two just people from among you; This is to enlighten those who acknowledge God and the Last day. Whosoever reveres God, He will look out for him.[6]

In her elaboration of the verses, she emphasised the principles of compassion (*raham*) and justice (*insaaf*) that one must abide by because this is what the Quran stood for. On one occasion, Niaz said, 'So the principles of Islam that we talk about have not come out of thin air. This (the Quran) is where we got it from. So the two words that have been used are justice (*insaaf*) and compassion (*rehemdili*).'

Niaz and her colleagues are engaged in a larger project of challenging gendered hierarchies in the everyday functioning of Muslim personal law in neighbourhoods in Mumbai. The BMMA is also invested in a more elaborate and detailed codification of Muslim personal law to do away with cultural practices that are inimical to gender equality. In the everyday construction of marriage and divorce rights, rights are not merely conceptualised as abstract legal entitlements. The process of claiming rights is linked to ethical conduct on the part of both the spouses. In Niaz's training sessions, the discussions are not merely about rights but about notions of good, ethical conduct that are associated with the reward and the claiming of these rights. Giving women what is due to them when the marriage fails is considered ethical conduct. Marriage and divorce rights are derived from this imperative on men to act in ethical ways.

It is important here to delineate how the notion of ethical conduct, compassion and justice squares with gendered roles in the heterosexual family. The verses of the Quran that are cited in the training sessions emphasise the importance of parting ways in a just fashion as also behaving in an ethical, compassionate and just way at the point of breakdown of the heteronormative family rather than on the preservation of the family as such. Hence, the Quranic verses referred to in the discussion on marriage and divorce refer to divorce or the point of breakdown in marriage. There were no discussions in the training sessions on the sacrosanct nature of marriage or the family but rather on what rights couples might claim when there was a crisis in the family.

In a similar training session, Suraiya Shaikh, one of the members of the BMMA, in her interaction with her students said that the Quran was their faith (*iman*) and that as Muslims it was their duty to abide by the Quran. In this workshop, Shaikh spoke about the rights (*huq*) granted to women by the Quran while critiquing the practice of arbitrary, oral, unilateral divorce given by men, popularly known as triple *talaq*. She introduced her training session as one where students would be taught about the rights (*huq*) granted by God in the Ayats of the Quran:

> These are the Ayats of the Quran where Allah has spoken about the rights (*huq*) of women. We are giving you the meaning and translation of those Ayats here.

In an interaction with men and women in a neighbourhood where she tried to recruit students for the movement, Shaikh said that God had sent human beings on earth so that they could worship (*ibadat karna*) Allah and that each of us is duty bound to work as God's agents. I reconstruct Shaikh's interventions in this moment below. Shaikh introduced the work of the BMMA in a workshop. She mentioned that the movement had a presence in 13 states and reached more than 1 lakh people. She said at the start of the session that Allah has created both men and women from the same *nafs* and hence both men and women are entitled to read the namaz (*Allah tala ne aadmi aur aurat ko ek nafs se banaya hai. Namaz dono padhte hai.*).

She then recounted a story that had been told to her by the *maulvi* (religious scholar) who taught her Arabic:

> Gaffar Janab told me a story. There was a man who used to pray day and night but he always spoke ill of people. Then there was another man who would not pray but would constantly help people. Then Allah talah said that the second man is going to Heaven and the first one is going to Hell. But I also feel that you shouldn't go around telling people that you should go to Jannat [heaven], and you should go to Jahannam (hell). I said Allah talah has made such a beautiful world for us. There are such beautiful, lush greens, rains that replenish the earth. There is the beauty of changing seasons. There is nature and there is God. We will *have* to love nature and God.

In this extract, submission to God is not presented as a choice. Working as God's agents on earth and loving God is what constitutes the agency and personhood of the pious person. Shaikh also took great care in training her students how to read the Quran, how to distinguish between the different Ayats and where to pause. For example, she pointed to the sections of verses that needed to be stressed in particular ways during the recitation. She also provided illustrative examples from the Sunnat or the Prophet's way of life from time to time. Shaikh's interlocutors usually demonstrated a lot of excitement and enthusiasm about reading and discovering the verses of the Quran. Shaikh often understood her project of conducting workshops and training women as part of the divine duty to share knowledge (*ilm*). She often said, 'The Quran keeps talking about sharing knowledge. Whatever *ilm* (knowledge) you have, convey it to people in a correct manner (*sahi tareeqa*). Nothing else increases if you share it. But *ilm* is something that grows as you share it.'

The training sessions emphasised the importance of creating spaces where Muslim women could come together to empower one another. This was a function of the particular social location of Muslims and Muslim women as a religious minority. In one of her training sessions, Niaz argued that though all women had similar concerns, Muslim women had particular issues related to their social (*samaj*) and religious, communal (*mazhab*) location. Muslim communities in India have remained socio-economically marginalised because of persistent discrimination against and violence towards religious minorities by the state and the Hindu right-wing non-state actors. Niaz argued that a backward community meant that women felt the brunt of unjust forms of domination in the family even more acutely. The fight for the rights of Muslim women, she argued, were mediated by this social context.

In an expository statement to members attending her workshop, Niaz said that the BMMA sought to create a narrative of claiming the rights of Muslim women guaranteed by the Constitution and the rights (*huq*) guaranteed by the Quran. This narrative of rights claims is conflated with creation of spaces where Muslim women could come together to empower each other and talk about their problems without any fear or hesitation:

> Now if a community is backward, can the women of the community progress? No, the women are then even more backward. They are not supposed to study or work or step out of the house. As soon as she comes of age, she is married off and then she's expected to reproduce 5–6 kids.

This is her domain. We wanted to build an organisation where Muslim women could come together and talk about their [Muslim women's] problems without any fear or hesitation. They would help each other get stronger (*Aapas mein ek dusre ke saath taqat badhaye – apas mein ek dusre ki taaqat badhaiye*).

There were discussions about the positions of the movement with respect to marriage, divorce and maintenance, and they were with reference to the text of a proposed draft bill that demands a more gender just Muslim personal law. The draft bill that Noorjehan Safia Niaz used in her workshops spoke of Muslim women as members of a community who needed a more gender-just codified Muslim law as other religious minority communities had their own laws.[7] The statement of objects and reasons talks about how the draft has been formulated in keeping with the 'human rights framework of the Constitution' and the 'spirit of gender justice' in the Quran. The demand for codifying a gender-just Muslim personal law as well as popularising it in community spaces is considered an attempt to safeguard their rights 'as Muslim women'. The objects and reasons in the statement of the Bill argued that 'if Muslim women do not draft the law, nobody will. We realised that neither the community religious leadership nor the state have any interest in the subject.'

This draft Bill asked for enhanced divorce rights for Muslim women, limits to men's rights to divorce and regulation of polygamy. It invokes the constitutional principles of religious and gender equality as enunciated in Articles 14 and 15 of the Indian Constitution. It enhances women's rights to divorce as it includes 'irretrievable breakdown' of marriage as a ground for divorce in addition to the existing grounds for divorce, bans oral, unilateral divorce pronounced by men and enhances the woman's right to initiate divorce without the consent of her husband (*khula*). In order to regulate arbitrary authority of men over women, it also introduces a Quranic method of divorce that is informed by the principle of compassion (*raham*) and includes methods of arbitration. At the same time, the draft Bill asks for compulsory registration of marriages, sets a minimum age of marriage at 21 and prevents polygamy.

Constituting minority rights

In my exploration of the training sessions of the BMMA on Muslim personal law and the fundamental rights guaranteed in the Indian Constitution,

I have traced the ethical ways in which women negotiate the domain of minority rights. We conceptualise minority rights as a bouquet of rights including marriage and divorce rights under Muslim personal law and some fundamental rights, such as the right to freedom of religion, the right to equality and the right to freedom of association guaranteed under the Indian Constitution. Women bring together an Islamic feminist ethics and an ethical commitment to collective mobilisation against gendered discrimination in Muslim law in their negotiations with the domain of minority rights. Their ethical commitment is conceptualised using the language of duty (*zimmedari*) towards creating a more just world as God's agents, which informs their construction of the right to religious freedom. The right to religious freedom is conceptualised as a right that enables women to carry out their duty as God's agents. This right is conceptualised by the women participating in these workshops and the activists of the BMMA in embodied ways in public meetings, rallies, conferences, demonstrations and protests through particular uses of the body. The right to religious freedom, therefore, needs to be conceptualised in terms of embodiment of this right in moments of collective organisation of Muslim minorities.

Marriage and divorce rights within the framework of Muslim personal law are conceptualised in terms of everyday ethical conduct of the spouses towards one another in moments when they claim these rights. This chapter has thus highlighted how a range of ethical commitments and bodily ways of inhabiting rights constitute engagements with minority rights and other liberal rights. The language of rights is used to challenge the authority of male *qazi*s, collectively demand enhanced access to public services, emphasise the importance of respectful conduct at points of breakdown in the marriage, emphasise the divine duty to share *ilm* (knowledge) and create spaces for collective communal solidarity among Muslim women. The ethnographic vignettes draw attention not only to the substantive rights claims but also to *how* women claim their rights; the vignettes show the ethical and everyday motivations that shape their engagements with rights and the law.

My ethnographic exploration here illuminates how we might think about minority rights and liberal freedoms beyond textual approaches. I have delineated here a range of rich negotiations with rights. My exploration establishes the salience of everyday ethics and the conceptual architecture and the modes of practice of the same. Such explorations advance our understanding of minority rights, gender and liberalism in novel directions.

The discourse and practice of duty is constituted in these moments of negotiation with texts as well as collective mobilisation against particular practices such as oral, unilateral divorce and gendered hierarchies in neighbourhoods. An ethnographic exploration allows us to reconstruct and theorise this complex field of interaction between minority rights and other liberal freedoms such as the right to freedom of religion. My ethnographic exploration here brings out how minority rights can be theorised in these moments of interaction between sets of rights. Ethnographic approaches allow us to advance our knowledge of minority rights beyond the abstractions of normative theorising and also enrich our understanding of minority rights and liberalism in a non-Western context. There can be ways of exploring and conceptualising minority rights that do not align with the standard tensions between the individual and community or the language of state accommodation of minority rights by the liberal state that animates scholarship on liberal multiculturalism.

In theorising minority rights and their entanglements with other liberal freedoms from a grounded perspective, as well as analysing the way in which ethics and the notion of duty play an important role in the everyday construction of minority rights, this chapter advances my overall aims of decolonising debates on minority rights in political theory. In reconstructing the everyday life of the legal domain of minority rights in India through an ethnographic exploration of the workshops of the BMMA, this chapter advances our understanding of minority rights beyond reified, textual legal categories. Debates on minority rights and gender often replicate a reified conception of minority cultures and religion. This reification becomes particularly apparent in a legal, juridical construction of Muslim family laws relating to marriage, divorce and maintenance. My ethnographic approach unhinges minority rights from a textual understanding of the law and legality. In my exploration of the workshops of the BMMA, Muslim personal law and its links with a range of liberal freedoms can be understood in terms of a range of registers such as ethics, duty and lived everyday processes such as embodiment and collective, communal assertion of agency. This is borne out by the way in which notions of duty towards God, everyday ethical conduct, compassion and embodied collective action are brought to bear on the conceptualisation of Muslim family law and its interactions with liberal freedoms, such as the right to freedom of religion. In analysing these processes through ethnographic exploration, my approach aims to dismantle reified, colonial forms of knowledge about the law and legality and minority communities, especially in relation to the study of Muslim family law and minority rights in India.

I pay attention to the details of everyday negotiations and also speak to the context within which the meaning of minority rights is framed by my interlocutors. These moments, I argue, are moments where the praxis of minority rights gets a new lease of life as it is reclaimed by Muslim women. The interventions of Muslim women resonate with a tradition of liberalism in India focused on state action to address social inequality and mobilise group-differentiated rights, even though their interventions reconstitute and reconfigure state power and bring it in conversation with transnational feminist activist ideas in the everyday.[8] Everyday negotiations with minority rights articulate particular grievances of Muslim women. The negotiations also become sites for ethical and gendered self-fashioning of Muslim women. Hence, it can be argued that religious minorities in these instances reimagine themselves as a political rather than merely a numerical and juridical category. This resonates with Dr Ambedkar's political conception of minorities as different from merely a territorial and numerical idea of minority.[9] Ambedkar clearly distinguished the political conception of minorities based on lack of social and economic deprivation from a numerical understanding of minorities.[10] In the moments of negotiations with the legal framework of minority rights discussed above, these frameworks are being imagined in novel ways to articulate gendered inequality within the Muslim family. A new ethical commitment to work collectively towards addressing inequality as aggrieved Muslim women is instantiated.

At the same time, by presenting the entanglements of ethics and bodies that constitute the domain of minority rights, my approach qualifies anthropological conceptions of minority rights and religious freedom as expressions of sovereign state power. The anthropological scholarship sheds light on minority rights as an expression of sovereign power and outlines the generative and disciplinary capacity of the liberal, secular state. But this scholarship runs the risk of reifying a Western European conception of the liberal, secular state. The story of minority rights and liberalism in India provides us with a far richer conception of how some liberal commitments are engaged in the everyday in ways that make us question a reified conception of the liberal, secular state. We also miss out on a fine-grained conceptual analysis of the lived life of minority rights in non-Western contexts if we merely focus on the sovereign power and authority of the state. In this chapter, my analytical labour has been to further a more nuanced everyday as well as conceptual understanding of minority rights that privileges ethics and embodiment and everyday articulations of the rights of minorities in a language of duty. This is, I argue, a project of decolonising the study of minority rights in political theory. Decolonising is not merely a project of critiquing the West or a form of nativism, but it also entails questioning predominant modes of theorising in political theory. In this chapter, my ethnographic investigations have charted new ways of conceptualising minority rights that build upon the everyday engagements with these rights in India as well as a range of materials that have not been traditionally explored as archives of political theory.

Notes

1. Amina Wadud, *Qur'an and Woman: Rereading the Sacred Text from a Woman's Perspective* (New York: Oxford University Press, USA, 1999).
2. Niaz, personal communication.
3. Triple *talaq* is a form of oral, unilateral divorce practiced in India. In this practice, the utterance of the word 'talaq' three times leads to the wife being divorced by the husband. This practice is recognized in the Hanafi tradition of Sunni Islam. Muslim women's mobilization around Muslim personal law in India recently has questioned the legality and constitutionality of this method of divorce.
4. Bharatiya Muslim Mahila Andolan, *The Legal Rights of Muslim Women: Protected and Promoted by the Quran* (n.p., n.d.).
5. Ibid.
6. Ibid.
7. *Muslim Family Law, 2017: Draft for the Bill*, 1.
8. Bajpai, 'Liberalisms in India'; Rao, *The Caste Question*.
9. Evidence of Dr. Ambedkar before the Indian Statutory Commission on 23 October 1928, in BAWS, vol. 2, 465.
10. Evidence before the Simon Commission, in BAWS, vol. 2, 465.

2

Becoming equals

Gender equality as an ethical commitment*

In a bustling neighbourhood in a bylane off the Western Express Highway in Mumbai, a small room houses the women's *sharia adalat* (alternative dispute resolution forum) of the BMMA. The women's *sharia* court, as it is popularly known, is presided over only by activists of the BMMA who have been trained as *qazi* who resolve marital disputes.[1] In the adjudication of cases, the *qazi* heard both the sides when a couple approached the court for resolving a matrimonial dispute. She often advised both men and women to demonstrate compassion (*raham*) in their everyday interactions even at the point of breakdown of a marriage. Suraiya Shaikh, a female *qazi*, conducted training sessions on Muslim family law on marriage, divorce and maintenance for women of the neighbourhood. In her training sessions, she often emphasised the spiritual equality of men and women and how they were equally obligated to lead a life of piety. Shaikh would invoke this notion of equality to critique social and legal inequality between men and women.

In this chapter, I analyse the concept of gender equality as it is constituted by activists and adjudicators of the BMMA. In doing so, I delineate how notions of ethics are brought to bear on the concept of gender equality. While the previous chapter showed how the right to religious freedom is constituted in ethical ways using the language of duty by activists while they navigate the framework of minority rights and Muslim family law, this chapter

---

*This chapter is a reworked version of an article previously published as 'Becoming Equals: The Meaning and Practice of Gender Equality in an Islamic Feminist Movement in India', *Feminist Theory* 23, no. 4 (2022): 423–443.

focuses on the concept of gender equality. In debates on multiculturalism, gender equality has been a bone of contention. Liberal feminists have often been preoccupied with the question of balancing gender equality with the cultural and religious rights of minority communities. Theorists working within a liberal multiculturalist paradigm dwell upon the state regulation of minority cultural, ethnic and religious practices for the attainment of normative goods such as freedom, autonomy and gender equality.[2] There is, on the one hand, Okin's rather crude characterisation of cultures that are 'religious ones and those that look to the past – to ancient texts of revered traditions' – as discriminating against women.[3] Okin's work suffers from a careless characterisation of cultures and religions. Shachar, on the other hand, proposes a joint governance model where adjudicatory power is shared between the state and religious, cultural communities to balance gender equality and cultural accommodation.[4] In her recent work, Anne Phillips expands the ambit of this debate beyond the state to examine reformist social movements in the twentieth century shaped by religious beliefs that endorse 'gender, racial, and economic quality'.[5] Hence, Phillips expands the debate beyond state regulation of religion. But she does not eschew the liberal preoccupation with balancing group claims with individual rights and gender equality altogether. Recent feminist and anthropological scholars have engaged questions of religious reform and women's engagement with religion.[6]

Anthropological scholarship on women's ethical self-fashioning has traced the tension between ethical commitments to piety and liberal feminist notions of gender equality.[7] Mahmood's critique of liberal feminist conceptions of gender equality can be situated within similar scholarship in the postcolonial feminist theory tradition[8] and postcolonial anthropology[9] that questions the suitability of Western, liberal feminist categories for understanding women's concerns in other parts of the world. Mahmood traces this tension in her exploration of the piety movement in Egypt. She argues that women's religious participation in this movement was 'critically structured by, and serves to uphold, a discursive tradition that regards subordination to a transcendent will (and thus, in many instances, to male authority) as its coveted goal'.[10] Ethical self-fashioning, conceptualised by Mahmood within a Foucauldian tradition of ethics, requires subjects to 'transform themselves into the willing subjects of a particular moral discourse' by means of 'operations on their own bodies and souls, thoughts, conduct, and way of being'.[11] Mahmood contends that the Islamic discursive tradition that inspired the participants of an Islamic revivalist movement in twentieth-century Egypt has historically entailed subordination to a transcendent will, to male authority and to some notions of gendered segregation and has endorsed distinct roles for men and women in society.[12] Therefore, it is not compatible with liberal notions of gender equality. She argues that women's self-descriptions need to be taken seriously instead of merely reducing them to a 'secular-liberal register' and weighing them against the 'goals of progressive politics'.[13] Mahmood's work has inspired several anthropological and historical explorations of the disciplinary power and myriad articulations of the secular state.[14]

Hence, ethical self-fashioning, as conceptualised by Mahmood, works on a register that is different from the universe of the law and liberal, legal languages and traditions. Minority rights and religion-based family law systems are also considered by some anthropologists of secularism as perpetuating the disciplinary power of the sovereign state.[15] Separate religion-based family laws are often considered a marker of minority cultural rights protected and accommodated by the liberal, secular state. Religion-based personal laws or the family laws work through entrenching a public–private divide. In this schema of the public–private divide, religion is consigned to the private sphere.[16] The domain of gendered family relations such as marriage, divorce and maintenance is considered by the state to belong in the private sphere as well as in the sphere of religion. The state both defines and regulates religion through religion-based family laws. The gendered ideology of the state shapes the private sphere of the family and religion. This mechanism of confining religion to the private sphere as well as the state regulation of the private sphere purportedly amplifies the legal, juridical dimensions of religion and ignores the moral, ethical realm.[17] Hence, the state's gendered ideology shapes the politics and praxis of minority rights.[18] Consequently, religion-based family law is considered the domain where gender equality is compromised. Hence, a lot of liberal feminist concerns about multiculturalism, especially about religion-based personal laws, revolve around gender equality.

Yet in these debates on multiculturalism, minority rights and gender equality, a grounded conception of gender equality is missing. In this chapter, I deparochialise the concept of gender equality with respect to family law and minority rights. My project of deparochialising gender equality entails addressing the postcolonial critique of the universality of the ideal of gender equality as conceptualised by liberal feminists. While some postcolonial scholarship has focused on the liberal feminist moorings of gender equality, I provide in this chapter a grounded conception of gender equality. This ethic and practice of gender equality emerges in a specific juncture in India at the intersection of social location, everyday gendered struggles and a transnational Islamic feminist ethic. This grounded notion of gender equality is constituted in moments when activists navigate the domain of Muslim family law that is constituted by multiple state and non-state actors. Paying close attention to this category of gender equality enables us to expand our scope of enquiry into gender equality beyond a mere critique of its putative Western liberal universal mooring. This can be achieved by exploring multiple registers such as moral, ethical commitments and practices that constitute this domain instead of reducing them to an abstract normative liberal definition of gender equality.

Delineating the meaning and practice of gender equality also helps us nuance our understanding of how the legal domain of Muslim family law as well as minority rights is constituted in the everyday. We move the conversation on minority rights beyond multicultural accommodation by a purported neutral, liberal state to an analysis of various aspects of the legal framework of minority rights and their ethical and everyday conceptual dimensions. In the subsequent section, I briefly outline the organisational structure of the BMMA and the role of female *qazi* and activists in the movement. In the next two ethnographic sections, I analyse the practical, ethical and conceptual dimensions of gender equality vis-à-vis Muslim family law. In the final section of this chapter, I analyse how my ethnographic exploration can contribute to deparochialising gender equality and decolonising political theory debates on minority rights.

Organisational structure of the BMMA

Founded as a movement advocating for gender justice within the legal framework of Muslim family law in India in 2007, the BMMA began its sharia *adalat* programme in 2013.[19] Members of the BMMA were already prominent activists in neighbourhoods where the *sharia* courts came into being. In 2013, sharia courts were founded by members of the BMMA in Mumbai, Pune, Ahmedabad and Dindigul. In the run-up to the establishment of the *sharia* courts, activists of the BMMA were trained as female *qazi*s (Islamic judges).[20] Activists had not been formally trained in Islamic law or in state law. The training sessions included lessons in the basic tents of the Quran, the various schools of Islamic law, principles of the Constitution and an introduction to other legislation focused on gender justice, such as the Domestic Violence Act 2005. The *sharia* court in Mumbai was always abuzz with activity and frequented by several Muslim women in the neighbourhood as well as from other parts of the city. There was the odd case of a Hindu couple approaching the forum, but the litigants who approached the forum were predominantly Muslim women. The office that housed the *sharia* court was managed by several members of the BMMA. Members of the BMMA took on multiple roles in the neighbourhoods where they were active. In addition to performing the role of the *qazi*, members of the BMMA noted down details of cases in a register, carried out data entry of cases on a computer, sent summons to husbands against whom a complaint had been filed, liased with the local police station, and so on. Some members who had been trained as *qazi* also frequented neighbouring localities to sensitise women on various aspects of Muslim family law and gender justice.

Practising pious equality

Suraiya Shaikh, an activist and a female *qazi* associated with the BMMA, a resident of Mumbai, grew up in Behrampada, a poor, now predominantly Muslim neighbourhood in Mumbai. Most people living in this neighbourhood had migrated to Mumbai from parts of Uttar Pradesh. Suraiya grew up in a slum with six other siblings. Her father was a religious scholar (*maulana*). She did not receive much of a formal education but was trained to read the Quran by a religious scholar. When she was growing up, she witnessed several incidents of everyday misogyny, violence and discrimination against women in her neighbourhood, including domestic violence, men divorcing women arbitrarily, and so on. As a believer, she would often ask herself how God could allow women to be subjected to such injustice. She was married off when she finished school. Thanks to a supportive husband, she was able to pursue higher education and study for her graduation. Suraiya had witnessed the violence and mayhem caused by the Mumbai riots in 1992.

On several occasions following the riots, she along with other women in her neighbourhood, protested police excesses such as arbitrary detention of youth from her neighbourhood. Subsequently, she joined a women's organisation (Mahila Shakti Mandal) in 1998 that engaged in community adjudication of marital disputes in the neighbourhood. Suraiya and other activists of the BMMA were part of such initiatives in Mumbai. In 2001, Suraiya joined the Women's Research and Action Group (WRAG), a voluntary organisation which trained women on issues of public health, Muslim personal law and the provisions of the Constitution. In 2001, as she started working with the WRAG, Suraiya got to know Noorjehan Safia Niaz. She was introduced to Quranic exegetical traditions, and in 2013 she trained as a *qazi* (a female Islamic judge) as part of an initiative of the BMMA.[21]

Suraiya conducted workshops and training sessions in neighbourhoods in Mumbai, such as Bharatnagar, Golibar and Navpada, with Muslim women aged between 15 and 40 years. These neighbourhoods, with mostly mixed populations, became predominantly populated by Muslims following the riots in 1992–1993.[22] They are characterised by poor civic amenities, a lack of proper roads and a very high density of population. Suraiya's workshops on the Quran and Muslim personal law took place against the backdrop of heated debates in the public sphere about the legal reform of Muslim personal law and the criminalisation of cultural practices such as oral, unilateral divorce.[23] The participants of these workshops were mostly women working in the informal economy from neighbourhoods with a large Muslim population where the BMMA activists had networks. The workshops would usually be held in the homes of one of the BMMA activists, where she would invite women from the neighbourhood to participate. Some women would be drawn to the concerns discussed in these workshops and would in turn recruit more women to the movement; they would also offer their homes for organising similar workshops.

At the start of the workshops that I observed, Suraiya distributed pamphlets containing verses of the Quran that spoke to women's marital rights, including Surah Nisa and Surah Al-Baqr, and encouraged students to read and memorise these verses.

She emphasised the pious obligations of both men and women to God as proof of their equal status in society and urged them to cultivate piety. She took great pains to impress upon her female students, including young girls and women from the neighbourhood attending the workshop, the importance of reading and memorising some of the verses of the Quran. Her students showed enthusiasm for learning and discovering these lessons and understanding the values of the Quran that Suraiya tried to impress upon them. But they also brought up instances of social interaction where women were discriminated against.

Her students would refer to various kinds of social taboos in these neighbourhoods around older women marrying younger men, the employment of women and power exercised by men over women through sudden pronouncement of divorce. Suraiya would usually emphasise the socially (*samajik*) constructed nature of these forms of gender discrimination and offer an alternative vision of gender relations premised on meanings of the Quranic values of equality (*barabari*), compassion (*raham*), justice (*insaf*) and reason (*aql*). She then spelt out the correct form of conduct for persons involved in these social interactions by linking gender equality (*barabari*) with the attributes of everyday justice (*insaf*) and compassion (*raham*). These values should guide the conduct of persons, who must treat one another as equals. In the domain of marital discord and divorce, honouring the values of justice and compassion meant parting ways peacefully in the event of a divorce without any ill-feeling, resentment, or intention to harm each other. Suraiya also advocated for women taking up work and repudiated social norms that stopped them from doing so. She cautioned her students against self-proclaimed scholars (*alim*) who boasted of their knowledge of religion. She scoffed at the arrogance of the male custodians of religion (*dharm ke thekedar*).

On one occasion, one of Suraiya's students mentioned that men often divorced women in a fit of rage, and if women retorted angrily, people cast aspersions on the character of the woman. Suraiya responded, 'So this is wrong. In Allah's eyes, both are equal.' The student replied that men in the neighbourhood do not brook such reasoning. At this point, Suraiya pointed to the leaflets with the verses of the Quran and emphatically said, 'After all we will die one day, we are all Muslims, so we *must* follow the Quran. We are not making up these rules ourselves.'

Subsequently, she referred to a proper method of divorce and mentioned the purpose of the observance of the *iddat* period.[24] She said that this period was necessary to provide some calm (*sukoon*) to the mind of the woman and help her come to terms with the changed circumstances of her life. Invoking Surah 2:221, Suraiya would argue that men and women should either stay together or part ways in a just fashion (*insaf se rahiye ya insaf se alag rasta apnaiye*). This meant that they should not indulge in casting aspersions on one another's character. Spouses should not hurt each other (*nuksan pahuchana*), say unkind words (*galat lafz*) or indulge in resentment and enmity (*dushmani*) towards each other. There will be no blame game because in Allah's eyes everyone is equal, and they need to be just towards each other.

In Suraiya's understanding, the *iddat* period is part of a larger scheme of a proper method of divorce where men and women as spiritual equals are to be guided by the tenets of justice (*insaf*) in their actions. When one of her female students asked her if women could go to work during the *iddat* period, Suraiya replied in the affirmative. She said that if the woman was the only breadwinner and needed to provide for her children, she could go to work and need not observe *iddat*. The question of women not being allowed to work during the *iddat* came up on other occasions too. Suraiya appreciated the situation of economic precarity of women in these situations. On one occasion, one of her students rhetorically asked her, 'If she [a divorced woman] sits at home will anyone pay for her expenses?' Suraiya asserted that a woman was free to go to work during the *iddat* period. In fact, she clarified that the *iddat* period was traditionally observed to determine whether the woman was pregnant after the death of her husband or after a divorce. Today, this practice was not necessary, and the purpose of *iddat* was only to provide women peace of mind (*sukoon*). If some women enjoyed (*dimag ko accha lagta hai*) going to work, there was no harm in doing so.

In Suraiya's pedagogical interventions, we can discern various aspects of *barabari*. First, the category of *barabari* is premised on the spiritual equality of men and women. At the same time, both men and women have the duty to honour pious obligations to God.[25] Second, in the conversations between Suraiya and her students, she underlined how the spouses, as spiritual equals, should both observe particular forms of ethical conduct, such as avoiding being hurtful to each other (*nuksan pahuchana*), avoiding utterance of unkind words (*galat lafz*), eschewing an attitude of resentment or enmity (*dushmani*) and being compassionate (*raham*) towards each other. Hence, *barabari* (gender equality) had a clear practical as well as an embodied dimension to it and was not merely an abstract legal category. She also repudiated too much arrogance and pride because of one's knowledge. Third, the notion of spiritual equality between men and women was used by Suraiya to critique the everyday gendered discrimination faced by women because of social and cultural norms, such as the social taboos around working during the *iddat* period. In these instances, Suraiya creatively reinterpreted the meaning of these norms to align them with a discourse of proper conduct. These social norms were reinterpreted within an overall scheme of everyday ethical conduct whereby humans, irrespective of gender, were required to be just towards each other and create conditions conducive to justice. This was not merely a choice but an imperative for pious persons. The provision of *iddat* in some schools of Islamic law is meant to determine whether the divorced wife is bearing her husband's child. Suraiya was aware of this norm and its conventional interpretation, but in her conversation with her students, she framed the *iddat* period as time needed for the woman's peace of mind (*sukoon*). The observance of *iddat* was discussed in relation to the need for proper, respectful conduct of spouses towards each other following a divorce.

Suraiya conflated this ethic of proper conduct with concerns of the precarity of working-class Muslim women to repudiate social taboos regarding the employment of women. This is evinced in moments when she advocates for women going to work during the *iddat* period when faced with economic precarity. We can read Suraiya's pedagogical interventions vis-à-vis gender equality in the light of forms of everyday gendered discrimination and surveillance in community spaces and the economic precarity of Muslim minorities, especially women, in these neighbourhoods.[26] Islamic feminist scholars and activists have emphasised the importance of everyday ethical conduct. In *Quran and Woman* and subsequent works, Amina Wadud argues that humans, as agents of God on earth, have the responsibility to maintain a relationship of reconciliation, unity and equality in their lives.[27]

Adjudicating equality

In this section, I explore the meaning of gender equality in the adjudication of marital disputes in a women's *shariat adalat* run by the BMMA. The women's *sharia adalat* is part of a network of such courts run by female *qazi*s trained by the BMMA, which are meant to challenge the predominance of men in male-run *dar-ul-qaza*s (community adjudication forums) in India.[28] The adjudication of these courts can be understood in relation to the emergence of local alternative dispute resolution forums in India in the late 1980s–1990s that exist at the intersection of state and society and are meant to challenge gender discrimination and patriarchy in both forums.[29] These sharia courts were established in Mumbai, Ahmedabad, Dindigul and Kolkata by members of the BMMA in 2013.[30] Senior leaders of the BMMA train female Islamic judges (*qazi*s) in various aspects of Muslim personal law, including provisions in the Muslim Women's (Protection of Right to Divorce) Act 1986, the Dissolution of Muslim Marriages Act 1939, sections of the Quranic text, various schools of Islamic law as well as the Indian Constitution, and secular statutes that deal with women's rights in India, such as the Protection of

Women from Domestic Violence Act 2005. As of 2019, 16 women across India had been trained as *qazi*s by the BMMA.[31]

In the adjudication of disputes in the *sharia adalat*, the female *qazi* heard both sides when people approached the court at a designated hour. The *qazi* asked the couple initially if they wanted to consider reconciliation, but she did not harbour any moral judgment towards women who asked for a divorce. In instances where men wanted a divorce, the *qazi* advised them to follow the method of *talaq-e-ahsan* where divorce was pronounced over a period of three months and the woman was given a reasonable maintenance, *iddat* and dowry (*mehr*) that was due to her.[32] In instances where a woman wanted a divorce, the *qazi* would ensure she received a female-initiated form of divorce (*khula*). She would also ensure that the woman was not deprived of the *iddat* and *mehr* payments due to her.

When men were unwilling to pay maintenance or appear in the courts, the *qazi* approached the local police station and other lawyers who attended the *sharia* court to get him to pay. Thanks to the prominence of the BMMA as an organisation that worked avowedly within an Islamic ethical framework, and the networks that the local *qazi* had with the police, lawyers and members of other male adjudication forums in these neighbourhoods, most men respected the judgments of the *qazi*. When addressing husbands to fulfil their obligations in a marriage, the female *qazi* tried to persuade them by invoking Quranic principles. The *qazi* also resorted to veiled and sometimes direct threats of police action or legal consequences if husbands did not follow the *diktat* of the *sharia* court.

In what follows, I focus on the figure of Khatun Shaikh, a prominent female *qazi* of the BMMA, and the adjudication of marriage, divorce and maintenance disputes in BMMA's women's *sharia* court.

Khatun Shaikh hailed from a working-class Gujarati Muslim family. She grew up in Bhindibazaar, a neighbourhood in South Mumbai. She was one of three siblings in a poor household; she could not study beyond seventh standard in primary school. She married early and was a victim of domestic violence. Khatun's first brush with the resolution of marital disputes happened when she approached the police to seek help for a domestic violence case in her extended family. She had moved to Navpada, a neighbourhood in Bandra East, by then. She gradually came to know activists in her neighbourhood working on women's rights and providing legal aid.[33]

She had witnessed the mayhem caused by the 1992 Mumbai riots in the areas around Bandra. She was involved in various rehabilitation activities in the neighbourhood following the riots.³⁴ In 1995, Khatun, along with other activists and women working in the neighbourhood, founded a women's organisation (*mahila mandal*) which offered counselling and legal aid to women experiencing marital problems such as domestic violence, arbitrary divorce and lack of maintenance from husbands. This women's organisation was housed initially in Khatun's house in Navpada. Khatun recalls that there was massive resistance from the *qazi* and other elderly males in the neighbourhood. They branded the women who were associated with these spaces home-wreckers (*talaq-dilani waali auratei*). Khatun and her fellow activists continued running the *mandal* in the face of harassment, intimidation and threats from local goons, *qazi*s and men in the neighbourhood. Khatun later also came to be associated with the MCMT, an initiative led by the police and civil society activists in Mumbai to foster a relationship of trust between citizens and the police following the Mumbai riots in 1992. Following her meeting with Noorjehan, she was introduced to the discourses and practices of Islamic feminism and feminist ways of interpreting the Quran. In 2007, Khatun joined the newly formed BMMA. She subsequently trained as a *qazi* as part of the initial drive of the BMMA to train women as *qazi*s.

In her adjudication of cases of marriage and divorce in the *shariat adalat*, Khatun often invoked the figure of the Prophet and his personal qualities that Muslim men and women were urged to emulate. Khatoon asked men to be compassionate (*rahamdil*) towards their wives as their Creator was compassionate. Women who visited the court were also asked by Khatun to be respectful, polite and kind. Khatun discouraged overt displays of anger. This was often a concern in cases of desertion and oral, unilateral divorce, where men treated women poorly.

Yet it is important to distinguish the quality of compassion that Khatun invoked from a notion of paternalist charity of men towards women. According to Khatun, men were urged to be compassionate as it was one of the virtues of the Prophet that they needed to emulate as pious subjects. For instance, on one occasion Khatun told a man who refused to pay post-divorce maintenance to his wife that he ought to be compassionate (*rahamdil*) as he was a follower of Allah (*Allah ka banda*). Allah was a fount of compassion (*raham*). Hence, as Allah's follower, he could not be otherwise. The attribute of *raham* was not ostensibly gendered.

In addition to emphasising compassion, Khatun stressed how maintenance payments during and after marriage were a reward for women's domestic labour and not an act of charity by the husband. Referring to sections of the Quranic verse Surah Talaq, she argued that the husband was instructed by the text to employ a nurse and pay her if the wife was unable to nurse her child.[35] Therefore, maintenance could be construed as a reward and compensation for the wife's labour (*Dudh pilani waali aurat hai us ka bhi kharcha do*).[36]

While adjudicating cases of marriage and divorce, Khatun often enlisted the help of the local police station. Some activists of the BMMA routinely visited police stations to interact with the police and took up issues of everyday misogyny and Islamophobia that Muslim women faced when filing their complaints with the police. The case of Shabana illustrates this phenomenon. Shabana, a 25-year-old woman, approached the *shariat adalat* of the BMMA on 1 January 2018. This was an instance of polygamy. She wanted her marriage to be restored. She claimed that her husband had deserted her and gone back to his first wife. She filed a complaint with the police for cruelty.[37] But conversations with her revealed that she meant to use this complaint as a bargaining tool to get back together with her husband. She approached the *shariat adalat* when the police refused to register her complaint; she claimed that the police were uncooperative and had cast aspersions on her character.

At the *sharia adalat*, she filed a petition for restoring her marriage. Khatun was empathetic to her plea. She disapproved of the action of her husband. Khatun felt that the husband had not acted in accordance with the principles of the Quran; she emphasised that the husband should have shown compassion (*raham*) and parted ways in a just manner. A case was filed by Shabana in the *shariah adalat* against her husband for non-payment of maintenance and desertion. At the same time, Khatun asked her colleague to get the police to register her complaint and called an activist of a human rights organisation to ask what the best possible course of action might be if the police refused to listen to her. Khatun herself accompanied Shabana to the police station and tried to reason with the police officer who had been refusing to file her complaint. In the everyday functioning and adjudication of the *sharia adalat*, we see how notions of ethical conduct are interlaced with concerted local struggles against gender discrimination in state and non-state forums such as the police station and the family.

The collective struggle for gender equality was conceptualised by the activists as an ethical commitment. This ethical commitment was shaped by a motivation to emulate the qualities of the Prophet, such as dedication and perseverance. On days when the *shariat adalat* would not be hearing cases, Khatun conducted reading sessions where she and her colleagues from the BMMA read Quranic commentary (*tafsir*) literature. In these reading sessions, Khatun and her colleagues emphasised the ordinariness of the Prophet and reflected on the need for an everyday relationship with Him. On one occasion, Khatun reflected on her and her colleagues' struggles for Muslim women's rights (*ḥuq*). She said that their endeavours mirrored the meditation, contemplation and perseverance of the Prophet which prepared him to receive the revelation. She described the physical privations and long spells of the contemplation of the Prophet that prepared him to receive the first verse of the Quran in Ghar-e-Hira. This intimate relationship with the Prophet can be discerned in a moment of self-reflection:

> 'Our Prophet was not very educated. The Angel asked him to read. Then he said, 'How can I read? I am not that educated.' Similarly, now Noorjehan is training all of us (as *qazi*s and activists). Some of us are struggling with the training, but Noor keeps insisting that we must apply ourselves. Then we will succeed. Some of you might feel that she is being forceful, but this is how the Prophet fashioned himself too. After three years of contemplation, he received a revelation again. This is significant. I had never thought that I would read the Quran so closely with translations.[38]

This ethnographic vignette brings out how Khatun and her colleague conceptualised their everyday struggles against gender inequality as a pious ethical commitment. Taking part in this struggle for gender equality in the everyday adjudication of the *sharia* court is therefore likened to nurturing some of the qualities of the Prophet. Hence, fighting for gender equality is enmeshed with a project of ethical self-fashioning. Much Islamic devotional literature dwells upon the relationship of intimacy experienced by Muslims with the Prophet and his immediate family.[39] In this literature, the Prophet is revered as a moral exemplar whose 'words and deeds' are not merely commandments but ways of 'inhabiting the world, bodily and ethically'.[40] The Prophet is not merely an external icon to be revered; those who follow him aspire to emulate his behaviour and his virtues in everyday life.[41] Scholarship on alternative dispute resolution forums in India show how state and non-state law are entangled in multiple ways –in terms of both the actual circulation of cases and the commonality of gendered ideologies – in the everyday functioning of these forums.[42] The ethnographic vignette presented in this section shows how this navigation of state and non-state forums is shot through with notions of everyday ethical conduct, in this instance an imperative to emulate the qualities of the Prophet.

Deparochialising gender equality

This chapter has shown how notions of moral, ethical conduct as well as everyday ethical commitments and bodily practices constitute the meaning of gender equality (*barabari*). Gender equality is not merely an abstract legal category. It is constituted through practice in moments when women navigate the domain of Muslim family law. The domain of Muslim family law is constitutive of the larger category of minority rights in India. Within this framework of minority rights, gender equality means more than just equal rights guaranteed by the law within a liberal, legal framework. Gender equality connotes an everyday practice of ethics. In the ethnographic vignettes presented in this chapter, we encounter notions of ethical conduct that are invoked in moments of breakdown of the heterosexual marriage and divorce. The spouses are both expected to be just towards each other. Justice is not merely an abstract concept and is not reducible to the rights and claims that the parties owe to each other. It entails ethical, compassionate conduct that involves using and also not using the body in particular ways, such as not uttering unkind words, avoiding overt displays of anger, not harbouring resentment, and so on. The practice of gender equality involves reinterpretation of existing social norms and forms of social and legal inequality in the light of the imperative towards everyday ethical conduct. Hence, unjust social norms are reinterpreted and reconstituted by focusing on what might be a more ethical and a just way of conducting oneself. Gender equality is hence a category that is inhabited through everyday practice and concerted, collective political action. This is borne out in the moment when the practice of *iddat* and its particularities are reconstituted within a broader scheme of ethical conduct that requires spouses to be just towards each other through the divorce proceedings.

In exploring the alternative dispute adjudication of Khatun Shaikh, I have shown how an emphasis on ethical conduct goes hand in hand with concerted struggles against gender inequality in state and non-state forums. In the ethnographic vignettes presented above, I have traced the everyday life of gender equality as it is constituted by negotiations with local struggles with state and non-state actors as well as a project of ethical self-fashioning. The collective struggle for gender equality is inspired by the urge to emulate the qualities of the Prophet in everyday life, such as dedication and perseverance. My overall argument in this chapter further contributes to a project of decolonising the debates on minority rights and gender in political theory. Through a grounded theorising of gender equality, I have drawn attention to a range of ethical commitments, everyday practices and bodily ways of inhabiting a scheme of gender equality within the everyday practice of Muslim family law and, hence, minority rights.

In doing so, I have shown how debates on gender equality in liberal multiculturalism often limit our understanding and the conceptual apparatus available to us for theorising gender and minority rights. In the ethnographic examples in this chapter, the standard debates of individual versus community rights, state regulation of gender and minority rights do not quite mediate the struggle for gender equality. I have delineated a range of other ethical commitments that mediate how people constitute and fight for gender equality in creative ways. We can only analyse the conceptual architecture, the moral and ethical dimension, and the everyday ethics and practice of gender equality through an ethnographic exploration of Muslim family law and the legal framework of minority rights. Non-textual sources help us broaden our horizons of thinking and conceptualising how gender equality might be conceptualised within the practice of minority rights.

This is particularly important in an Indian as well as a global context where gender equality often becomes a stick to beat minority communities with. The discourse of gender equality is often appropriated by neo-imperialist and racialised discourses about the backward, culturally regressive other. A delineation of the rich moral, ethical obligations of Muslim citizens that mediate their construction of gender equality is indeed an important exercise that dismantles essentialised binaries of gender equality and religion as well as individual rights and minority rights.

This exercise is an important contribution towards decolonising the discourse on minority rights, gender and liberalism. My careful analysis of gender equality and the creative construction of the same within a legal framework of Muslim family law shows how the debate on minority rights and gender can move beyond a textual, essentialised and reified conception of the law and religious community. This way of reifying and conceptualising Muslim law as a set of texts and prescriptions informs a lot of current debates on minority rights. Understanding Muslim law only in terms of a set of rights or textual prescriptions essentially perpetuates a colonial project of minoritisation of Muslims as well as a liberal nationalist project of conceptualising Muslims as a discreet community identified by a set of well-defined cultural practices. In this chapter, I have demonstrated how we can move beyond this impasse through an analysis of ethical commitments, everyday practices and embodiments that shape the everyday life and understanding of gender equality in Muslim family law. These commitments and practices are contingent and shaped by a range of factors, such as social location, economic precarity and cultures of engagement with state and non-state actors. The interventions of Muslim activists foreground a political conception of minority rights rather than a logic of minority rights that is based on any essentialised, reified idea of a minority community. Muslim activist interventions here echo Dr Ambedkar's political conception of minorities as based upon social and economic deprivation of a group rather than on a territorial or a numerical logic.[43] Muslim women's rights activists collectively reimagine themselves as part of a community while making claims based upon gender equality and their social location. In doing so, they challenge a reified and static understanding of a Muslim minority community.

This chapter provides us a vantage point for thinking about how grassroots movements led by Muslim women conceptualise gender equality; this is not necessarily an approximation of neo-imperial discourses or mere liberal apologia. The everyday practices of ethical conduct in this movement constitute in important ways the discourse and practice of gender equality.

Minority rights in India show a complex domain of interaction of an ethic of piety, collective organisation and activism. Minority rights and religion-based family law are therefore not merely an expression of the sovereign, regulatory power and authority of the secular state. While the critical scholarship on minority rights helps us explore the constructed category of the minority and the gendered ideology that animates religious family law,[44] my exploration of the everyday life of Muslim family law in India brings out a more layered narrative of minority rights. The law is not merely confined to the text and state institutions but comes alive in everyday interactions in alternative dispute resolution forums and neighbourhoods where discussions on Muslim family law take place. In these moments, a range of registers mediate negotiations with legal categories. Being alive to these multiple everyday ethical ways in which family law is constituted helps us move beyond reified, textual and codified conceptions of family law and minority rights and thereby contributes to a project of decolonising debates on minority rights and gender in political theory.

Notes

1. The BMMA has trained women as *qazi* (dispute adjudicator). These trainings are part of the larger aims of the BMMA to challenge gender inequality in the domain of Muslim personal law on marriage, divorce and maintenance. The adjudication of Muslim family law includes alternative dispute resolution forums that have been traditionally run by men. The BMMA has made a concerted effort to promote women's leadership roles in these spaces. In the everyday functioning of the *shariat adalat*, women *qazi*s of the BMMA engage a range of state and non-state actors to fight against everyday sexism and gendered domination in the family as they navigate the legal-pluralist domain of Muslim personal law. The female *qazi*s of the BMMA are trained in various schools of Islamic law, the Constitution and secular statutes that guarantee rights of women in marriage, such as the Domestic Violence Act 2005.
2. Okin, 'Is Multiculturalism Bad for Women?'; Benhabib, *The Claims of Culture*; Shachar, *Multicultural Jurisdictions*.
3. Okin, 'Is Multiculturalism Bad for Women?', 21.
4. Shachar, *Multicultural Jurisdictions*.
5. Anne Phillips, 'Religion: Ally, Threat or Just Religion', in *Religion, Secularism and Constitutional Democracy*, ed. Jean L. Cohen and Cecile Laborde, 49 (New York: Columbia University Press, 2015).
6. Shahra Razavi, 'Islamic Politics, Human Rights and Women's Claims for Equality in Iran', *Third World Quarterly* 27, no. 7 (2006): 1223–1237; Lila Abu-Lughod, *Do Muslim Women Need Saving?* (Cambridge, MA: Harvard University Press); Phillips, 'Religion: Ally, Threat, or Just Religion'.
7. Mahmood, *Politics of Piety*.
8. bell hooks, *Feminist Theory: From Margin to Center* (Boston, MA: South End Press, 1981); Maria C. Lugones and Elizabeth V. Spelman (eds.), 'Have We Got a Theory for You! Feminist Theory, Cultural Imperialism, and the Demand for "The Woman's Voice"', *Women's Studies International Forum* 6, no. 6 (1983): 573–581; Gloria Anzaldua, *La Frontera/La Frontera:*

The New Mestiza (San Francisco, CA: Aunt Lute Books, 1987); Aunt Lute Books, Chandra Talpade Mohanty, Anne Russo and Lourdes Torres (eds.), *Third World Women and the Politics of Feminism* (Bloomington, IN: Indiana University Press, 1991).

9. Lila Abu-Lughod, 'Orientalism and Middle East Feminist Studies', *Feminist Studies*, 27, no. 1 (2001): 101–113; Abu-Lughod, *Do Muslim Women Need Saving?*
10. Mahmood, *Politics of Piety*, 3.
11. Ibid.
12. Ibid., 36.
13. Ibid., 38.
14. Mayanthi Fernando, *The Republic Unsettled: Muslim French and the Contradictions of Secularism* (Durham, NC and London: Duke University Press, 2014); Julia Stephens, *Governing Islam: Law, Empire, and Secularism in Modern South Asia* (Cambridge: Cambridge University Press, 2018); Katherine Lemons, *Divorcing Traditions: Islamic Marriage Law and the Making of Indian Secularism* (Ithaca, NY: Cornell University Press, 2019).
15. Mahmood, *Religious Freedom in a Secular Age*; Agrama, *Questioning Secularism*.
16. Mahmood, *Religious Freedom in a Secular Age*.
17. Ibid.
18. More recent empirical work on *dar-ul-qaza* in India has in fact shown how the state's patriarchal and paternalist gendered ideology is replicated in alternative dispute resolution forums. See Lemons, *Divorcing Traditions*.
19. Jones, 'Where Only Women May Judge'.
20. Ibid.
21. All personal information on Suraiya Shaikh is based on an interview conducted in Mumbai, 30 March 2018.
22. Hansen. *Wages of Violence*, 8.
23. The Supreme Court of India declared the practice of oral, unilateral divorce unconstitutional in *Shayara Bano v. Union of India* on 22 August 2017. This judgment was welcomed by most Muslim women's groups. However, a subsequent proposal to criminalise oral, unilateral divorce by the Union government witnessed a chasm between Muslim women's groups. For a detailed account of the debates around Muslim women's movements against oral, unilateral divorce, see Jyoti Punwani, 'Muslim Women: Historic Demand for Change', *Economic and Political Weekly* 51, no. 42 (2016): 12–15;

Jyoti Punwani, 'Triple Talaq Judgment and After', *Economic and Political Weekly* 53, no. 17 (2018): 12–16. .
24. The *iddat* period refers to a period of rest of about three months after divorce. Men are expected to provide for women during this period according to most schools of Muslim law.
25. The notion of men and women created from the same *nafs* is a mainstay of Islamic feminist thought. In *Quran and Woman* and subsequent works, Amina Wadud uses this trope to argue against traditional constructions of men as guardians (*qawamun*) of women in some readings of the Quran. For example see Wadud (1999).
26. Sameera Khan, 'Negotiating the Mohalla: Exclusion, Identity and Muslim Women in Mumbai', *Economic and Political Weekly* (2007): 1527–1533.
27. Wadud, *Qur'an and Woman*, 37.
28. A network of sharia courts is managed across several states in India by the Sunni organisation Imarat-e-Shariat (Houses of Dispute Settlement) and the All India Muslim Personal Law Board (Mahmood, 1995: 108–109; Jones, 2019: 441). The women's sharia court of the BMMA regularly interacted with networks with the *dar-ul-qaza* and the local male *qazi* that catered to the neighbourhoods where they worked, as well as the *dar-ul-qaza* run by members of the All India Muslim Personal Law Board. For a detailed elaboration on this, see my earlier work: Sagnik Dutta, 'Competing Allies: Legal Pluralism, and Gendered Agency in Mumbai's Sharia Courts', *Law and Social Inquiry* 47, no. 2 (2022): 514–534.
29. Jones, 'Where Only Women May Judge'.
30. Ibid.
31. Interview, Noorjehan Safia Niaz, 14 April 2015.
32. Section 125 of the Criminal Procedure Code enables married women in India to claim maintenance from their husbands. Apart from this section, there is an elaborate legal framework available to divorced Muslim women who seek to claim maintenance from their husbands under the Muslim Women's (Protection of Rights to Divorce Act), 1986. Section 3(1) (a) of this Act mandates that the husband pay a 'reasonable' and 'fair provision' and maintenance to the wife during the *iddat* period.
33. Interview, Khatun Shaikh, Mumbai, 4 April 2018.
34. Interview, Khatun Shaikh, Mumbai, 9 November 2017.

35. The relevant verse of Surah Talaq (65: 6) reads as follows: 'You shall let them reside in the home you were in when you were together, and do not coerce them to make them leave. If they are pregnant, you shall spend on them until they give birth. Then, if they nurse the infant for you, you shall pay them their due for such. You shall maintain the amicable relations between you. If you disagree, then another woman may nurse the child'. This extract is taken from the translation by Yuksel et al. (Edip Yuksel, Layth Saleh al-Shaiban and Martha Schulte-Nafeh, *Qur'an: A Reformist Translation* [United States: Brainbow Press, 2007], 359). The pamphlets and booklets of the BMMA that are distributed in workshops refer to this text.
36. Regular meetings were conducted in the shariat adalat with local civil society activists who trained members of the BMMA and other women in the neighbourhood in accessing the law and addressing gender discrimination by the police and family members. In these meetings, a member of the Commonwealth Human Rights Initiative (CHRI), an independent, international human rights organisation, distributed pamphlets and leaflets in Hindi and Urdu to women participants which outlined their rights (huq) in instances of domestic violence. Women spoke about the difficulties they faced in filing a report with the police in instances of domestic violence or other forms of cruelty by their spouses. Activists of the CHRI then trained them in navigating the institutional hierarchy of the police and informed them about their rights with respect to filing a police complaint.
37. Muslim personal law in India works within a complex legal framework. While Muslim women have access to statutes to gain a reasonable post-divorce maintenance from their husbands, such as the Muslim Women's (Protection of Rights to Divorce) Act 1986, they are also able to access provisions of criminal law such as Section 498A of the Indian Penal Code in instances of domestic violence and cruelty by their husband.
38. Fieldnotes, Mumbai, 1 August 2018.
39. Ali Sultaan Asani, Kamal Abdel-Malek and Annemarie Schimmel, *Celebrating Muḥammad: Images of the Prophet in Popular Muslim Poetry* (Columbia, SC: University of South Carolina Press, 1995); Saba Mahmood, 'Religious Reason and Secular Affect: An Incommensurable Divide?' *Critical Inquiry* 35, no. 4 (2009): 836–862.
40. Mahmood, *Religious Reason and Secular Affect*, 847.
41. Ibid.

42. Solanki, *Adjudication in Religious Family Laws*; Srimati Basu, 'Judges of Normality: Mediating Marriage in the Family Courts of Kolkata, India', *Signs: Journal of Women in Culture and Society* 37, no. 2 (2012): 469–492; Lemons, *Divorcing Traditions*.
43. Evidence before the Simon Commission, in BAWS, vol. 2, 465.
44. Mahmood, *Religious Difference in a Secular Age*; Agrama, *Questioning Secularism*.

Part II

Spaces

3
Remaking the ghetto
Sites of resistance

When they (the police) were taking away the men (during the 1993 riots in Mumbai), then women wouldn't understand anything. Then they got together and approached the police. When we approached the police in a group, we were be able to rescue our men. We then realised that we could do things – there were many things that we were capable of. This is how the seven *mahila mandal*s (women's organisations) were created in 1998. Women realized they could get together to do something. They started learning many kinds of work. Then many self-help groups were formed.[1]

On 6 December 1992, following the demolition of the Babri Masjid in India, communal riots broke out in several parts of the country.[2] Mumbai witnessed a horrific bout of communal riots in the months between December 1992 and January 1993, which saw enormous violence against Muslim minorities in the city. This violence was accompanied by the Hindu right-wing political party Shiv Sena's attempts to reconfigure the city as a sacred Hindu space.[3] According to official statistics, the death toll exceeded 800, and 1,50,000 residents, mostly Muslims, left the city.[4] About 100, 000 Muslim refugees took shelter in camps constructed in neighbourhoods that were predominantly populated by Muslims in central Mumbai.[5] The role of the police in the riots was widely criticised by civil society actors and later by an investigating committee as they were accused of being mute spectators and at times active participants in the excessive violence against Muslims, especially in the city's slums.[6] The riots transformed the social geography of Mumbai drastically. Mumbai was a city with a high proportion of ethnically mixed neighbourhoods with the Muslim population spread across the city.[7] After the riots, the Muslim population became far more concentrated in central Mumbai and in slums in north Mumbai. This violent spatial reorganisation of the city because of a concerted attack against Muslim minorities catapulted several Muslim women into the public sphere. They were involved in the rehabilitation of riot victims. Subsequently, they began participating in several initiatives that spoke to concerns of gender justice within the family and ultimately became a part of a project for addressing gender equality in the domain of Muslim family law. This project of remaking the city led by women also coincided with a global narrative of Islamic reform in response to the rise of Islamism. This chapter shows how the domain of minority rights is constituted through particular gendered negotiations with spaces in a ghettoised city. Attempts to reclaim the legal and quasi-legal domain of minority rights by Muslim women are closely tethered to reconfiguring the use of urban spaces and particular ways of inhabiting such spaces.

In this chapter, I show how the spatial marginalisation and ghettoisation of Muslims in the city and state-directed and right-wing violence against Muslim minorities are negotiated by women to forge novel forms of communal solidarity and new intimacies with the state. I also show how gendered negotiations with minority rights are constituted by a gendered negotiation with the politics of ghettoisation and resonates with a global politics of Islamophobia and Islamic reform. The practice of minority rights is made in moments of gendered reconceptualisation of the Muslim ghetto. I trace how alternative dispute resolution forums come into being in moments of Hindu right-wing violence against Muslim minorities. In these very moments, Muslim activists reconceptualised their relationship to the spaces of Muslim neighbourhoods. They transformed the home, the police station and the neighbourhood into sites of resistance against the patriarchy of both the state and non-state actors. Alternative dispute resolution forums functioned within this altered geography of new relationships of women to space.

This chapter is divided into three sections. The first section discusses the emergence and consolidation of Muslim ghettoes in Mumbai following the communal riots of 1992–1993. The second section draws upon my close enmeshment with the lives of two activists who have multiple affiliations with social movements and political parties such as the BMMA, the MCMT and the Congress party. In the final section, I show how women's grievance redressal cells of the MCMT became spaces where new relationships between the state, religious minorities and non-state actors were staged.

Processes of ghettoisation

In the last two decades, the frequent occurrence of communal violence in India has led to the violent reconfiguration of the social geography of several cities.[8] Sociologists and policy-makers have taken note of the emergence of the Muslim ghetto in Indian cities in the late twentieth and twenty-first centuries.[9] The Sachar Committee report, which was drafted by a committee to study the socio-economic status of Muslims in India appointed by the United Progressive Alliance government, observed that Muslims in India, fearing for their security, were increasingly resorting to living in ghettoes across the country.[10]

Sociologist Loic Wacquant defines a ghetto as a 'bounded, ethnically, or religiously uniform socio-spatial formation born of the forcible regulation of a negatively stereotyped population'.[11] Jaffrelot and Gayer expand this definition to point out five major characteristics of socio-spatial formations that can be termed ghettoes:

1. 'social, political constraint' that dictates the residential options available to a population;
2. the regrouping of individuals of different social backgrounds and caste and class on the basis of 'ethnic or religious ascribed identities';
3. neglect of neighbourhoods by state authorities which leads to a lack of infrastructure and educational facilities;
4. lack of public transportation and limited job opportunities that alienate the locality and its residents from the rest of the city;
5. limited access to public spaces beyond the locality ;
6. 'subjective closure of residents' which have to do with 'patterns of estrangement from the rest of the city'.[12]

The political and social marginalisation of Muslim minorities in Mumbai started long before the communal riots happened in 1992–1993.[13] According to Hansen, decline in employment prospects in the organised sector of the textile industry through the 1960s isolated Muslims from the rest of the city in 'socio-economic and political terms'.[14] Labour migration of Muslim youth from UP and other parts of north India to smaller industrial units in Mumbai continued through the 1980s.[15] But the communal riots in 1993 altered this trend as several migrant labourers and their families left

Mumbai for good.[16] The changing fortunes of Muslims in Mumbai coincided with the rise in the chauvinistic cultural nationalist assertion of the Shiv Sena, staged in its xenophobic regionalism, violent public spectacles and its virulent anti-Muslim rhetoric.[17] Following the communal riots in 1992–1993, the urban geography changed drastically as Muslims who lived in enclaves in predominantly Hindu areas fled to areas where Muslims were a majority, such as Nagpada in Central Mumbai and its adjacent neighbourhoods.[18] More recent work has confirmed that the riots had a lasting impact on the social geography of the city.[19] As a result of the violence, new boundaries around communal identities were formed in neighbourhoods in the city.[20] Sociologists have read these moments of community boundary drawing and ghettoisation as moments that increased community surveillance on women's behaviour and restricted their access to public space.[21] Sameera Khan notes that Muslim women's access to public space is more closely policed by their families and their community because of the ever-looming threat of violence towards religious minorities in public spaces.[22] The assertion of religious identities in this literature is understood in relation to 'neo-fundamentalist forces' entrenching themselves in Muslim ghettoes, rise in veil, or *purdah*, among women and the expanded role of '*sharia jamaats* in solving domestic disputes and addressing community grievances'.[23] Hansen notes that Muslim assertion in Mumbai through the 1980s entailed a dual strategy of a quest for 'internal purification and unity of Muslim community' across barriers of sects and interpretations and a 'plebeian assertion' expressed through 'enterpreneurial spirits and lifestyles' related to small industry and informal businesses.[24]

But violence also reconfigured ongoing everyday relationships and the way in which people related to the community and the nation in more intriguing and unexpected ways.[25] The predominantly Muslim ghettoes became sites where women reconceptualised the home, the police station and public spaces in novel ways by challenging gendered hierarchies in these spaces and reconstituting them as spaces of activism. While some existing scholarship takes note of the porosity of boundaries between the state and non-state adjudicatory forums, this chapter explores entanglements between the politics of ghettotisation and minoritisation and new ways in which Muslim religious minorities conceptualise and inhabit spaces.[26] This chapter draws out the spatial aspects of collective organisation of minority groups as well as the ways in which a global politics of Islamic reform is lived out in everyday contexts in India.

In the years after the riots, several texts were being discussed in middle-class Muslim circles in Mumbai which foregrounded the question of gender justice vis-à-vis a Muslim identity based on the Quran. Some of the interlocutors of this movement were part of a collective called Centre for the Study of Society and Secularism. Among the important figures in this circle were the reformist Bohra Muslim, scholar Asghar Ali Engineer, Irfan Engineer, and journalist, scholar and activist Javed Anand. Asghar Ali Engineer published voluminously on Islam and gender throughout the 2000s. His Urdu pamphlet *Quran mein Aurato ka darja* (*Women's Status in the Quran*) published in 2000 was read and discussed in these circles widely. Engineer was an inspirational figure for most women who were part of activist networks that were active in Muslim neighbourhoods in Mumbai.[27] He travelled extensively during this period in the slums and Muslim neighbourhoods of Mumbai to talk about the Quran. As Khatoon Shaikh, a member of the BMMA, recalled in an interview, 'Asghar Ali Engineer brought the Quran to our neighbourhoods.'[28] This sentiment was shared by most other women who encountered him.

Engineer published a great deal on Islam and gender, including journal articles and books throughout the 2000s. He wrote in Hindi, Urdu and English. Some of his journal articles were published posthumously in the journal *Islam and Modern Age*, which is brought out by the Centre for Studies of Secularism and Society. Other journal articles published by the Centre also provide commentaries on contemporary debates on reforming personal law. In Engineer's articles on the Quran and gender equality, gendered roles in the family are dependent on particular circumstances. In an article originally published in 2001 and reprinted in 2004, Engineer argued that the Quran was committed to creating a 'new ethics, a new liberated society transcending the given situation'. Hence, the Quran described the given situation as well as guided 'the faithful as to what ought to be'. As proof of gender equality, Engineer argued that the Quran made it obligatory for both men and women to 'enforce what is good and prevent what is evil'. Engineer observed, 'It is only through fulfilment of this obligation that a society can be completely transformed and women are equally responsible for this transformative project. It is on this basis that eminent jurist like Imam Abu Hanifa opined that a woman can also become a *qadi*.'[29] In the same article, Engineer argued that the Quran envisaged men and women as *awliya* (friends) of each other.

As a journalist and activist, Javed Anand was actively involved in reporting on the riots during 1992–1993. He later wrote extensively in the popular press on Islam and gender. In 2009, a special issue of the fortnightly magazine called *Communalism Combat* edited by Anand was devoted to resurrecting a nineteenth-century text called *Huquuqun Niswan*, written by a nineteenth-century religious scholar Maulana Mumtaz Ali. Anand published an English translation of the Urdu text. This text written by a religious scholar from Lahore in 1898 demolished theological arguments offered by *ulema* of the time to justify male supremacy. In addition to Anand's translation, this special issue also carried an article by Asma Barlas, a Pakistani-American scholar of Quranic hermeneutics who has written extensively on gender and the Quran, titled 'Muslim Women and Sexual Oppression'.

The Muslim ghettoes became important sites where global ideas of Islamic reform circulated. Following the 9/11 terror attack and the global war on terror, the US State Department has persistently focused on programmatic efforts to 'reshape and transform "Islam from within"'.[30] In 2003, the White House National Security Council (NSC) established a new program called Muslim World Outreach, which aimed at promoting organisations and intellectual currents in Muslim-majority countries that the US government considered 'moderate, tolerant, and prone to democratic values'.[31] The Muslim world outreach and similar programmes advocated a strategy of reading the Quran which was based upon an 'empiricist notion of history', whereby the true meaning of the Quran must be abstracted through individual interpretation and human labour.[32] Several liberal Muslim thinkers in the Middle East echoed this vision of Quranic interpretation as they advocated for a contextual, individualist interpretation of the Quran. Nasr Hamid Abu Zayd, an academic at Cairo University, argued that the Quran when 'subjected to human reason' loses its 'fixedness and its meanings proliferate'.[33] Hence, the Quran was also subject to 'historical and sociological laws or regularities'.[34] Hasan Hanafi, an Egyptian writer, similarly historicises the Quran by arguing that the Quran needs to be detached from an abstraction as the eternal word of God; the Quranic text became materialised in a human language at a particular moment in human history.[35] Mahmood critiqued these reformist thinkers for their proximity to a neo-imperialist, American project of secularising and modernising Islam on the lines of a Protestant reformation of Christianity. In an Indian context, however, the everyday iterations of this global discourse of Islamic reform took far more complex shapes that defy any easy slotting into a hegemonic, neo-imperial project of Islamic reform. In the ghettoes of Mumbai, women's engagements with an everyday rhetoric of Islamic reform are tethered to their renegotiation of gendered spaces in the city. As we shall see in my exploration of the everyday life and activism of some members of the BMMA and the MCMT in the following sections, activists use Quran as an instrument for challenging gendered oppression as well as reconceptualising how they might reconstitute spaces in the city. Women assert their Muslim identity through new spatial negotiations and novel engagements with the Quran at a time when an assertion of Muslimness in public spaces is exposed to both the violence of the state and other right-wing political actors.

Home-makers: reclaiming the ghetto

I trace the emergence of a distinct Muslim identity and a narrative of gender justice within the Muslim family shaped by the relationship of activists to Behrampada, a neighbourhood predominantly populated by Muslims. Thanks to notorious press coverage, Behrampada became infamous in the public imaginary as a den of 'Muslim fundamentalists' and a threat to the security of the neighbouring Hindu community.[36] The slum is tucked away in a narrow stretch between Khar, Bandra and Santacruz railway stations on one side and the Western Express highway on another side. Behrampada and its neighbouring slums were volatile during the riots. These neighbourhoods witnessed several incidents of police violence against minorities.[37] It is surrounded by similar slums in Bharatnagar, Golibar and Navpada. The demography of these neighbourhoods changed after the riots.[38] They became areas populated predominantly by Muslims. These areas are characterised by very poor civic amenities, lack of proper roads and a very high density of population. During my fieldwork, the state neglect of these neighbourhoods was visible. There were large garbage dumps which lay uncleared for days on end and the lack of proper sanitation facilities. Roads, especially in Behrampada, are extremely narrow, and illegal construction is rampant. The occurrence of fires because of electrical short-circuits was very common as naked wires providing electricity to illegal constructions criss-crossed the neighbourhood.

The story of X, an activist with the BMMA, shows how new kinds of spatial reconfigurations in the Muslim ghetto constituted alternative dispute resolution forums in Behrampada and its adjacent neighbourhoods.[39] I followed X to a range of training sessions that she conducted mostly in low-income, predominantly Muslim neighbourhoods in Mumbai. I developed a good friendship with her during my fieldwork. X has also been a single parent for some time now, and as a queer single person I was very sympathetic to her struggles. X grew up in a slum in Behrampada with six other siblings. Most people living in this neighbourhood had migrated to Mumbai from parts of Uttar Pradesh. X had witnessed the violence and mayhem caused by the Mumbai riots in 1992. On several occasions following the riots, she along with other women in her neighbourhood protested police excesses such as arbitrary detention of youth from her neighbourhood. Subsequently, she joined a women's organisation (Mahila Shakti Mandal) in 1998 that engaged in community adjudication of marital disputes in the neighbourhood. X and other activists of the BMMA were part of such initiatives in Mumbai.

X's story is one of several ordinary working-class Muslim women being catapulted to public places during and after the Mumbai riots. Accounts of the process of ghettoisation primarily highlight the socio-economic marginalisation of Muslims and the violence of the state. X's narrative and her everyday activities in Muslim neighbourhoods in Mumbai presents more complex insights into how Muslim women's relationship to spaces responded to violence, ghettoisation, and minoritisation.

Police surveillance and violence against Muslim youth in Behrampada were also a moment when women, hitherto confined to the home, were catapulted to the public sphere. Negotiating police violence entailed occupying public space in particular ways. Police violence and targeting of minorities inaugurated a culture of protest and resistance as women occupied public spaces to protest excesses of surveillance and police violence. X shared a vivid memory of one occasion when women stopped the police from entering the neighbourhood in Behrampada:

> We all gathered together in the street in Behrampada and stopped the police vans. We told the police that we wouldn't allow them to enter the locality unless our kids were released.... The police had picked up many Muslim youths from the locality after the riots. They would pick up the youths at 2 AM–3 AM at night. So this is how the situation was – even when a number of youths would gather in the neighbourhood for a chat, the police would say that they were hatching a plan to riot. The police colluded with the Shiv Sena. They would come to our locality and pick up the guys. The mothers wouldn't know where their kids were. Which is why the parents would ask them to stay close to their homes and not go anywhere. But even then they would come at around 2 or 2.30 and

pick up the youths. They would beat them up. Then *we all got together and stopped the police from entering the locality.*⁴⁰

This culture of occupying public spaces and negotiating the police and other law enforcement agencies shapes everyday activism in this neighbourhood. As X observed, the violence and rioting were a moment of self-making for women who realised that they could organise collectively:

When they were taking away the men [during the riots], then women wouldn't understand anything. Then they got together and approach the police. When we approached the police in a group, we would be able to rescue our men. We realized that we could do things – there were many things that we were capable of.⁴¹

These moments of collective organising also made women question the violence at home. X herself was drawn into activist networks and women's groups (*mahila mandal*) that facilitated access to the police and legal remedies for women in local communities.

This kind of activism is instantiated not only in alternative dispute resolution forums run by women's organisation but also in the homes of activists. X organised training sessions on Muslim law, the Constitution and criminal law in the houses of her colleagues and other women whom she meets through her networks in the neighbourhood. Most of these houses were located in the slums in and around Behrampada. In Behrampada and neighbouring localities, the houses usually have a single room, a kitchen and a toilet shared by about four to five members of a family. X had first joined a Mahila Shakti Mandal that was started in the house of one of the activists in Navpada, a project supported by the charitable organisation Anjuman-e-Islam. In the training sessions held at home, activists would usually invite women from the neighbourhood to participate. Some women would be drawn to the concerns discussed in these workshops and would in turn recruit more women to the movement; they would also offer their homes for organising similar workshops.

In a typical workshop, X would discuss the message of the Quran, the *huq* (rights) with respect to marriage, divorce and maintenance granted to women by the Quran as well as the aims of the BMMA to bring about greater sensitisation regarding Muslim personal law. Women would usually be seated in a circle around X and listen carefully to her comments. These training sessions were attended by women aged between 20 and 60, sometimes along with their children. Women showed a great deal of enthusiasm when X elaborated on the Ayats of the Quran and also issues of women's rights under Muslim law. But these were also spaces where women discussed everyday gendered hierarchies in the domain of Muslim law and the challenges that women faced in accessing their marriage and divorce rights.

X would distribute leaflets and booklets with excerpts from the Quran in Hindi and Urdu as well as a document with the BMMA's proposed draft bill on Muslim personal law. Women would often bring up complaints of polygamous unions, corrupt practices of male *Qazi*s, cultural practices that worked against women and arbitrary power exercised by men over women in community adjudication forums.[42] X would adopt a conversational and interactive style in her training sessions. Women would point out the challenges that they faced in the neighbourhood when they tried to introduce these ideas, especially to men.

X would then elaborate on her ideas further with references to the Quranic text and her own elaboration of the principles of the Quran. Hence, the home became a space where contestations over religious authority as well as the everyday challenges in accessing marriage and divorce rights faced by working-class Muslim women were staged. The home emerged as a space where everyday practices of gender inequality in Muslim law were discussed and debated. X's training sessions in the houses of Muslim women provided an enabling space for women to discuss various kinds of discrimination that they faced in the domain of the family in relation to marriage, divorce and maintenance.

As I became intimately involved with the organisation and scheduling of these training sessions, I realised what kind of challenges this project faced. At times, X would find it difficult to recruit participants for these training sessions. Sometimes, participants would refuse to provide space for the training session after the first session had been held. There would be resistance from some quarters in these neighbourhoods against X's workshops and conversations on gender equality and marriage and divorce rights.

Other than houses, training sessions would also be organised in local schools in the neighbourhood at times. These sessions would usually be held after the school got over. X would be seated on a chair facing a bunch of women from the neighbourhood seated in wooden benches. In this space, there would be free-flowing conversations on marriage and divorce rights,

Muslim law, and the tenets of the Quran. The space allowed for informal interactions between X and her participants.

I argue that the organisation of training sessions at home gestures towards a very fundamental challenge to the gender dynamics of the community and the home. The home, an abode of the heterosexual family, became a site where marital disputes are discussed and debated collectively by women of the neighbourhood. Organising such events in the homes challenges the gender dynamics of the family as well as the neighbourhood.

My enmeshment with the everyday life and activism of Y, another activist of the BMMA and a member of the MCMT and the Congress party, helped me explore the entanglement between processes of ghettoisation, violence against minorities and novel forms of women's activism.[43] Y gained prominence as an activist in Behrampada in the years following the riots. Y was involved in several collective acts of resistance against police atrocities on Muslim youth in Behrampada during the riots.[44] Y witnessed police atrocities in the neighbourhood during the riots and was herself brutalised in the process.

The moments of resistance to police excesses were fresh in Y's memory. In several interactions with people in the neighbourhood, she recalled a particular incident vividly:

> The police were arresting a lot of Muslim youths from the neighbourhood [Behrampada]. I stood up to the police once as this series of arrests continued. On this occasion, the police shot at me. He was an officer. His name was K.[45] I still remember his name. He was an officer. He shot at me. 'Tu hatengi nahi, chokro ko nahi le jane denge toh tere ko firing karenge' (If you don't move, you will be shot at). I was unperturbed. 'Kar le na toh karoge toh koi wanda nahi' (You can do what you want. I won't budge). I didn't let the police arrest the youths. I was shot at by the police. [She kept repeating this throughout the interview.]

Subsequently, Y became a part of the MCMT, an initiative that was meant to restore the trust of religious minorities in the police following the riots.[46] As a member of the Mahila Shakti Mandal and the MCMT, Y approached the police with many instances of domestic violence in the neighbourhood where she felt that the police did not take appropriate action against the guilty.[47] She would mobilise women in Behrampada to collectively organise and claim their rights when the police refused to address their grievances. On one occasion, she urged the women in the neighbourhood to fight for their rights:

> You need to step out and ask for your own rights. If you won't come to rallies, protests, how can you demand your (*huq*) rights?

She would intervene on behalf of female victims of domestic violence in the neighbourhood. She would agitate along with other women at the police station for appropriate action in such cases. Y's activism, hence, involved reconstituting and reclaiming the police station as a space where women could articulate their grievances. The act of occupying the police station reconstituted gendered hierarchies in the neighbourhood and reworked the relationship between the police and religious minorities. Following the riots, novel forms of mobilisation of Muslim citizens took place in the neighbourhood. These are spatial negotiations with the law as women occupy spaces that had been denied to them and also reconfigure the meaning of those spaces. The experiences of religious minorities with the police had been shot through with violence. Y's activism shows how this relationship is reconstituted as one of gendered resistance as well as moments where Muslim minorities articulate a set of claims to the police and the state. Hence, processes of ghettoisation and minoritisation produce unexpected and intriguing relationships of intimacy with the police and the state. In the next section, I trace how we might think about these gendered spatial negotiations in another neighbourhood. I am particularly attentive to the relationship between a women's grievance redressal cell of the MCMT and the police in this neighbourhood.

Courting the police: women's cells in Mumbai

Many neighbourhoods in Mumbai witnessed a gradual 'ethnic-religious segmentation' with the decline of employment prospects of Muslims in the organised textile industry through the 1960s.[48] In the 1970s, changing trends in the textile industry and the labour market and the emergence of the Hindu nationalist Shiv Sena led to Muslim workers being laid off from mills.[49] This led to Muslims being employed in smaller units and workshops which recruited workers through kinship networks in north India.[50] The 1993 riots seemed to have reversed this trend of labour migration as a number of families left for UP and only some men returned.⁵¹ Through the 1970s–1980s, there was an increasing trend of isolation of Muslim entrepreneurs from the socio-economic and political life of the city.⁵² Central Mumbai became home to an 'impressive array of religious entrepreneurs', several of whom claimed to speak for the community.⁵³ These included the Ulema Council, a group of preachers inspired by the Deoband school of thought in north India, All India Tablighi Seerat and Tablighi-e-Jamaat.⁵⁴ More recent ethnographic work has noted that ghettoisation in central Mumbai is linked to both security and identity issues as people move to 'areas, neighbourhoods or buildings where people of their own community live, not only for greater security but also as a way of preserving their identity'.⁵⁵

Nagpada was one such neighbourhood in central Mumbai which was affected by the communal riots. Subsequently, the Mohalla Committee movement, an initiative of the police to restore the confidence of citizens, especially minorities, took shape in several neighbourhoods in Mumbai, including Nagpada. As part of this initiative, Muslim middle-class citizens took part in meetings to restore dialogue between citizens and the police. This included sessions where riot victims recounted their suffering to the police, and the police attended long sessions on Islam and Muslim culture conducted by activists.⁵⁶ The Mohalla committees expanded their remit to address issues of marital discord, domestic violence and other forms of gendered oppression that women were facing in these neighbourhoods.⁵⁷ Women' grievance redressal cells of the committee were founded with this aim in 1998. Some of these cells then become quasi-legal sites where lawyers would advise Muslim women on the best course of action available in disputes related to unilateral divorce, arbitrary divorce, post-divorce maintenance and domestic violence. There are eight such cells of the MCMT spread across the city.

The location of the women's grievance redressal cell and its relationship to a range of state and non-state actors shed light on how spatial negotiations constitute the domain of Muslim family law, and hence the practice of minority rights. The women's grievance redressal cell is housed in a tiny rectangular room in a bylane off the main road in Nagpada. The grievance redressal cell symbolised the creation of a new relationship between the state and religious minorities produced by the processes of ghettoisation.⁵⁸ On the other side of the main road lies a *dar-ul-qaza* (alternative dispute resolution forum run by Islamic judges) of the AIMPLB. Several litigants who approach S are women who are dissatisfied with the verdict of the *dar-ul-qaza*. The cell is a joint initiative of the Mohalla Committee and the local police. Yet it is not located inside the Nagpada police station but a couple of blocks away. S, a lawyer, attended to women's complaints at the women's grievance redressal cell in Nagpada.[59] S was drawn into the Mohalla committee movement in the backdrop of targeted violence of the police against Muslim minorities. This violence saw neighbourhoods in central Mumbai such as Nagpada become spatially recognised in the city as 'Muslim' neighbourhoods. S used a range of techniques of mediation and counselling to resolve cases of marital disputes for women who frequent the cell. She was also a practising lawyer and was engaged in litigation related to matrimonial disputes at both the high court and the family courts. She presided over cases in the legal aid cell, a tiny room with four chairs and a table and a portrait of Indira Gandhi, India's first woman prime minister, on the wall. There was a notice board which declared that this service was free of charge and that women should not pay anyone who asks for a fee. She assiduously took notes as women narrated their marital disputes. Women waited for their turn in a bench outside the room. The lawyer was assisted by two assistants who helped in maintaining a register where the details of the cases were recorded.

In the everyday running of the women's cell, the police were not directly involved. Yet S derived her authority from her association with the police. As a member of the MCMT, she helped in the rehabilitation of locals affected by the riots and hence became intimately involved with the local community. S recounted that while helping people who had been afflicted by the police, she came to know of several women who had been victims of domestic violence or other cultural practices such as an oral, unilateral divorce. According to S, Muslim law meant only the set of statutes adjudicated by state courts that regulated the Muslim family as well as criminal laws on domestic violence. In several cases where women approach S with their marital disputes, S invoked both secular laws adjudicated by the state courts and criminal laws as a pressure tactic to get the husbands to pay maintenance due to their divorced wives. Her invocation of criminal laws as well as her ability to summon errant husbands was a function of her close links with the neighbouring police station. These links, as I have argued earlier, were forged in moments of a violent reorganisation of urban space and targeted violence against Muslim minorities.

I will now discuss a case of a marital dispute where S negotiates multiple forums to get a favourable verdict for a female litigant. This case, involving a woman called Nasreen, involved interactions with multiple state and non-state actors, Muslim personal law and criminal law. These interactions shaped the everyday functioning of the women's grievance redressal cell. Nasreen was a graduate and a middle-class woman in her forties who had got married in 1998. She was a teacher at a local English-medium school. She had been educated in a college and a university in Mumbai. Nasreen was given a house by her natal family at the time of marriage. Her husband was a doctor who had just started his practice in Mumbai and had moved there from a village in Uttar Pradesh. Nasreen's family had helped in setting up his practice. Nasreen's husband allegedly had a series of affairs during their marriage and eventually got married to a cousin during a trip to his native village. Following his second marriage, the husband wanted to divorce Nasreen and take over ownership of the house where they were residing. Nasreen had two daughters at this point and was still working at the school in the neighbourhood.

At this point, Nasreen approached the women's cell to get advice from S, the lawyer. Nasreen's was a case of polygamy, but she was more concerned about ownership of her property and security for her children rather than preserving the marriage or repudiating the act of polygamy itself. S advised her to file a complaint under Section 498A of the Indian Penal Code with the local police station alleging cruelty as well as a plea for maintenance under Section 125 of the CrPC.[60] These measures were deployed as a way to prevent the husband from deserting her or usurping the matrimonial home to which Nasreen's natal family had contributed. S used her local networks with the police to make sure that the husband was not able to arbitrarily remove her from her property while the cases were being heard in the court.

In my conversation with Nasreen, she always emphasised her attachment to her home, which had been given to her by her natal family. She stressed how she wanted to retain possession of the home as a form of security for herself and her children. It seemed that her husband marrying a second time did not come as a surprise to her as such. Her husband had a series of affairs even before his second marriage. But she was more discomfited by his efforts to dislodge her from her home. The women's grievance redressal cell enabled her to voice her grievances without fear. It was easier for her to access this space than either a state court or a male-run *dar-ul-qaza*.

This case panned out in the backdrop of a fierce debate on Muslim personal law reform and the Hindu right-wing government's stated aims to reform and criminalise some aspects of Muslim law, such as an arbitrary, oral, unilateral divorce known as triple *talaq* in popular parlance. While debates in the popular press increasingly focused on aspects of Muslim law such as polygamy and triple *talaq* that were deemed inimical to gender justice, the narrative of everyday negotiations with these aspects of Muslim law presents a far more complicated picture of gendered spatial negotiations. The space of the women's grievance redressal cell is one where a relationship of intimacy is constituted with the female lawyer who presides over the negotiations. Nasreen specified that she had approached the female lawyer, who she fondly called *apa*, as the latter had a reputation in the neighbourhood for facilitating favourable settlements for women who were dealing with marital disputes.

Nasreen's case shows us the overlapping jurisdictions of state and non-state actors, as well as the intimate connections between them that shape the adjudication of marital disputes in alternative dispute resolution forums. These intimate connections, however, are shaped by an overarching narrative of a Muslim identity that comes into being through processes of ghettoisation and violence of the state and non-state actors against Muslim minorities. Various iterations of the state are constituted and negotiated by non-state actors in the spaces of women's grievance redressal cell. It is important to note here that state law itself is not a concrete, monolithic entity, and it is continually constituted by non-state actors in multiple, heterogeneous ways. These acts of construction and everyday constitution of state law are linked intimately to particular histories of ghettoisation and violence which unexpectedly lead to entanglements between a violent state and religious minorities. My contribution here is hence far more attentive to historical processes of ghettoisation, minoritisation and the shaping of urban spaces in response to the same that mediates the construction of the state in particular, unexpected everyday ways by the non-state actors than is allowed for by existing models of joint adjudication of marital disputes.

Nasreen's case is an example of how Muslim personal law often intersects with criminal laws on domestic violence and state laws on maintenance. The lawyer used provisions of state law as a bargaining tool to prevent the desertion and dispossession of the wife. These entanglements with the coercive apparatus of the state are inhabited and performed in very mundane ways. For example, in her interactions with me and the lawyer, Nasreen narrated the facts of her ongoing case as well as her husband's second marriage in a matter-of-fact way. As her husband was known to have several extramarital affairs, his contracting a second marriage was only expected. Nasreen was concerned about her economic rights in the marriage and securing the future of her children. In her conversations with the lawyer, Nasreen did not display any emotions of anger or sadness. Her primary concern was obtaining access to the house and receiving a monthly maintenance.

S's interactions with clients as well as her invocation of her contacts with the police are characterised by a routine, matter-of-fact and occasionally playful demeanour. S joked around with Nasreen's husband as she reminded him of the time when he almost went to jail. In these interactions in alternative dispute resolution forums, novel relationships between the police and Muslim minorities are staged. Despite the history of violence of the police towards religious minorities in the city, interactions with the police are shaped by a sense of everyday familiarity.

As several state and non-state actors were involved in the resolution of matrimonial disputes, there were tensions between them. S was often at loggerheads with the neighbouring male-run *dar-ul-qaza*. Clients who had visited the *dar-ul-qaza* of the AIMPLB and had not been able to procure a favourable judgment with respect to their matrimonial dispute would show up at the women's cell. S unequivocally asserted that she was the authority on Muslim personal law as she had been trained as a lawyer. She dismissed the *dar-ul-qaza* of the AIMPLB as well as other sharia courts run by women's groups as spaces that were not aware of the intricacies of the law. With her arsenal of legal acumen and her networks with the local police, S felt empowered to challenge the diktat of the local *dar-ul-qaza*. On one occasion, she expressed her exasperation with the proliferation of *dar-ul-qaza*:

> See if you go to Behrampada, if you go to Mumbra, every shop has a *dar-ul-qaza*. There everybody is trying to do social work. There are some *mahila mandal* in Behrampada. These members will go to the husband's place and ransack everything. There is no end to all this. But as a legal officer of the court, I know what is wrong and what is right.[61]

The women's cells become new spaces of contesting religious authority even while women lawyers negotiate the state and consolidate a unified, juridical conception of Muslim community.

Reframing rights in the ghetto

In this chapter, I have illuminated the story of how processes of ghettoisation and minoritisation produce and interact with new spatial ways of inhabiting the legal framework of minority rights. The innovative negotiations of Muslim women with minority rights need to be understood in terms of their creative reconstitution of spaces. This chapter presents some of these negotiations. While ghettoisation has been understood as a social phenomenon that consolidates community boundaries and increases surveillance on women's activities, in this chapter I have presented a range of novel ways in which women conceptualise space. These conceptualisations are tethered to a reworking of relationships between the state, religious minorities and non-state actors. A range of such reconceptualisations emerged in the Muslim 'ghetto'. For example, the home, the conventional abode of the gendered, heterosexual family, becomes a site of pedagogy, debate, discussion and activism on marriage and divorce rights. The home became a site where the practice of Muslim law and minority rights is remade.

The practice of Muslim personal law is not just restricted to state courts and alternative dispute resolution forums but is staged in police stations and local communities where women stage protests, demonstrations and rallies that challenge gender hierarchies in state and non-state law. Processes of ghettoisation and minoritisation produced unexpected and intriguing relationships with the state and the police. For example, the everyday activities of women's legal aid cells show how existing gender hierarchies in the community and community adjudication are reworked with the help of the police. A relationship of everyday familiarity with the police enables the adjudication of marital disputes in women's legal aid cells. Yet the cells themselves are not a part of the police station as such. Intimacy and familiarity with the police reconstitutes gender hierarchies between non-state alternative adjudication forums. Processes of ghettoisation, hence, produce new vocabularies of negotiations with the state and non-state actors.

Studying these reconfigurations of power in spaces enriches our understanding of minority rights. These non-textual modes of exploring minority rights contribute significantly to our understanding of novel relationships between the state, religious minorities, gender and other non-state actors. Moving away from a monolithic conception of a liberal nation state and questions of 'accommodation' of religious minorities in discussions on multiculturalism, minority rights and gender, I develop a grounded understanding of minority rights through my ethnographic exploration in this chapter. The legal domain of minority rights is constituted by minority communities through renegotiations with gendered spaces in the city even in moments of violence against minorities. Considering these gendered negotiations with minority rights illuminates new conceptual possibilities for explorations of minority rights and gender. In this chapter, I have highlighted some of these conceptual possibilities that might help us envisage minority rights and gender in spatial ways. Minority rights are not merely abstract guarantees made by the liberal, nation state. The meaning and practice of these rights are tethered to gendered negotiations with spaces in the city. Ethnographic explorations illuminate this range of meanings and practices. The everyday practice of Muslim law is tethered to a reclaiming and reconstruction of gendered spaces such as the home and the police station. The process of inhabiting and negotiating these rights also brings forth new everyday intimacies with the state and reorients the power dynamics between non-state actors who negotiate the domain of Muslim personal law. These insights into how minority rights are conceptualised could not have been generated through textual, politico-theoretic approaches.

My exploration of these complex and layered spatial negotiations with the legal domain of Muslim family law and minority rights also contributes to a decolonial approach to the study of minority rights, liberalism and gender. It unsettles the idea of a static, reified, religious personal law, which is largely a legacy of colonial processes of codification and consequently the postcolonial nation state's minoritisation of Muslims, against which liberal claims of rights need to be measured. My spatial exploration of Muslim family law shows instead how gendered spatial negotiations with neighbourhoods in the city produce the domain of minority rights. They show the domain of minority rights can be understood through a gendered reconstitution of the meaning of homes, the police station and public spaces where women engage Muslim family law. These processes of gendered reconstitution intersect with a global politics of Islamic reform as texts and ideas of Islamic reform circulate in Muslim neighbourhoods. These spaces show how the relationship between the state and non-state actors is constituted in multiple spaces in moments of gendered negotiations with family law. I also show how the state itself is often constituted in multiple spaces and iterations through everyday gendered negotiations as well as shaped by histories of ghettoisation and violence and through interactions with global ideas of Islamic reform. Hence, minority rights, religion and the state are co-produced through spatial negotiations.

Notes

1. Interview, Suraiya Shaikh, Mumbai, 30 March 2018.
2. Hansen, *Wages of Violence*; Laurent Gayer and Christophe Jaffrelot, *Muslims in Indian Cities: Trajectories of Marginalisation* (Comparative Politics and International Studies Series) (London: Hurst, 2012).
3. Hansen, *Wages of Violence*, 121.
4. Ibid., 122.
5. Ibid., 122.
6. Ibid., 123.
7. Ibid., 128.
8. Christophe Jaffrelot and Laurent Gayer, 'Introduction', in *Muslims in Indian Cities: Trajectories of Marginalisation* (Comparative Politics and International Studies Series), ed. Laurent Gayer and Christophe Jaffrelot (London: Hurst, 2012), 21; on sexualised violence against the Muslim other in urban spaces, see Manali Desai, 'A History of Violence: Gender, Power, and the Making of the 2002 Pogrom in Gujarat', in *States of Trauma: Gender and Violence in South Asia*, ed. Piya Chatterjee, Manali Desai, and Parama Roy, 293–313 (New Delhi: Zubaan, 2009); Martha C. Nussbaum, *The Clash Within: Democracy, Religious Violence, and India's Future* (Cambridge, MA London: Belknap Press of Harvard University Press, 2007).
9. Jaffrelot and Gayer, 'Introduction', 21.
10. Sachar Committee Report, Prime Minister's High Level Committee Cabinet Secretariat, Government of India, November 2006, 14.
11. Lois Wacquant, *Urban Outcasts: A Comparative Sociology of Advanced Marginality* (Cambridge: Polity Press, 2008, 9).
12. Gayer and Jafferlot, *Muslims in Indian Cities*, 22
13. Hansen, *Wages of Violence*, 160.
14. Ibid., 166.
15. Ibid., 164.
16. Ibid., 164.
17. Ibid., 11.
18. Ibid., 160.
19. Qudsiya Contractor, '"Unwanted in My City" – The Making of a "Muslim Slum" in Mumbai', in *Muslims in Indian Cities: Trajectories of Marginalisation*, ed. Laurent Gayer and Christophe Jafferlot (London: Hurst and Company, 2012), 25; Mustansir Dalvi, 'Mumbai Two Decades After: Landscapes of

Exclusion, Mindscapes of Denial', *Economic and Political Weekly* 48, no. 7 (2013): 24–26.
20. Contractor, '"Unwanted in My City"', 27.
21. S. Khan, 'Negotiating the Mohalla, 1529; Shilpa Phadke, 'Dangerous Liaisons: Women and Men – Risk and Reputation in Mumbai', *Economic and Political Weekly* (2007): 1510–1518, 1513.
22. S. Khan, 'Negotiating the Mohalla', 1529.
23. Ibid., 1530.
24. Hansen, *Wages of Violence*, 172.
25. Veena Das, *Life and Words: Violence and the Descent into the Ordinary*. (Berkeley; London: University of California Press, 2007), 9.
26. Solanki, *Adjudication in Religious Family Laws*.
27. Interview, Zakia Soman, New Delhi, 21 June 2018; interview, Noorjehan Safia Niaz, Mumbai, 19 October 2017; interview, Khatoon Shaikh, Mumbai, 4 April 2018.
28. Interview, Khatoon Shaikh, Mumbai, 4 April 2018.
29. Asghar Ali Engineer, *Quran ko samajhne ki paddhati In 21wi sadi ki chunotiya aur Islam* (Mumbai: Centre for Islamic Studies, 2004). All translations from Engineer's text are mine.
30. Mahmood, 'Secularism, Hermeneutics, and Empire'.
31. Kaplan, 'Hearts, Minds and Dollars', cited in Mahmood, 'Secularism, Hermeneutics, and Empire'.
32. Mahmood, 'Secularism, Hermeneutics, and Empire', 336.
33. Ibid., 337. Nasr Hamid Abu Zayd, *Naqd al-khitab al-dini* (Critique of Religious Discourse) (Cairo: Maktabat Madbuli, 1995), 9 (translation by Saba Mahmood in her article).
34. Mahmood, 'Secularism, Hermeneutics, and Empire', 337.
35. Ibid., 338.
36. Flavia Agnes, 'Two Riots and After: A Fact-finding Report on Bandra (East)', *Economic and Political Weekly* (1993): 265–268.
37. Ibid., 265.
38. Dalvi, 'Mumbai Two Decades After', 25; Noorjehan Safia Niaz, *Women's Shariat Court: Muslim Women's Quest for Justice* (Chennai: Notion Press, 2016), 25.
39. A pseudonym has been used here because of the sensitivity of the material and the descriptions of violence involved.
40. Ibid (emphasis mine).

41. Ibid.
42. Ibid.
43. The name has been redacted because of the sensitivity of the interview material.
44. Interview, N, Mumbai, 27 March 2018.
45. Some names have been redacted deliberately because of the sensitive nature of this information.
46. Ibid.
47. Ibid.
48. Hansen, *Wages of Violence*, 160.
49. Ibid., 162.
50. Ibid., 163.
51. Ibid., 164.
52. Ibid., 165.
53. Ibid., 172.
54. Ibid., 174.
55. Radhika Gupta, 'There Must Be Some Way Out of Here: Beyond a Spatial Conception of Muslim Ghettoization in Mumbai?' *Ethnography* 16, no. 3 (2015): 352–370, 356.
56. Ibid., 155.
57. The Mohalla Committee Movement Trust, *Towards Gender Justice and Peace: Ten Years of Women's Grievance Redressal Cell* (Mumbai: Ujjval Press, 2008).
58. Scholars writing on the adjudication of family law have focused on the interpenetration of state and non-state laws. See Solanki, *Adjudication in Religious Family Laws*. My attempt here is not merely to discuss the relationship between state and non-state actors but rather draw out through ethnographic descriptions and analysis how processes of ghettoisation and violence constitute the 'non-state' and the religious minority itself and how these moments of violence are reconstituted through ethical and spatial engagements by Muslim activists.
59. Pseudonyms have been used here to protect the identity of the lawyer.
60. Section 498A was inserted into the IPC in 1983 to provide a remedy for married women subjected to cruelty by their husbands and in-laws. The section provides for imprisonment which may extend up to three years and a fine for the accused husband and in-laws.
61. Interview, Mumbai, 18 August 2018.

4

Estranged attachments

The carceral state and the everyday life of Muslim law

A small room at the end of a courtyard housed the *sharia adalat* of the Indian Muslim Women's Movement (BMMA) in Mumbai. A group of men and women waited inside the room as the female judge (*qazi*) presided over cases. The female *qazi* usually sat in one corner of the rectangular room surrounded by some other activists of the BMMA as she heard cases of divorce, marriage and maintenance. Though this was an alternative dispute resolution forum meant to adjudicate Muslim personal law, the cases often included instances of criminal violations such as domestic violence. On the days when the *shariat adalat* was not hearing cases, this space hosted meetings with human rights organisations that trained women in approaching the police in instances of domestic violence. Stacks of leaflets and pamphlets provided by this human rights organisation lay in one corner of the *sharia adalat*. These resource materials provided details of how women citizens could access the police, how an FIR might be filed in a police station, and so on. These materials circulated within and beyond the *shariat* court. Activists of the BMMA distributed these materials to women who frequented the *sharia* court. They also distributed these materials in neighbourhoods in Mumbai where they conducted workshops on issues of gender equality and Muslim law with women. Some activists of the BMMA were also part of other activist networks. They frequented the meetings with senior police officials organised and facilitated by the members of the MCMT. In these meetings, activists exchanged pleasantries with police officials even as they recounted the difficulties that they faced in approaching the police. These events were held once a month in an auditorium where several activist groups and non-governmental organisations would assemble.

During the hearings of the cases, state laws were often invoked rhetorically by the *qazi* to convince men to pay post-divorce maintenance to their wives. The coercion of the state and state law remained an imminent threat, under the shadow of which marriage, divorce and maintenance claims were adjudicated by the female *qazi*. Deliberations on criminalising a certain form of oral, unilateral divorce by the right-wing BJP government found their way to the *sharia adalat*. The female *qazi* warned errant husbands that ill-treating their wives would soon attract a jail term. In instances where husbands refused to turn up at the *sharia adalat* or refused to pay maintenance, the female *qazi* often sought the intervention of the local police to get the husbands to appear at the *adalat* and pay maintenance.

This *shariat* court is a part of a network of alternative dispute resolutions known as women's *shariat* courts run by activists of the BMMA in various cities in India. These courts are christened women's sharia courts (*auraton ki sharia adalat*). They are a part of the BMMA's efforts to challenge the hegemony of men and male *qazi*s in alternative dispute resolution forums that administer Muslim personal law in India.[1] These alternative dispute resolution forums are not formally recognised by the Indian state.[2] Yet they share adjudicatory authority in the administration of Muslim personal law. The women's sharia courts of the BMMA bear resemblance to a network of alternative dispute resolution forums in India that emerged in early twentieth- and late twenty-first-century India and which included both religious and secular institutions, even though they claim to be more explicitly situated within a Quranic ethical framework. These forums challenged the misogyny and patriarchy of both formal judicial institutions and community adjudication forums such as *dar-ul-qazas* run entirely by men.[3]

In this chapter, I trace the insidious, shadowy, material and intimate ways in which the state is constituted in the networks of alternative dispute resolution forums and the multiple interactions of activists with state actors. This chapter is based on participant observation in the sharia courts of the BMMA as well as the interactions between BMMA activists, the police and activists of the MCMT. In doing so, I illuminate yet another spatial dimension of the practice of minority rights. In the previous chapter, I traced how the politics of ghettoisation and state violence against minorities produced and shaped the domain of alternative dispute resolution and minority rights. In this chapter, I further elaborate on the spatial politics of minority rights by exploring how the state is constituted in the everyday life of both alternative dispute resolution forums or *sharia* courts, interactions between activists of the BMMA and the police, as well as in interactions organised with members of the MCMT. This chapter traces the relationship of estranged intimacy of Muslim activists and adjudicators of alternative dispute resolution forums with the state, manifested in everyday interactions with the police and everyday engagement with materials such as leaflets, booklets and manuals outlining legal remedies and police action in domestic violence cases.

Recent scholarship on alternative dispute resolution forums has explored the entanglements between the state and such forums.[4] This chapter advances existing scholarship by exploring the myriad forms in which the state is instantiated in alternative adjudication forums. It thereby contributes to a spatial and affective understanding of the relationship between the state, minority rights and gender. I trace three kinds of such iterations: (*a*) the state as a shadow and an imminent threat that mediates adjudication of marriage, divorce and maintenance in alternative dispute resolution forums, (*b*) material manifestations of state legalities in the form of leaflets and booklets that circulate in these forums, (*c*) the state as a form of estranged familiarity both inhabited intimately and contested by women in alternative dispute resolution forums and in activist networks. Here, we stand to benefit by incorporating some insights from feminist geopolitics. A feminist geopolitical approach is premised upon the idea that state policy and political ideology are produced and materialised in everyday life and bodies[5] as the intimate and the global are connected registers. We can use this approach as a heuristic for understanding everyday iterations of the state in alternative dispute resolution forums and for enriching our understanding of the relationship between minority rights and the liberal, nation state. The state is instantiated not only discursively in cases, laws and intersecting legal regimes; its shadow is ever present in everyday interactions within and outside the courts and in the material forms that circulate in these spaces.

In contrast to existing scholarship on alternative dispute resolution forums, my chapter is focused more on how the state is constituted in everyday interactions, spaces and materials and not just in discursive or ideological ways. I use a feminist geopolitical lens to explore how the state is not only instantiated in a top-down manner but also mobilised in the everyday lives and interactions of non-state actors in alternative dispute resolution forums and in activist networks. This chapter is divided into five sections. The first section situates my enquiry in relation to the scholarship on alternative dispute resolution. The second, third and fourth are ethnographic sections which trace the iterations of state power in non-state forums. The final section outlines how my conceptualisation of the state in material, affective and spatial registers advances our understanding of minority rights and gender.

Alternative dispute resolution forums

Scholarship on non-state adjudicatory forums explores the wide range of legal bases for such forums and their complex relationship with the state.[6] Some recent scholarship on India has explored how intersecting legal regimes constitute the domain of adjudication of personal laws on marriage, divorce and maintenance.[7] In her ground-breaking ethnography, Lemons has advanced the argument that alternative dispute resolution forums replicate the gendered ideology of the liberal, secular state as they entrench the public–private divide and consolidate notions of gendered roles in the conjugal family.[8] Redding argues that the secular, liberal state in India depends upon non-state Islamic legal actors to carry out functions that it is unwilling or unable to perform, such as divorce.[9] In fact, recent empirical evidence suggests that few Muslim women access the formal legal system in India.[10] The secular state in India builds upon both an 'exclusionary, otherising' stance towards Islam and a 'radically absorptive stance' towards it.[11] This scholarship on alternative dispute resolution forums is concerned with the category of the legal case as it explores the discursive iterations of the state. This chapter draws out the iterations of the state in everyday interactions in alternative dispute resolution forums, where it is present both in shadowy and material forms.

It is particularly useful here to use a feminist geopolitical lens to understand the presence of the state in alternative dispute resolution forums. A feminist geopolitical approach shows how the production and materialisation of 'state policy and political ideology are dependent upon everyday life and bodies'.[12] Recent research argues that the Indian secular state's governance of Muslim minorities is premised upon a 'geopolitical instrumentalisation' of Muslim women's plight by the Hindu nationalist state to further its own agenda of framing Muslims as a cultural other within the territory of the nation state.[13] State law is deployed ostensibly to 'protect' Muslim women. At the same time, the state represents Muslim men as 'hypermasculine and security threatening'. While protecting Muslim women, the state requires them 'to perform an abject relation to Muslimness'.[14] Hence, laws that are ostensibly meant for the protection of Muslim women, minorities and other marginalised communities can further a project of state-building and territory making where Muslims are marked out as 'outsiders'.[15] This chapter draws upon these insights to further explore how this process of secular governance and othering of Muslim outsiders is instantiated in everyday processes of the construction of the state.

The state as shadow and threat

In the adjudication of disputes of marriage, divorce and maintenance at the women's *sharia adalat*, the shadow of the state was ever present. Women adjudicators invoked the state as an imminent threat in instances where husbands refused to show up in the *sharia adalat* or pay maintenance that was due to their divorced wives. The female *qazi* and the activists of the BMMA had strong networks with the local police station, women's legal aid cells and sympathetic lawyers who would often frequent the *sharia adalat*. Ongoing discussions about reforms in Muslim personal law, especially the proposal of the Hindu nationalist BJP government to criminalise oral, unilateral divorce, were often invoked by women adjudicators in this space. The adjudication of cases that involved an oral, unilateral divorce pronounced by a man was particularly salient. In these cases, the female *qazi* invoked the impending law to discipline errant husbands and get them to reward the maintenance that was due to their divorced wives. One of the activists of the BMMA was engaged in building networks with the local police. She would visit the local police station every day to converse with local police officers. In the following ethnographic vignette, I sketch the details of a case involving an oral, unilateral divorce that was adjudicated in the backdrop of efforts to criminalise the practice by the Hindu right-wing state.

Rahima approached the women's *sharia adalat* as she had been divorced by the pronouncement of an oral, unilateral divorce by her husband. She complained of routine domestic violence. She said that her husband would beat her up and not allow her to approach a police station to file a complaint. He then divorced her suddenly in a fit of rage. Rahima then approached the *sharia adalat* to claim some post-divorce maintenance for her and her children. During the hearing of the case in the *sharia adalat*, Shaikh, the female *qazi*, seemed agitated at the husband's conduct.[16]

At one point, the husband said that he had consulted several *maulana*s and *mufti*s (religious scholars) who had advised him to issue a triple *talaq*. At this point, Shaikh got extremely agitated. She said in a moment of exasperation, 'Muftis and maulanas! Which one of them asked you to give a triple *talaq*?'

She then asked the husband if he had prepared the 'papers' (documentation) for the *talaq*. She further reprimanded the husband for pronouncing triple *talaq*. She asked him if he had thought about his kids when he divorced his wife in a fit of rage. In a moment of exasperation, Shaikh said:

> Now what will this woman do? If he [the husband] has done wrong, shouldn't he be punished? Look at *qazi*s and *mufti*s. They are delivering such judgments. Why is it? He must suffer the consequences of his deeds (*Jaise usne talaq diya waise usko bhugatna padhega*). Therefore, the BMMA has raised its voice (*Isi liye awaaz uthai hai BMMA ney*).

On another occasion, in a similar case of triple *talaq*, Shaikh reprimanded a husband and a father-in-law who asserted that 'Muslim law' permitted triple *talaq*. In this instance too, the woman had been a victim of routine domestic violence and had then been divorced by an oral, unilateral divorce. As the husband and his family defended the husband's conduct, Shaikh cautioned the man about an impending law, 'A new law will be in place soon. You just cannot pronounce *talaq*. It will invite a prison term. You must provide maintenance and *jurmana* [compensation].'

When the father in-law continued to assert that Muslim law permitted oral, unilateral divorce, Shaikh said in a moment of exasperation, 'To hell with Muslim law (*Muslim law gayi dabbe mei*). According to the new *law*, there will be a three-year prison term for pronouncing triple *talaq*.'

These cases pan out in the backdrop of the proposal of the Hindu nationalist BJP government to criminalise the practice of triple *talaq*.[17] In the everyday adjudication of Muslim personal law in the *shariat adalat*, the impending legislation to criminalise this practice is invoked as a putative threat to discipline errant husbands. Thus, the shadows of the Hindu nationalist state mediate everyday negotiations with Muslim law in alternative dispute resolution forums. We also see how the female *qazi* uses the language of retribution to frame Muslim men as dangerous and therefore deserving of punishment. The female *qazi*'s rhetoric thus echoes some of the Hindu right-wing rhetoric about Muslim men as threats that need to be contained by the state; Muslim women emerge as victims who need to be protected against this threat.

Yet the state remains a shadow or an elusive presence. At the time when the cases were being heard, the law had not yet been enacted. In both the cases cited above, women were also brutalised by routine domestic violence. They only demanded a proper post-divorce maintenance and had no wish to get back together with their husbands. Yet, in adjudicating these cases, Shaikh emphasised the egregious nature of triple *talaq* and invoked the criminal legislation to be enacted by the state which according to her was proportionate to the violation of triple *talaq*. The possibility of criminal legislation against Muslim men is invoked by Shaikh. The gendered ideology of the Hindu nationalist state, hence, can be conceptualised as a shadow. State violence against Muslim men is ever present as a possibility, even though it is not always apparent in concrete forms.

These ethnographic vignettes help us trace how the gendered ideology of the state is a shadow that is evoked by female adjudicators in the alternative dispute resolution forum. The state mediates the space of alternative dispute resolution in insidious, shadowy ways. The vignettes illuminate the complex relationship between the state and religious minorities. The state is constituted in an ever-present yet elusive manner by religious minorities who negotiate the legal domain of alternative dispute resolution and, hence, minority rights. The state's presence is not merely discursive or ideological but also elusive and paradoxical. These aspects of the state and its entanglement with legal cultures of religious minorities can become apparent only through ethnographic investigations. As is borne out by the ethnographic vignettes, this mode of conceptualising the state plays an important role in the political practice of minorities and minority rights. Unlike some of the forums explored by Lemons and Basu, state ideology is not necessarily concretised as a discourse or practice but is present as a shadow and a possibility.[18] It is present in these vignettes as the possibility of criminal legislation, the threat of coercion and police action against Muslim men. A feminist geopolitical lens is useful here for furthering our understanding of the presence of the state in non-state adjudication forums. As feminist geopolitical scholarship suggests, state ideology is concretised in everyday lives and bodies.[19] The ethnographic vignettes further show the ways in which Muslim women themselves constitute the state and thereby shape the relationship between the state and religious minorities.

A state of booklets

The *sharia adalat* was not merely a forum for adjudication of marital disputes. It was a space frequented by lawyers, civil society activists and human rights practitioners who interacted with activists of the BMMA. It was a space where the fluidity of the boundaries between state and non-state adjudicatory forums became apparent. The practice of minority rights is tethered to this porous relationship between state and non-state actors. The state is constituted not only in moments of adjudication but also in a range of interactions between state and non-state actors. In this section, I delineate the material aspects of the state that is constituted and in circulation in these neighbourhoods.

The sharia *adalat* is often frequented by other civil society activists who trained members of the BMMA in how to access state law and the police. Members of the Commonwealth Human Rights Initiative often frequented the sharia *adalat* to conduct trainings for activists of the BMMA on legal rights (*qanooni huq*). A range of booklets and leaflets were distributed during these workshops that were printed in both Hindi and Urdu. Activists of the BMMA then distributed these materials to both women who came to the *sharia adalat* and other Muslim women in the same neighbourhood. The booklets were rectangular in shape. The booklet that was most popular had a cover that contained an image of a burly policeman with a huge moustache surrounded by people from various walks of life holding petitions. The booklet was titled '101 Things about the Police that You Would Like to Know But Were Afraid to Ask' (101 *Baatei jo aap police ke baare mei janna chahte hai lekin puchne se ghabraate hai*). The booklet is in the form of a series of frequently asked questions about the police with answers that clarify legal terminology in a lay person's terms. Some of the questions include how to lodge an FIR, jurisdictions of police stations, special provisions available to women who might want to lodge an FIR, and so on.

The preface to the booklet stresses that it is meant to be a practical guide for people approaching the police. It emphasises the importance of law and order. The preface underlines the responsibility (*zimmedari*) of the police towards citizens and the responsibility of citizens towards upholding law and order (*qanoon*). The booklet stressed the importance of citizens becoming aware of their rights (*huqooq*) as well as their responsibility (*zimmedari*). Here, law (*qanoon*) and the preservation of the law is seen as of utmost importance and the police and citizens seen as working together to preserve the law.

Hence, the rights emphasised here are rights claims of individuals against other individuals who violate the law. Moreover, the booklet sets up a rights framework in relation to a duty of active citizenry to preserve and uphold the law. The following extract underlines the message of the leaflet:

> It is significant that we know about our rights and our duties. This would ensure that neither the police nor the citizens would be able to break the *law*. This is the true meaning of abiding by the law.[20]

In trainings conducted by the activists of the CHRI, activists of the BMMA were trained in how to call and approach the police in instances of domestic violence. Dolphy D'Souza, an activist of the CHRI, often conducted workshops with activists of the BMMA. He usually provided tips to the audience on how to increase citizen access to the police. These pamphlets were used to emphasise how activists could cultivate an everyday equation with the police. D'Souza would inform the activists about how to file an FIR, how to approach more senior officials if a police official was unwilling to lodge a complaint on behalf of women, and so on. D'Souza provided activists with contact details of senior police officials in the neighbourhood.

These booklets were usually stacked in a pile beside the case register in the *sharia adalat*. The size and shape of the booklets made it easy for them to be slipped into a handbag while activists travelled to neighbourhoods in Mumbai where they held training sessions on Muslim family law and gender equality for other women.

These circulating materials demonstrate how the state is constituted in material and intimate ways in the domain of alternative dispute resolution. State power travels in tactile, concrete modes that activists and citizens mobilise in their everyday negotiations with gender inequality. While existing scholarship has focused on case law and adjudication in alternative dispute resolution forums,[21] I trace the material presence of the state that circulates in alternative dispute resolution forums.

State and estranged intimacy

As mentioned before, the alternative dispute resolution forums had networks with the state and were enmeshed with various manifestations of state power, such as the police, the law and materials that constituted state power. In this section of the chapter, I delineate everyday interactions between the activists and the police. I trace here the attempts by the activists to cultivate a relationship of familiarity and intimacy with the police based upon my close enmeshment with the lives of activists of the BMMA as well as my participant observation in interactions with the police organised by the MCMT. This relationship of familiarity and trust often turned into antagonism and confrontation as activists approached the police with cases of domestic violence or non-payment of maintenance. I term this a relationship of estranged intimacy. There is a long history of hostility by the police towards religious minorities in the city.[22] Yet this history of antagonism and hostility is interlaced with an ethic of everyday cooperation and camaraderie with police officials.

Some activists of the BMMA were assigned the task of coordinating with the local police stations. I accompanied Bharati, one such activist, to the local police station. She usually had the contact numbers of local police officers. She called them once or twice a week. The conversations involved easy banter. The activist also interacted with female counsellors who were part of the women's legal aid and grievance redressal cells in the police stations. These legal aid cells had been set up by members of the Mohalla Committee Movement, a voluntary citizens' initiative formed following the communal violence that damaged the social fabric of Mumbai in 1992–1993. These women's grievance redressal cells worked in tandem with the police to address problems of marital discord that women faced in the neighbourhoods where they functioned. There was a traffic of cases between the sharia *adalat* and the women's grievance redressal cells, as the latter often referred Muslim women to the former. At the same time, members of the *shariat adalat* often called up the police in instances where the men were unwilling to show up in the *adalat* or when there were other violations related to domestic violence or cruelty. In these interactions, the ethic of everyday familiarity and cooperation could often transform into one of antagonism and hostility. When the police were uncooperative with filing a complaint, activists often became aggressive and asserted the rights of women to legal redress.

Members of the MCMT frequently organised interactions between various civil society organisations associated with the movement. Senior police officials, such as present and former commissioners of police, would be present at such events. These events were usually held once a month in an auditorium. These were forums where members of civil society organisations could interact with the police. These were informal settings where there would be an opportunity for women to interact with senior police officials. The auditorium consisted of several rows of seats where activists from various organisations would be seated. There was a podium where senior police officials and organisers of the MCMT would be seated. These events would usually include the distribution of awards for cultural performances in various neighbourhoods, members from various neighbourhoods sharing their thoughts on communal violence and former and present police officials addressing the public. I attended these meetings along with activists of the BMMA. At the end of the meetings, there would be an opportunity for informal interactions between the activists and the police. In these interactions, women would point to instances where the police had been inattentive to the marital problems of Muslim women. There would often be delays at the local police station. At times, the police would refuse to file an FIR in cases of domestic violence. I describe in detail one such interaction to show how intimate interactions between the police and activists were structured.

On 4 November, activists of the BMMA and community leaders of the MCMT organised an interactive session with the police officials, which was attended by officials from the Bandra Kurla complex police station, former police officials and other local civil society activists. This interaction was held in a small auditorium, which would normally be hired for weddings and other religious festivities in the neighbourhood. In this interaction, the police officers and the organisers were seated on a podium, which had a few chairs and microphones. The female activists were seated in chairs in two rows inside the hall. The event started with one of the activists of the BMMA thanking the police officers for attending the event and spelling out how this was an occasion for activists and ordinary women from the neighbourhood to learn more about how the law worked. The police officers and some of the organisers were then presented with bouquets of flowers by the activists. In the interaction that followed, some of the activists pointed out the problems that women faced when they approached the police, such as long delays in the police station and the lack of cooperation on the part of the police when filing a complaint. One of the police officers, a woman, encouraged women in the neighbourhood to freely approach the police whenever they had a problem. The officer mentioned that women, children and youngsters were all free to approach the police whenever they needed help. The police officer was patient in her response to queries from the audience. Responding specifically to questions of delays at a police station, the officer mentioned that this was a function of the vast area that it catered to. She said that there was a bigger problem with the lack of enough police officers. In police stations that were well-staffed, it was possible to file a complaint with relative ease.

Dolphy D'Souza, the human rights activist who also conducted trainings for activists of the BMMA, mentioned that people were often unaware of the mechanisms available for approaching the police in an emergency situation. He mentioned the police helpline number 103. One of the activists remarked that, indeed, the number worked very well. In fact, when one files a complaint using the number, the police usually call to ask for feedback and enquire whether timely action was taken. D'Souza also informed that when an FIR was lodged, an SMS confirmation was sent to the complainant. He stressed the importance of building cordial relations with the police. He told the activists that the work of the police often went underappreciated, and people should make an effort to speak to the police when they are responsive. One of the activists quipped that in recent times they have focused on building cordial relations with the police. Once the formal interaction with the police officials was over, the activists interacted in a more informal way with the human rights activist from CHRI. In this interaction, the activists huddled around D'Souza in chairs as he shared the numbers of various police officers with them.

The interactions between the police, the activists and the organisers of the event show how there is an attempt to cultivate a relationship of everyday intimacy and familiarity with the police. Even so, these interactions evince a hierarchical relationship between citizens and the police. As we see in the vignette above, the police were seated on a podium and presented with flowers on this occasion, and the citizens were seated in chairs in rows facing the podium. The interaction hinged on respect and gratitude towards the police for finding time to participate in the interaction. During the interactive session, the consensus was on the need to sensitise citizens to issues of access to the police and cultivate an everyday, cordial relationship with the police. The coercive, carceral state is hence constituted in everyday, intimate ways in these interactions between the religious minorities and the police. Alternative dispute resolution forums became sites where the everyday state apparatus is constituted in intimate ways. This is a salient aspect of how Muslim minorities negotiate their rights that is ignored when we merely conceptualise minority rights in relation to abstract liberal categories.

This relationship of everyday familiarity is a tortuous one, and it often slips into antagonism and conflict between the activists and the police.

Hence, I call this a relationship of estranged intimacy. A relationship of estranged intimacy is staged in multiple spaces, such as the police station and alternative dispute resolution forums where the litigants travel. I will trace one such interaction with the police to bring out the relationship of estranged intimacy and familiarity between the police and the activists of the BMMA. In a particular case, Shaista, a 25-year-old woman, had approached the *sharia adalat* with a complaint about torture and intimidation by her husband's first wife, followed by desertion by her husband. She had initially approached the sharia *adalat* to get some relief. As the absconding husband refused to turn up at the sharia *adalat*, activists of the BMMA helped the woman approach the police station. In a letter addressed to the Superintendent of Police, the woman alleged a threat to her 'life and limbs' by her husband, his first wife and her relatives. I accompanied the woman, along with one of the activists of the BMMA, to the local police station. We visited the police station a few times and interacted extensively with the officer on duty. Initially, the BMMA activist tried to persuade her to summon the husband to the police station and register an FIR. Bharati's initial tone was one of persuasion, coaxing and cajoling.[23] She tried to impress upon the police officer that this was a genuine case and the husband needed to be booked. The police officer then accused Shaista of cheating on her husband. The husband had apparently informed her that Shaista was having an affair with another man. After two visits, when the police still refused to file an FIR, Khatun Shaikh, a *qazi* of the BMMA, herself accompanied Shaista to the police station. During the interaction with the female police officer, Shaikh's demeanour and tone changed. Initially, she tried to persuade the police officer. When this did not yield any results, she became more and more assertive and angry in her approach to the police officer. As Shaikh initially approached the police official, she stressed that both activists and the police were involved in implementing the 'law' and that they should help each other.

When the police official continued to question the narrative of Shaista, Shaikh lost her cool. She raised her voice and waved her arms in an agitated manner. She threatened the officer that she would approach the Deputy Commissioner of Police if the official did not act against the errant husband. As part of the training imparted by civil society activists, Shaikh had learnt how to negotiate the institutional hierarchy of the police.

In this ethnographic vignette, we see how a relationship of everyday familiarity with the police is interlaced with moments of antagonism where activists assert the rights due to women. Bharati tried to cultivate familiarity and intimacy with the police by visiting the police station regularly, engaging in small banter and occasionally trying to coax and cajole the police into filling out a complaint. In fact, in many instances, the cooperation of the police helped enable errant husbands to attend the sharia *adalat*. But this relationship of intimacy turns into one of antagonism and confrontation, where a more aggressive stance towards the police is adopted by the activists. Hence, I call this entangled relationship a form of estranged intimacy.

Alternative dispute resolution, feminist geopolitics and the state

The three ethnographic vignettes above draw out three ways in which state power and ideology find expression in alternative dispute resolution forums and everyday interactions with the police. These vignettes point to the insidious, material and intimate ways in which the state is constituted in the domain of political practice of minority rights. As Muslim minorities engage the complex legal domain of state and non-state actors, Muslim personal law and criminal law, they constitute the state in myriad ways in a range of spaces. An ethnographic exploration of this domain illuminates these conceptions of the state and its relationship to minorities. I traced how the state can be conceptualised as shadowy, elusive yet ever present in alternative dispute resolution forums. This is evinced by the ways in which the adjudication of oral, unilateral divorce in the women's *sharia adalat* is mediated by the evolving state rhetoric on criminalisation of oral, unilateral divorce by the Hindu nationalist right-wing state. Building upon a feminist geopolitical lens here helps us understand the articulation of state power and ideology in non-state adjudication forums. State policy and ideology are articulated in everyday lives and bodies.[24] Bodies reproduce and transform the boundaries of those who belong and those who do not belong within the nation state.[25] In this instance, the rhetoric of the Hindu right-wing state paints Muslim men as errant and dangerous subjects whom the state needs to control and thereby consolidates the Muslim other within the boundaries of the nation state. Muslim women are also enlisted as pliant subjects within this project of the construction of the Muslim other.[26]

In the first ethnographic vignette we see how the rhetoric of the Hindu nationalist right-wing state on the criminalisation of triple *talaq* and the need for retributive action towards erring Muslim husbands is echoed in the activist rhetoric of the BMMA. Yet the rhetoric of the activists about the criminalisation of triple *talaq* remains a shadow, a possibility which is not completely concretised in the adjudication of the *sharia adalat*. It is always presented as a future possibility and an imminent threat. The state is not only an active presence that shapes the discourses of marriage and family in alternative dispute resolution forums[27] but also a shadow and an imminent threat that makes its presence felt in everyday adjudication.

Notions about state power also circulate in material forms of alternative dispute resolution forums. These are mobilised and negotiated by women in the alternative dispute resolution forums in myriad ways. Hence, everyday interactions and materials make up the state in alternative dispute resolution forums. State power is entangled with the everyday in alternative dispute resolution forums in ways that combine everyday familiarity with antagonism and friction.

Understanding the state and its iterations in non-textual ways advances our knowledge and theorisation of minority rights in novel directions beyond the standard debates of liberal multiculturalism focused on individual rights versus community rights and the liberal nation state's accommodation of minority rights. My ethnographic exploration has laid bare several nuances of the state and its relationship to minorities that remain under-theorised in abstract liberal debates on minority rights. In this chapter, I have presented new ways in which we might conceptualise the legal domain of minority rights by paying attention to spaces, materials and everyday intimacies that are inhabited by the subjects of the legal regulation of Muslim minorities in India. My analytical labour using ethnographic observations has been to bring out this range of spatial, material and affective aspects of the state as they are experienced and constituted by religious minorities. My theorisation of minority rights considers these aspects of the state and hence complicates both an abstract understanding of a liberal nation state, qua theorists of liberal multiculturalism, and an understanding of the state, minority rights and religion that emphasises the sovereign, generative power of the secular state. As is evinced by my ethnographic vignettes here, the state is not merely symptomatic of sovereign power that generates the category of the minority using instruments of the law. Our conceptual understanding of the relationship between religious minorities and the state can be enriched through an exploration of these tortuous entanglements and intimacies, as well as the multiple everyday aspects of the relationship between the state and religious minorities. This chapter also furthers my broader project of a decolonial approach to minority rights, gender and liberalism. An important way of undoing textual, codified and reified interpretations of Muslim family law as well as the category of minority rights in India is to underline affective, material and everyday aspects of Muslim family law as it is constituted through an ongoing dialogue and interaction with various iterations and manifestations of the liberal state. More importantly, I have shown how the liberal state itself is not a monolithic apparatus but is constituted in a range of spaces through affective registers, everyday interactions and interactions between multiple state and non-state actors.

Notes

1. Jones, 'Where Only Women May Judge'; Dutta, 'Divorce, Kinship, and Errant Wives.
2. Jones, 'Where Only Women May Judge'.
3. Sylvia Vatuk, 'The "Women's Court" in India: An Alternative Dispute Resolution Body for Women in Distress', *Journal of Legal Pluralism and Unofficial Law* 45, no. 1 (2013): 76–103.
4. Lemons, *Divorcing Traditions*; Jeffrey A. Redding, *A Secular Need: Islamic Law and State Governance in Contemporary India* (Washington, DC: University of Washington Press, 2020); Solanki, *Adjudication in Religious Family Laws*.
5. Jill Williams and Vanessa Massaro, 'Feminist Geopolitics: Unpacking (In)Security, Animating Social Change', *Geopolitics* 18, no. 4 (2013): 751–758; Deborah P. Dixon and Sallie A. Marston, 'Introduction: Feminist Engagements with Geopolitics', *Gender, Place and Culture* 18, no. 4 (2011): 445–453.
6. Marc Galanter, 'Justice in Many Rooms: Courts, Private Ordering, and Indigenous Law', *Journal of Legal Pluralism and Unofficial Law* 13, no. 19 (1981): 1-47; Erin P. Moore, 'Gender, Power, and Legal Pluralism: Rajasthan, India', *American Ethnologist* 20, no. 3 (1993): 522–542; Shalini Randeria, 'Entangled Histories: Civil Society, Caste Solidarities and Legal Pluralism in Post-Colonial India', in *Civil Society: Berlin Perspectives*, ed. John Keane, 213–242 (New York: Berghen Books); Mitra Sharafi, *Law and Identity in Colonial South Asia: Parsi Legal Culture, 1772–1947* (Cambridge: Cambridge University Press, 2014).

7. Lemons, *Divorcing Traditions*; Redding, *A Secular Need*; Mengia Hong Tschalaer, *Muslim Women's Quest for Justice*.
8. Lemons, *Divorcing Traditions*, 89.
9. Redding, *A Secular Need*, 4.
10. Catherine Larouche and Katherine Lemons, 'The Narrowness of Muslim Personal Law: Practices of Legal Harmonization in a Delhi Family Court', *Journal of Legal Pluralism and Unofficial Law* 52, no. 3 (2020): 308–329.
11. Redding, *A Secular Need*, 9.
12. Dixon and Marston, 'Introduction: Feminist Engagements with Geopolitics'.
13. Pallavi Gupta, Banu Gökarıksel and Sara Smith, 'The Politics of Saving Muslim Women in India: Gendered Geolegality, Security, and Territorialization', *Political Geography* 83 (2020): 1–10, 7.
14. Ibid., 8.
15. Ibid., 6.
16. Mumbai, 27 November 2017, fieldnotes.
17. The BMMA and several other organisations representing Muslim women, including Bebaak Collective, a secular Muslim women's organisation, and the Centre for the Study of Society and Secularism (CSSS), an organisation founded by reformist scholar Asghar Ali Engineer, led a campaign to get the Supreme Court to declare the practice of triple *talaq* unconstitutional. For more details, see Saptarshi Mandal, 'Out of Shah Bano's Shadow: Muslim Women's Rights and the Supreme Court's Triple Talaq Verdict', *Indian Law Review* 2, no. 1 (2018): 89–107, 95. This movement was not just aimed at state institutions. It was accompanied by concerted campaigns in neighbourhoods and public spaces by members of the BMMA advocating against the practice (Interview, Noorjehan Safia Niaz, Mumbai, 9 October 2017). On 22 August 2017, a five-judge bench of the Supreme Court of India declared the practice of triple talaq to be illegal. While the judgment on the triple *talaq* was welcomed by all the petitioners and most Muslim women's organisations, a subsequent move to criminalise the practice by the ruling right-wing Bharatiya Janata Party saw a chasm within the Muslim community. Punwani, 'Muslim Women', 12. The BJP government's move to criminalise the practice of triple *talaq* needs to be understood within the context of the long-standing opposition of the Hindu right to the legal pluralist system of adjudication of religion based personal laws in India. Menski, 'The Uniform Civil Code Debate in Indian Law'; Nivedita Menon, 'A Uniform Civil Code in India: The State of the Debate in 2014', *Feminist Studies* 40, no. 2 (2014): 480–486.

The Hindu right has for long advocated the implementation of a Uniform Civil Code to replace personal law systems based upon religion which they perceive as a form of minority appeasement. Menon, 'A Uniform Civil Code in India', 481. The Hindu right's advocacy for criminalisation of oral, unilateral divorce squares with the image of the oppressed Muslim woman, a marker of regressive cultural practices of Muslim communities in the Hindu right's imaginary. Menon, 'A Uniform Civil Code in India', 484. This proposed legislation was opposed by women's groups and civil society organisations such as Bebaak Collective and the Centre for the Study of Secularism, who thought that the move was meant to target Muslim minorities. On the other hand, some women's groups felt that the law would act as a necessary deterrent to stop the practice or oral, unilateral divorce. The BMMA, along with the All India Women's Muslim Personal Law Board, supported the legislation. This move has attracted some criticism of the BMMA's institutional position as being co-opted by the Hindu right. Flavia Agnes, 'Triple Talaq: Gender Concerns and Minority Safeguards within a Communalised Polity: Can Conditional Nikahnama Offer a Solution', *National University of Juridical Sciences Law Review* 10 (2017): 427–450.

18. Basu, 'Judges of Normality'; Lemons, *Divorcing Traditions*.
19. Dixon and Marston, 'Introduction: Feminist Engagements with Geopolitics'; Williams and Massaro, 'Feminist Geopolitics'.
20. *Batein Jo Aap Police Ke Baare mei Jan na Chahtey Hai, Lekin Puchne Se Ghabraate Hai* (New Delhi: Commonwealth Human Rights Initiative, 2014), 4.
21. Solanki, *Adjudicating Religious Family Laws*; Lemons, *Divorcing Traditions*; Redding, *A Secular Need*.
22. Thomas Blom Hansen, *The Saffron Wave* (Princeton, NJ: Princeton University Press, 1999); Gyan Prakash, *Mumbai Fables* (Princeton, NJ: Princeton University Press, 2010).
23. Fieldnotes, Mumbai, 1 January 2018.
24. Dixon and Marston, 'Introduction: Feminist Engagements with Geopolitics'; Williams and Massaro, 'Feminist Geopolitics'.
25. Gupta, Gökarıksel and Smith, 'The Politics of Saving Muslim Women in India', 2.
26. Ibid.
27. Lemons, *Divorcing Traditions*; Solanki, *Adjudicating Religious Family Laws*; Redding, *A Secular Need*.

5

Between the home and the world

The many publics of Muslim law

I have been frustrated for five years now. I just want *chutkara* [riddance] from my husband. Nothing else.¹

When will this issue [triple *talaq*] be resolved? When will this issue be resolved? For how long will poor helpless women keep approaching us with issues of *talaq*? Will we keep running such *adalat* [women *shariat adalat*s] forever? At some point, this must become the law. At some point, people like us [Muslim women] need to be involved in law-making.²

On 22 August 2017, the majority judgments of the Supreme Court of India pronounced oral, unilateral divorce, known in popular parlance as triple *talaq*, un-Islamic and hence illegal.³ A few months following the Supreme Court judgment, the right-wing BJP government proposed a legislation to criminalise the practice of triple *talaq*. While the fight to declare triple *talaq* unconstitutional had united most Muslim women's groups, the move to criminalise the practice saw a wide chasm between multiple voices seeking to represent Muslim women and a Muslim community. Across the country, a public sphere of fierce debate about law reform was shaped by competing voices that sought to speak for the Muslim community. However, this debate did not fundamentally challenge the idea of a homogenous Muslim community whose identity rests on a state-defined conception of Muslim personal law based on a gendered division of labour in the heterosexual family. Against the backdrop of this fierce debate, women navigating the legal domain of the women's *shariat adalat* in Mumbai – a space which is also a part of the BMMA's struggle for gender justice in community spaces – continually challenged the narrative of a homogeneous Muslim community founded on a Muslim family. The logic of the *shariat adalat* was based on a recognition of the violence and fragility of the family and the fluidity of gendered roles in the family. It provided women with a space of comfort where they could openly talk about the violence of the family and fight for a divorce at points of crisis in the heterosexual family. In that sense, the alternative dispute resolution forums were semi-public spaces situated in between the public sphere of debate on law reform and the home. These spaces provided a supportive environment where women could talk about the violence at home. Moreover, these spaces were frequented by lawyers, civil society activists and researchers. There were lively discussions about the current state of Muslim law and the range of legal remedies available to women. To that extent, alternative dispute resolution forums emerged as spaces where the violence of the home and the fragility of the heterosexual family were staged. In the previous chapter, I traced the elusive, intimate and material ways in which the state is constituted, as well as the ways in which the blurred boundaries between the state and non-state spaces are negotiated in alternative dispute resolution forums that constitute the domain of Muslim personal law in India. In this chapter, I show how the public–private divide is challenged in alternative dispute resolution forums through publicising the hurt and violation experienced in the private domain. This chapter draws out the tensions between the high discourse and rhetoric of personal law reform in the public sphere and its categories, as well as the refusal of the same in the everyday negotiations with the law.[4] I also trace how gender and the heterosexual family are constituted differently in multiple spheres of debate on Muslim law.[5] The relationship of the litigants to the gendered roles in the family is only momentary and contingent. As they navigate the law, they carve out new roles for themselves, rejecting the logic of gendered roles in the family. This negotiation with the legal domain can be traced by paying attention to the performance of women's pleas and claims in the *shariat adalat* as they experience the institution of the family mostly in violent ways. I show how a range of emotions, affects and desires constitute gendered negotiations within the Muslim family in the spaces of *sharia adalat*, which do not map neatly onto a reified understanding of the Muslim family in public discourse.

In tracing these gendered reconceptualisations of the public–private divide, this chapter enriches our understanding of the everyday, conceptual life of religion-based personal laws on marriage, divorce and maintenance and its relationship to the public–private divide. In recent critical approaches to minority rights, religion-based personal laws are considered a function of the relegation of religion to the private sphere.[6] Family law based on religion is not merely a repository of religion and tradition; it is a modern invention. Family law is closely tethered to the regulatory capacities of the modern state. It is one of the 'central techniques of modern governance and sexual regulation'.[7] In conceptualising family law based on religion, the modern state concretises the public–private divide and relegates religion to the private sphere. The institution of the family law itself is premised upon the idea that the family is a domain of intimacy, care and nurturance that needs to be governed by a logic different from the cold rationality of market and contract. Therefore, family law needs to be a separate domain of the law.[8] The modern state's regulation of family law is based upon a public–private divide where the private sphere is governed by a different logic than the public sphere. The private sphere then is both the 'juridical expression of the liberal state's regulation of sexual and domestic relations' and the vehicle for 'intervening and reordering the private sphere'.[9] Anthropological work on family courts and alternative dispute resolution forums has shown how the gendered ideology of the state and its imaginaries of gendered roles in the heterosexual family permeate the adjudication of the private sphere of the family. The state's gendered ideology shapes the adjudication of family law in both family courts run by the state and alternative dispute resolution forums.[10]

An ethnographic exploration of the everyday practice of Muslim law and minority rights shows how the edifice of the public–private divide on which Muslim personal law rests is reconstituted. Violations in the private sphere of the family are publicised in multiple ways. They become a matter of debate, discussion and consultation in community spaces, which are also open to lawyers, researchers and journalists. Hence, the private sphere spills over into the public sphere.

The structure and logic of interactions in alternative dispute resolution spaces defy slotting these into the public–private divide. I refer to these as semi-public spaces. These community spaces of alternative dispute resolution are different from the home as well as the public sphere. These spaces led by women adjudicators are geographically situated in community spaces outside the home. Yet not everyone has access to these spaces, and in that sense, they offer a greater degree of privacy than public spaces such as courts, state institutions and other shared open public spaces. This chapter is divided into three sections. In the first section, I explore the semi-public nature of alternative dispute resolution forums by tracing the relationship between female litigants and this space. In the second section, I trace the public sphere of debate on Muslim law reform that pans out in open public spaces. In the final section, I outline how rethinking the public–private divide can help us reconceptualise our conceptions of minority rights, gender and the liberal state's role in regulating religious minorities.

Publicising violence, refusing the family

In her recent ethnography of *dar-ul-qazas* in Delhi, Katherine Lemons argues that these alternative dispute resolution forums further entrench the secular state's logic of regulation of the family based on a public–private divide and privatise the family as a domain governed by religion.[11] These spaces, according to Lemons, are hardly alternative legal forums but are, in fact, closely tied to the regulative labour of the secular state and its gendered definition of the family. In the *shariat adalat* run by women that I study, the state's gendered ideology of the family is challenged even while this forum remains entangled with several state and non-state actors and is located within the wider discourse of Muslim personal law reform. The ethnographic sections in the subsequent paragraphs will explore the logic of the interactions between the litigants and the *qazi* as well as the ways in which the litigants fashion their pleas and petitions to the *shariat adalat*.

In the interactions between the *qazi* and the women who approach the *sharia adalat*, the *adalat* emerges as a place where the family can be publicised. In my enmeshment with the lives of the litigants and activists, it became clear that women expected everyone present in the space to empathise with them as they narrated incidents of violence that they had experienced at home. At the start of my fieldwork, I asked Noorjehan Safia Niaz and Khatoon Shaikh if my presence in court would intimidate women given my identity as an outsider in terms of class, gender and religion. Both Niaz and Shaikh allayed my concerns. Niaz argued that the idea of space as divided into private and public was a 'Western' construct which most of these women did not share. Shaikh suggested that I could help litigants with reading documents that were written in English and get involved in other ways with the work of the court, such as data entry of cases using a computer. During my fieldwork, I got more and more involved with the multiple lives of the cases and the litigants as I accompanied many of them to the police station, the courts of other *qazi*s and the legal aid cell of the state women's commission.

In the space of the *shariat adalat*, the women and men would address the *qazi* during the hearing. But at the same time, there was an expectation that the gathered audience, including me, would understand and sympathise with their situation. The conversation between Shaikh and the women would often extend to everyone else present in that space. Not only were there no concerns about privacy, but there was an expectation that everyone present would participate in an unfolding narrative of sorrow and grief. The space was frequented by lawyers, journalists, civil society activists and researchers. Researchers and journalists would conduct interviews with some of the female litigants and activists of the BMMA. Civil society activists would carry out training sessions for activists of the BMMA in an adjacent room in the vicinity of the *sharia adalat*. Female litigants who visited the *sharia adalat* would be unperturbed by the presence of outsiders and would often share stories of grief and suffering with outsiders. Hence, this alternative dispute resolution forum was a space where both Muslim female litigants and outsiders participated in discussions about the violence and injustice experienced at home.

Women who approach the forum with a plea for a divorce often complain of routine domestic violence as a ground for divorce. In most instances, they demand post-divorce maintenance, but this is not based on any presumption of wifely duty or benevolence of the husband but rather on a legal remedy that is available to them in conditions of precarity. Most of the women who approach these forums are not educated beyond high school and do not have the employment opportunities to enter the organised sector of the economy. Some of them work in the informal sector as domestic help, beauticians and make-up artists. Their husbands are engaged in the informal economy as well.

The female *qazi*s themselves argue that the demand for maintenance is a reward for the domestic labour put in by women. This stands in stark contrast to the paternalist, gendered arguments in the case law on post-divorce maintenance of the Supreme Court and High Courts in India, which link maintenance to the duties of the husband towards the wife.[12] Lemons argues that the state courts, by forcing husbands or the Muslim community to support women, preserve paternalistic family structures, reify a 'Muslim community as separate' and shy away from 'broader questions of gender justice and women's economic opportunities'.[13]

On one occasion, a woman who was subjected to routine domestic violence and then divorced arbitrarily by her husband hesitated to speak up. Khatoon Shaikh, the female *qazi*, said, 'Speak out. This is your space'.[14]

In another instance, a woman alleged that she used to be beaten up by her husband and sought a *khula* (a divorce initiated by the woman).¹⁵ When Nasreen approached the *shariah adalat*, she claimed that she had put up with domestic violence and abuse for six years. She worked and supported her family. Later, when she was summoned to the *shariat adalat*, Shaikh asked her why she had not approached the police when she was beaten up by her husband. Nasreen replied that her parents had asked her to 'adjust'. To this, Shaikh said in a tone of chastisement, 'But this is your life. Parents are in their own place (*Maa baap apne jagah pe hai*). Is this why your parents married you off? To get beaten up?'

Nasreen's mother insisted that she had not visited the police station due to social stigma. To this, Shaikh insisted that she should have filed a complaint with the police station. She chastised the husband, 'You have to answer. She has been tolerating this violence for so long. How can you not answer?' At the same time, she turned to Nasreen and said, 'Then why stay with him? God has given you two hands. You are already working. Take your kids and stay with your mother.'¹⁶

After the husband left the *adalat*, Shaikh planned a strategy. She said that if the man was not willing to sign a *khula*, then she would ensure that she got a *faksh-e-nikah* (a form of divorce available to Muslim women when the husband has gone missing). Shaikh said that they will send her to a *dar-ul-qaza* of the AIMPLB.

This ethnographic vignette sheds light on the nature of the alternative dispute resolution space and the kinds of interactions and conversations it facilitates. The fact that the *qazi* chastised the woman and her mother for not approaching the police is telling. In the *shariat adalat*, violations in the private sphere are not hushed up. On the contrary, the *qazi* emphasised the importance of approaching the police in instances of violence in the private sphere of the home. There is an effort in these interactions and negotiations in the *shariat adalat* to create a space of intimacy and comfort where women can talk about violence at home and think of ways of overcoming their vulnerability. Hence, Shaikh's suggestion to Nasreen was that she start a life on her own terms, as she was already a working woman. As I have contended earlier in this chapter, religion-based personal laws regulating the family are premised upon a public–private divide. Religion is relegated to the domain of the private sphere of the family. The private sphere of the family is considered a domain of nurturance, intimacy and care in this imaginary of family law. Family law is also said to be a domain where the state's gendered ideology is staged as normative gendered kinship roles are concretised in these spaces. In these spaces of alternative dispute resolution or *sharia adalat*, not only is the notion of the family as a space of care and nurturance challenged, but encouragement is given to women to make 'public' violations in the family. We can gauge this effort both in the encouragement given to the litigants to speak up in the forum of the sharia court as well as the *qazi*'s insistence on the litigant filing a police complaint.

In the interactions in the *shariat adalat*, women's domestic labour is not gendered. This is evinced by Shaikh's repeated references to a Surah in the Quran which emphasises payment due to a woman for nursing her child. The relevant Surah 65: 6 has been translated as follows:

> You shall let them reside in the home you were in when you were together, and do not coerce them to make them leave. If they are pregnant, you shall spend on them until they give birth. Then, if they nurse the infant for you, you shall pay them their due for such. You shall maintain the [*sic*] amicable relations between you. If you disagree, then another woman may nurse the child.[17](65:6)

In her interactions with litigants, Shaikh translated the Surah as follows:

> Even if your wife nurses your children you are supposed to pay her. If she is not able to nurse her employ someone else.[18]

On another occasion, she emphasised that paying the wife for her was the Prophet's command:

> The Paigambar said that when your wife refuses to nurse her child, the man is commanded (*usko hukm hai*, emphatically) to employ a help (*ki dai rakhe*).[19]

These iterations stand in stark contrast to the way in which the Muslim woman is imagined in case law pertaining to marriage, divorce and maintenance as a recipient of the paternalist benevolence of the husband and the family.[20] This refusal of the gendered logic of state regulation of the family is further evinced by the way in which points of crisis in the family are negotiated by the female *qazi* and the litigants. On one occasion, Shaikh was negotiating a maintenance amount for a woman whose husband wanted to divorce her.

After several meetings, it was clear that the man was not willing to be with the woman. When the woman's entreaties did not help, Shaikh advised her to claim maintenance and move on with her life: 'No point in pleading so much (*Itna girgira mat*). Just ask for whatever maintenance is due. Try to fix a sum that he will be willing to pay monthly. Finish it off (*khatam kar*).'[21]

In another case, the woman complained that she had been ill-treated by her husband for long.[22] He allegedly cheated on her, had multiple affairs and used to beat her up when she protested. At the time of her marriage, she was told that she would be allowed to study, but later her husband and in-laws went back on the promise. The husband had now taken a second wife. She approached the court with a plea for a *khula* (a woman-initiated divorce). Shaikh advised her to take a *talaq* instead, as this would help her claim a better maintenance amount from her husband.[23]

In these interactions between Shaikh and the female litigants who approached the *sharia* court, one can discern an everyday practice of Muslim family law that does not merely concretise a gendered conception of the private sphere of the family. The sharia court is a domain where women's gendered labour is recognised and valued. Some sort of a public logic of payment for a service and contractual obligations are imported into the private sphere of the family. This is in contrast to the way in which the state continued to regulate the private sphere using gendered language about the obligation and responsibility of husbands towards their wives.

The gendered performances of female litigants in this space defy strict categorisation into a neat division of gendered roles according to the schema of a public–private divide or a mere replication of the state's gendered ideology. Women's claims in the courts are not strictly circumscribed by the roles laid out by the logic of family law and state regulation of religion-based family law. In tracing the itineraries of these cases in the *shariat adalat*, one can discern how women's pleas are shaped by a range of desires and motivations at points of crisis in the family. As they perform multiple roles in inhabiting the law, they refuse to be fixed by the logic of the legal regulation of the family. In her insightful ethnography of a rape case in Delhi, Veena Das argues for undoing the 'solidity of the narrative that the court is obliged to fix' and looking at 'each micro-event that makes up the case'.[24] She argues that the law is made by rendering complex forms of violence legible in the language of the law and producing them as recognisable categories that the law 'in the courtroom might recognise and track'.[25] In the following ethnographic vignettes, I trace this refusal to be fixed by the logic of family law even while women navigate the domain of the *sharia adalat*. Instead of focusing on the outcome of the cases, I analyse the gendered performances that are instantiated in moments when women approach the court and when the cases are heard.

Women's claims change through the course of the hearing of a case in the *shariat adalat*, and they inhabit multiple roles when they perform their claims in this space. In the case of Nasreen, her husband had approached the *shariat adalat* and asked for a divorce on 7 November 2017.[26] Nasreen had not finished high school. Her husband worked as a *zari* worker. Her husband alleged that she kept fighting with her and did not want to stay with her. He said that he was ready to provide for the kids as long as they stayed with him. On 12 December 2017, when they were summoned to the *adalat*, she claimed that her husband beat her up and did not provide for her or her children. She said that she was ready to stay with her husband if he provided adequately for her and paid the school fees for her children. The husband, however, wanted a divorce.[27] Additionally, he wanted to retain custody of the children. When it was obvious that there was no possibility of reconciliation, Nasreen said that she was not ready to do away with the custody of her children. She said she could take up any odd job to fend for her and her children but that she was not ready to part with them (*Mei Bandra mei rahoongi, kuch bhi kaam kar ke apna baccho kaa pet bharoongi*).

At this point, Shaikh, the female *qazi*, asked the husband to be kind and compassionate and provide for the wife and the kids. On 14 November 2017, the husband said that he was ready to hand over the kids to their mother. He even agreed to provide monthly maintenance for the kids. On 24 November 2017, the husband approached the *shariat adalat* and declared that he had just lost his job. Nasreen said that if he could stay with him, she was ready to work as domestic help and support the family. But it was obvious that the man was just not interested in being with her. At this juncture, Shaikh asked Nasreen to get a divorce, demand some maintenance and carry on with her life.

This vignette shows the changing gender configurations that are performed in the space of the *shariat adalat*. Initially, Nasreen inhabited the role of the wife within the economy of the family and expected her husband to provide for her and her kids. When it was obvious that the husband was not willing to be with her, she was ready to be the breadwinner and provide for her kids. She was not willing to hand over the custody of the kids to her husband. When the husband lost his job and thereby his ability to provide for his family, she was willing to be the breadwinner of the family and even support him. Shaikh invoked the message of compassion in the Quran and urged the husband to be with her and provide for her. But when this strategy failed, she advised Nasreen to get a divorce and get on with her life. Hence, the gender role performed by Nasreen is not attached in an unchanging way to a particular gendered conception of the private sphere of the family or a statist gender ideology. Nasreen's gendered kinship role as a member of the family is malleable, and it changes with the alteration of both her relationship with her husband and her husband's ability to provide. The *sharia adalat* is a space where this changing relationship to gendered kinship roles is staged.

The demands of maintenance are often a function of the practical necessity for women in situations of economic precarity. These are not markers of any moral value attached to the family as such in these interactions. Even when women demand post-divorce maintenance or maintenance as legally wedded wives, they do not attach any moral worth to the institution of the family. Given the very low levels of education of most of the women who approach these courts and thereby the scarcity of employment opportunities, maintenance is a pragmatic necessity. This provides a contrast to the ethnographic evidence on *dar-ul-qazas* ruled by men, where women are said to perform the role of an obedient, submissive wife to get a favourable judgment.[28]

The case of Azra further bears out this fragility of gendered roles. Azra approached the *shariat adalat* on 30 November 2017. She worked as a domestic help and earned INR 3,000 a month. Her husband worked as a truck driver. She alleged routine domestic violence. Her initial plea when she approached the court is significant:

I would have liked to stay with my husband but since he doesn't want to be with me, I want him to pay for me and my children.[29]

During the hearings of this case in the *sharia adalat*, the husband said that he did not want to be with his wife. Azra said that he used to beat her up all the time, yet she would stay with him because she had kids who needed care. On 10 December 2017, when it was obvious that the husband didn't want to get divorced, Azra asked for a lumpsum amount as post-divorce maintenance so that she would be able to take care of the kids. The case then evolved into an argument about the amount of maintenance that would be agreeable to her.

The husband initially proposed INR 1.5 lakh (about GBP 1,000), but Azra said that this was not enough. She demanded INR 3 lakh (about GBP

3,000) as post-divorce maintenance. She said quite sternly in the course of the negotiations that a lot of money was needed to bring up kids (*Baccho ka kharcha kam lagta hai kya?*). On 5 May 2018, a negotiation was arrived at. The couple got divorced using a *talaq-e-bain* (divorce pronounced by the husband) provision, and Azra received INR 2 lakh as a lumpsum amount of maintenance. On the day when the divorce was finalised, Azra and her mother broke down in the *shariat adalat*. Shaikh and her colleagues consoled them and said that getting divorced was better than staying in a marriage and putting up with so much violence.

In this ethnographic vignette, Azra's initial hope of staying in a marriage gives way to a protracted battle for securing reasonable maintenance that would supplement her income and help her bring up her children. Hence, Azra's relationship to the institution of the family is not fixed by a particular gender ideology. While her initial hope of staying in a marriage evinces some emotional attachment to marriage and the institution of the family, this hope soon gives way to a more pragmatic approach. She inhabits the subject position of a woman who claims rightful maintenance for her and her children. Azra and the other members of the *sharia adalat* engage in this exercise of discussing and debating a just maintenance amount. Therefore, the space of the *sharia adalat* becomes a space where violations in the private sphere of the family can be discussed, debated and redressed without any emphasis on the sacredness of the institution of the family.

While performing this bargain, there is no moral judgment expended on Azra by the female judges of the *shariat adalat*. Instead, they facilitate this negotiation and create a space where she can talk about this violence. They consoled her mother in a moment of breakdown when the divorce was being finalised. In another case, where a woman called Shagufta had been divorced and thrown out of her house by her husband, she approached the *shariat adalat* with a demand for 'proper paperwork' so that she could claim post-divorce maintenance.[30]

Women who approached the *shariat adalat* to resolve marital disputes often got involved with the everyday running of the forum. Hence, the *shariat adalat* became a space where women were drawn into spheres of activity that were different from the private sphere of the home and the family. The *shariat adalat* was a space where we might observe these myriad aspects of the everyday life of family law. In one such case, Nazneen, who had approached the *shariat adalat* troubled by the harrowing experience of domestic violence, insistently claimed that she just wanted *chutkara* (riddance) from her husband.

In her passionate pleas to the *qazi*, she claimed, 'I have been frustrated for 5 years now. I just want *chutkara* from my husband. Nothing else.'³¹ She wanted a divorce and was not bothered about post-divorce maintenance as she was already working at the time as domestic help. She claimed that her husband was an alcoholic and never went to work. She worked to support the kids. In the next few months, her husband was summoned multiple times to the *shariat adalat* and wanted to be with her. But she didn't budge from her initial resolve of getting divorced. As the case dragged on and remained unresolved, Nazneen started working as a cleaner in the office of the *shariat adalat* in addition to her other regular commitments. I saw her coming in everyday in the morning to clean the office space. Nazneen also gradually got involved with the activist interventions of the BMMA. Through this ethnographic vignette, one can gauge how the everyday life of family law is not confined merely to the gendered and sexual regulation of the private sphere or to an establishment of the state's gendered ideologies. The space of the *shariat adalat* where family law is adjudicated serves as a site for reconstitution of the private sphere of the family. This shows how the everyday life of family law is not confined to the boundaries of the private sphere of the family and the home. It spills over these boundaries in unexpected ways. This happens in moments when the adjudication of the family in the *sharia adalat* brings forth new subjectivities in relation to that space. The alternative dispute resolution forums, or *sharia adalat*, are important spaces where we might trace these unintended consequences of the adjudication of family law. Hence, I argue that the everyday practice of Muslim family law, and hence minority rights, can be spatially conceptualised by considering these subjectivities.

Women's petitions and pleas in the *sharia adalat* are mediated by a panoply of desires and motivations that do not map on to a gendered division of labour in the heterosexual family. These desires elude the propensity of the law to reify gendered roles. The alternative dispute resolution forum becomes a site where a range of affects such as love, betrayal and sexual desire are staged. The practice of family law in these spaces, hence, overflows the vocabulary and the gendered economy of the private sphere as envisaged by the state. This phenomenon can be tracked by following the itineraries of the case of Ayesha, a woman who approached the *shariat adalat* with a plea for maintenance. Ayesha worked as a *mehendi* artist. She earned as much as her husband, about INR 10,000 a month. She filed a petition in the *shariat adalat* on 1 January 2018. Before approaching the *shariat adalat*, Ayesha approached the local police station, where she filed a complaint with the police about her husband not providing for her as his legally wedded wife.³² In the police complaint, Ayesha alleged that her husband had been married earlier and she was his second wife. On getting to know about their marriage, his first wife, who had apparently moved to Kuwait, returned to India and started harassing her. In the police complaint Ayesha alleged that her husband had deserted her and that he was not 'maintaining her as his legally wedded wife'. This case spanned multiple state and non-state actors and institutional spaces of both the *sharia adalat* and the police station.

While Ayesha filed a complaint alleging non-maintenance by her husband at the police station, her interactions with the female *qazi*s and other members of the *shariat adalat* showed a more layered narrative. In her petition to the *sharia adalat*, Ayesha stated that she wanted to stay with her husband even if he continued to be with his second wife. The activists and members of the *sharia adalat* visited the police station several times, requesting the police to take action against Ayesha's absconding husband.

While the negotiations revolved around the issue of maintenance in the police station, a very different narrative played out in the *sharia adalat*. In her petition to the *sharia adalat*, Ayesha stated that she wanted to be with her husband irrespective of whether he chose to be with a second wife (*Mujhe mere aadmi ke saath rahna hai, agar pehli biwi ke saath rakhna chahta hai toh bhi rahne taiyar hoon*). In the petition, there was no mention of maintenance. During the hearing, Ayesha seemed hurt by the fact of her husband's desertion. She was a working woman and did not demand any maintenance from her husband. She felt hurt and betrayed by her husband's behaviour. She could portray these emotions in the space of the *shariat adalat*.

In her narration of the events at the hearing in the *sharia adalat*, Ayesha seemed hurt by her husband's betrayal and his sudden disappearance. She said that they used to love each other, and they got married. She was aware of his first marriage at that time. She claimed that her husband told her that his first wife had left for Kuwait and wasn't going to return to India. Ayesha said that after a few days his attitude changed, and he began to be irritable and hostile towards her. He would pick up fights over minor things. She claimed that the first wife reappeared on the scene after a few days. This explained her husband's changed demeanour. He then started coercing her to get divorced. In an emotional moment, she said:

> I got married because I was in love with him. He is a liar. If he agrees to be with me, I am fine with a second or even a third wife (*Pyaar se shaadi*

*kari, chorne ke liye nahi kari. Jhuta insaan Mera poora karega toh 2nd ya 3rd accept kar ne ko mein taiyar hoon).*³³

She further claimed that he started accusing her of having affairs so that he could divorce her. He defamed her in the neighbourhood. She said that this is something that had hurt her even more. In an emotional moment she said, 'If he hadn't shamed me, I would have divorced him myself (*Agar yeh badnaam nahi karta toh mein khud isi chor deti*).'³⁴

In the adjudication of this case, the *qazi* and other women in the *shariat adalat* were confused as to how to arrive at a resolution that would be agreeable to both the wives. This confusion was exacerbated by the arrival on the scene of the first wife and her family at one of the hearings. The talking point between the *qazi*s and the woman in the *shariat adalat* became the issue of betrayal (*dhoka*). Everyone seemed to disapprove of the husband's betrayal of both the women. Members of the *shariat adalat* felt that he now needed to stay with both. The first wife did not find this outcome 'just' and threatened to challenge this in a court.

Ayesha's narrative is an illustration of the panoply of desires that motivate women to approach the *sharia adalat* and the ways in which legal categories fix these desires into recognisable gendered roles. In the police station, Ayesha presented herself as a woman who was petitioning for maintenance as a legally wedded wife, as this was the language that was legible to the police. In the performance of her grievances in the *sharia adalat*, she does not take up the issue of maintenance and hence abjured the image of the dependent wife. Her narrative in the *sharia adalat* is built around love and betrayal and her desire to be with her husband. The *sharia adalat* itself struggles to find a legal equivalent for this desire and reduces it to the husband's obligation to spend time with both wives. Ayesha was not perturbed by the fact of the second marriage as much as by the act of betrayal and the sudden disappearance of her husband. This presents a contrast to the debates on the codification of Muslim personal law, which construct polygamy as a practice that needs to be repudiated and even criminalised.³⁵ The alternative dispute resolution forum is a place where we might trace this affective, everyday life of family law. The practice of family law involves the staging of affects and desires for which the gendered subject might not always find a clear legal category. The *sharia adalat* becomes a site for the staging of such affects and desires. This is how the practice of family law overflows the boundaries of the private sphere of the home as well as the ambit of gendered state regulation of the private sphere.

In a similar case, Heena accused her husband of betraying her.[36] She claimed that her husband was unable to fulfill her sexual desires and had concealed the fact that he was undergoing medical treatment for the same.[37] She just wanted to end her marriage as she felt no relationship can be based on a lack of trust:

> He never touched me on the night of the wedding. I got to know that he is a *na-mard* [incapable of sexual activity] after a few days. Why should I stay on when I know that my husband is not suitable for me? I don't want to stay with my husband. Whatever money was given to him at the wedding, I want it returned.[38]

In the rest of this section, I trace the interactions between the litigants and the *sharia adalat* that revolve around the issue of oral, unilateral divorce, or *triple talaq*. They play out in the shadow of the debates on oral, unilateral divorce, or triple *talaq*, in the realm of the law. The move to criminalise oral, unilateral divorce and transform the practice into a legal category was premised upon the assumption that Muslim personal law needed to be a distinct body of laws regulated by the state. Both the reformers and the opponents of the move to criminalise triple *talaq* did not question the category of a unified Muslim minority community, which was regulated by a set of clearly identifiable personal laws on marriage, divorce and maintenance. While the move to legislate triple *talaq* is aimed at making divorce difficult, the everyday life of triple *talaq* is shaped by an awareness of the fragility of the institution of the family.

Amreen filed a petition in the *sharia adalat* on 11 December 2017. Amreen had not finished high school, and she worked as a homemaker. Her husband was a daily-wage carpenter who earned about INR 20,000. In her petition, she claimed that she used to be beaten up by her husband and her in-laws. On one occasion she was forced to leave her house. Subsequently, she moved to her mother's house, and her husband pronounced an oral, unilateral divorce at her mother's house. This case played out in the backdrop of the national debate on the proposed criminalisation of oral, unilateral divorce. In her petition, Amreen said that she did not want to stay with her husband. She requested maintenance provisions for herself and her children (*Mujhe apne shauhar ke saath nahi rahna, mujhe shadi ka kharcha, aur bacche ka kharcha, mera kharcha chahiye*).

In the first hearing of the case in the *shariat adalat*, Khatoon Shaikh repudiated the man for pronouncing a triple *talaq* and reminded him that a very strict law would soon come in place that will invite a prison term for pronouncing triple *talaq*. She also reminded him of the method of *talaq-e-ehsan* mandated by the Quran:

> You need to answer my question. Why did you give her a talaq? This is not a sport. Triple *talaq* is not valid. If you wanted to give her a divorce you should have followed the method mandated by the Quran. You should have given her *talaq-e-ehsaan*. You should have called two witnesses from each of your houses and sat them down and then called the *qazi*. You cannot just pronounce *talaq* at your whim. A new law is coming in place. It will invite a prison term. You have to give maintenance and *jurmana*.³⁹

At the same time, Shaikh gathered that the woman did not want to stay with her husband. Amreen herself seemed quite resolved about this:

> What is the point of talking now? Everything is over.⁴⁰

Shaikh then said that if Amreen didn't wish to stay with her husband, no one could force her. He would have to provide her maintenance according to his ability. Amreen's mother seemed upset about the pronouncement of the divorce and the social stigma attached to it. Shaikh urged Amreen's family to not think too much about the three words (triple *talaq*):

> Don't think too much about the three words [*triple talaq*]. But the issue is now the woman herself does not want to go. We cannot force her into an agreement if she does not want it.⁴¹

In her verdict, Shaikh pronounced the couple divorced but also insisted the husband pay a lump sum as post-divorce maintenance as well as pay for the child. Amreen decided that she did not want maintenance for the child but wanted complete custody. The terms of the divorce were altered accordingly. In the divorce papers, the occurrence of oral, unilateral divorce was never mentioned. The divorce papers said that the man had divorced his wife by the method of *talaq-e-bain* in the presence of witnesses.⁴² The divorce was said to have occurred because of the inability of the couple to attempt a reconciliation (*na-ittefaki*). The post-divorce maintenance amount and the amount of *mehr* were specified, and it was agreed by both parties that the amount would be paid to Amreen at the woman's *shariat adalat*. The woman was given custody of the child for her entire life. Her husband would have no custody rights but he would also not have to pay for the maintenance of the child.

In tracking the itineraries of this case, we notice how the event of arbitrary divorce accompanied by domestic violence reveals the fragility of the private sphere of the family. Moreover, the purported victim of the oral, unilateral divorce in this case here also wished to end the marriage. After being divorced arbitrarily, Amreen herself wanted to end her marriage and only demanded post-divorce maintenance. The female *qazi* in the *shariat adalat* not only repudiated this arbitrary act of divorce but also facilitated an end to what was already an abusive marriage.

In a similar case, Sana approached the *sharia adalat* after her husband divorced her arbitrarily following a quarrel by pronouncing *talaq* thrice. Sana approached the *shariat adalat* with a plea that her marriage be restored. She wanted to stay with her husband. While adjudicating the case, Khatun Shaikh was not able to convince her husband to stay in the marriage. However, she managed to secure post-divorce maintenance and custody rights for Sana. Responding to the case, Shaikh clearly expressed her disapproval of the practice of triple *talaq*. She outlined the problem of male *qazi*s (judges) endorsing such *talaq* without consulting women.

While Shaikh expressed her discomfort with triple *talaq* and spoke about the fight for regulating the category of triple *talaq* legally, she continued to negotiate a post-divorce maintenance that would be beneficial for both parties. Sana's initial plea requesting the restoration of marriage changed into a bargain for an enhanced amount of maintenance. Sana's husband tried to get her to sign a *khula nama*. But she refused, as this would deprive her of an enhanced post-divorce maintenance. Eventually, the couple agreed to a divorce. In the divorce papers, the female *qazi* who authorised the divorce changed the occurrence of triple *talaq* into a *talaq-e-bain* (a *talaq* that had been uttered twice), which was considered a more acceptable form of divorce. Sana was awarded a post-divorce maintenance as well as a dower (*mehr*) as per the divorce papers. Sana was also granted full custody of the children. The divorce documents stated that the couple were agreeable to these terms and that they had signed the papers without any coercion or pressure. Following the itineraries of cases on triple *talaq* in the *shariat adalat* shows the fragility of the institution of the family as well as the refusal of women to occupy this schema of community constituted by the gendered family. This is instantiated in moments of negotiation following an arbitrary divorce in the women's *shariat adalat*. In the ethnographic vignettes presented, the legal domain of the *shariat adalat* helps women negotiate a favourable divorce.

Law reform and the triple *talaq* debate

In this section, I will first briefly trace the genesis of the movement to collectively fight against oral, unilateral divorce given arbitrarily by Muslim men. I will then trace how debates about the criminalisation of this practice pan out in the urban space of Mumbai. I trace how the debates on Muslim family law reform are staged in public spaces by both the BMMA and the AIMPLB.

In these moments, many publics of debate and contestation around Muslim family law are forged. The public sphere of debate on Muslim law reform stages the public–private divide in multiple ways. In the interventions of activists of the BMMA in public debates, press conferences and public protests, the pronouncement of triple *talaq* becomes an act of violation in the private sphere. This act of violation is staged in the public sphere of press conferences, rallies and public meetings as an issue that requires urgent intervention in the form of state intervention and the enactment of a law. On the other hand, in the interventions of the AIMPLB Muslim family law is constituted as a private domain where the state is not supposed to intervene. The public–private divide that constitutes the edifice of family law is consolidated in the interventions of the AIMPLB. Ironically, the Muslim Law Board frames their demands for non-intervention in Muslim family law in terms of the need to protect the *sharia*. The AIMPLB's interventions do not take into account the fact that Muslim family law itself came into being through a process of codification, textualisation and standardisation of religion by the colonial state, as well as a process relegating religion to the private sphere of the family.

In February 2016, Shayara Bano, a Muslim woman from Kashipur in the north Indian state of Uttarakhand, approached the Supreme Court with a writ petition challenging the validity of the triple *talaq*, the practice whereby a Muslim male can divorce his wife arbitrarily by merely pronouncing the words *talaq* thrice.[43] Bano's petition also challenged the validity of polygamy and *nikah halala*, the practice whereby a divorced wife is required to consummate her wedding with another man before she can get married to her ex-husband. Bano alleged that she had been unilaterally divorced by her husband after being subjected to routine domestic violence. The petition challenged the constitutionality of Section 2 of the Muslim Personal Law (Shariat) Application Act 1937 and the Dissolution of Muslim Marriages Act 1939. The issue of oral, unilateral divorce has been at the forefront of several campaigns for Muslim personal law reform led by Muslim women's organisations before the filing of this petition.[44] Vatuk notes that since the 1990s, several Muslim women's rights networks, NGOs and social movements such as the Awaaz-e-Niswaan (Women's Voice [AeN] in Mumbai, Muslim Women's Rights Network (MWRN) and the BMMA had emphasised the importance of legal reform of Muslim personal law to regulate practices such as oral, unilateral divorce (triple *talaq*), polygamy and enhanced rights for women who initiated divorce (*khula*), more gender-just *nikahnama*s, whereby women will have greater bargaining power with respect to their marriage and divorce rights.

The petition to outlaw triple *talaq* can be seen within this wider context of Muslim women-led social movements demanding greater state regulation of Muslim personal law by the state as well as efforts to popularise more gender-just ways of adjudicating marriage and divorce in community spaces. The validity of triple *talaq* itself had not been adjudicated by the Supreme Court decisively before the Shayara Bano judgment in 2016. In 2002, in *Shamim Ara v. Union of India*, the Court did lay down conditions for the validity of a divorce but did not explicitly rule on the validity of triple *talaq*. Since then, the High Courts have delivered conflicting rulings on the issue.[45]

The filing of the petition itself witnessed an array of opinions on state regulation of the Muslim family and the marriage and divorce rights of Muslim women. Mandal notes that the organisations which supported the petition all had very different ways of envisaging the state regulation of Muslim personal law and the Muslim family. A submission by Bebaak Collective, comprising a number of autonomous Muslim women's groups and the Centre for the Study of Society and Secularism, argued against triple *talaq* as well as all divorces that were delivered by non-state actors as they led to non-state entities carrying out a state function.[46] Activists of the BMMA urged the Court to declare the practice of triple *talaq* invalid but did not want the adjudicatory structure of Muslim law, including alternative dispute resolution forums, to be disbanded.[47] A similar position was adopted by renowned feminist activist Flavia Agnes.

The five-judge Bench of the Supreme Court delivered three different judgments on the issue, which pursued very different lines of reasoning.

Justice Jagdish Khehar ruled that triple *talaq* was uncodified law and was therefore not amenable to a test of constitutionality and could not be weighed against fundamental rights provisions.[48] Justice Rohinton Nariman declared the practice invalid because it was manifestly arbitrary. Justice Kurian Joseph dwelled on the question of whether triple *talaq* was Islamic and reasoned that it was not in accordance with the tenets of the Quran and was hence un-Islamic.

After the triple *talaq* judgment, the Union government led by the ruling BJP proposed to criminalise the practice. Replacing Muslim personal law with a uniform civil code has been a part of the core agenda of the Hindu right for many years.[49] While the judgment had been welcomed by most Muslim women's groups and civil society actors who had led the movement against triple *talaq*, the move to criminalise the Act saw a wide chasm between these very entities.

Press conferences and public meetings

For activists of the BMMA, support for this controversial legislation was part of an ongoing attempt to codify Muslim law governing marriage and divorce rights of the Muslim family and a reclaiming of the legal apparatus that governs Muslim women's lives. In the meetings in the run-up to the announcement of the legislation by the BJP government, there was a lot of discussion and debate on how to mobilise further on the issue of triple *talaq*. Once the legislation was formally announced, the meetings held in Mumbai revolved around the issue of what stance the movement should take vis-à-vis the legislation. The legislation itself was seen as part of a step towards a more comprehensive codification of Muslim personal law. Niaz addressed several press conferences in Mumbai at this juncture, where she spoke of the proposed law as an outcome of the popular mobilisation against the practice led by Muslim women. In one such meeting, Khatoon Shaikh voiced the basis of the movement's demands for a law regulating the practice of triple *talaq*.

> For the last 10 years poor and hassled women have been approaching us (*shariat adalat*). They are always crying and helpless. They would ask 'When will this issue (triple *talaq*) be resolved?' When will this issue be resolved? For how long will poor helpless, crying women keep approaching us with issues of *talaq*? Will we keep running such *adalat*

(women *shariat adalats*) forever? At some point, this must become the law. At some point, people like us (Muslim women) need to be involved in law-making. So if there is a law that has come to prohibit this horrible practice, then for us it's a huge deal. Some people are saying that this is 'politics', Of course, this is politics. I agree that it's politics. Many people have been in power. They have been in the Parliament. But did anyone ever raise their voice against this?[50]

In meetings with other members, Niaz spoke about garnering support for the draft law in the neighbourhoods where the activists of the BMMA knew people. The neighbourhoods in Mumbai where BMMA members were most active were Behrampada, Navpada, Bharatnagar and Golibar. As I have noted in the last chapter, these were neighbourhoods that had been turned into Muslim ghettoes because of the riots. She mentioned that she had met members of Parliament, the chairperson of the women's commission, the Human Rights Commission and the Law Commission in Delhi to garner support for the law on triple *talaq*.[51]

For activists of the BMMA, support for the law to regulate triple *talaq* was a part of the larger movement towards a comprehensive codification of Muslim family law as per a draft that had been prepared by the organisation as a result of consultations with lawyers between 2008 and 2014. The draft, which had been the outcome of consultations with lawyers, academics and Muslim women across India, stated that a law was needed to ensure the 'dignity and rights' of Muslim women in matters of marriage and family.[52]

The press conferences and public meetings of the BMMA demanding the enactment of the law staged questions of dignity and rights within marriage and family in the public sphere. Therefore, the private sphere of family, marriage and divorce, as well as religion, became a topic of discussion, debate, and deliberation in the public sphere in the press conferences, public meetings and protests organised by the BMMA. These rights were also closely tied to forms of state regulation of marriage and cultural practices, as well as the presumption of a coherent, state-defined, juridical Muslim community regulated by a codified Muslim personal law. The draft code envisaged by the BMMA includes a demand to codify an appropriate method of divorce, ban unilateral oral divorce, polygamy and other cultural practices such as nikah *halala*.

In the interactions and meetings of BMMA activists, they raise a legitimate grievance of Muslim women's voices being underrepresented in the official discourse of law reform. A lot of scholarship points to the hegemony of male authority in the governance of the Muslim family in the legal domain of Muslim personal law.[53] This is amply borne out by the resistance of bodies such as the AIMPLB to the question of law reform. The imaginary of a Muslim community in the official discourse of the BMMA is firmly grounded in a conception of the heterosexual family as an entity defined and regulated by the state and a minority community defined by this mode of state regulation. Ultimately, this vision of a Muslim family is built upon the idea of a public–private divide. Within this scheme, family laws based on religion are defined by the state. This process entails a standardisation and definition of what religion is in legal, juridical terms, as well as a relegation of religion to the private sphere of the family.

One of the vocal critics of the move to legislate on triple *talaq* is the feminist scholar and activist Flavia Agnes. A vehement critic of the right-wing BJP government as well as Muslim women's groups such as the BMMA, Agnes questioned the logic that criminal laws against a cultural practice would prove to be a deterrent.[54] In an article published in the middle of ongoing debates on the triple *talaq* legislation, Agnes critiqued the hypocrisy of the right-wing BJP government, which only selectively took up the cause of triple *talaq* and projected itself as the 'saviour of Muslim women' while ignoring widespread violence and atrocities against Muslim minorities.[55] Referring to Zakia Pathak and Rajeswari Sunder Rajan's essay titled 'ShahBano', Agnes argued that the present controversy over triple *talaq* was indeed an instance of Hindu men 'saving Muslim women from Muslim men'.[56] She argued that to justify this kind of intervention, the Muslim woman must be projected as 'devoid of rights and lacking agency' and the Muslim male as 'premodern, lustful, polygamous, and barbaric'.[57]

She accused the BMMA of giving in to this narrative as it ignored other issues of poverty, illiteracy, marginalisation and denial of access to public resources affecting Muslim women and only foregrounded the issue of arbitrary divorce.[58] Citing a BMMA research publication, Agnes argued that the need of the hour was more access to public resources for Muslim women and not more stringent laws. Agnes highlighted findings from a study conducted by the BMMA titled 'Seeking Justice within the family'. She pointed out that 53 per cent of the women interviewed by the BMMA, who had been divorced unilaterally by their husbands, were subjected to various forms of domestic violence and would have been eligible for protection and maintenance under the Protection of Domestic Violence

Act. She further argued that as per the maintenance provisions under the Muslim Women's (Protection of Rights) to Divorce Act 1986, Muslim women were better protected than their counterparts from other religions.[59] Through a progressive interpretation of the Act, she argued, a Muslim wife has been awarded a lumpsum maintenance as 'fair and reasonable settlement'.

While Agnes critiqued the politics of the Hindu right and the denial of agency to Muslim women, her own conception of Muslim women as mere recipients of maintenance within the heterosexual, conjugal family reiterated a similar trope of the hapless Muslim woman in need of protection of the husband within a gendered structure of the conjugal family. Agnes did not question the notion of a unified Muslim community governed by a state-defined Muslim law. She was oblivious to the politics of framing the woman and the family within the imaginary of the nation. Institutions such as the AIMPLB are complicit in this politics.

Rallies of the AIMPLB: Azad Maidan

At the other end of the spectrum, members of the AIMPLB, the custodians of Muslim personal law in India, critiqued the legislation and gave a clarion call for preventing state interference in Muslim personal law and the *sharia*. Following the announcement of the government's aim to criminalise triple *talaq*, several rallies were organised by members of the AIMPLB across the country, where thousands of women participated. In one of these rallies organised in Azad Maidan in Mumbai, a clarion call was given by the members of the Board to Muslims to come forward for the protection of Muslim personal law and the *sharia*. In fiery speeches by leaders and women members of the Board, there was an emphasis on preventing state interference in Muslim Personal Law and the *shariat*.[60] Some of the posters carried by women protestors who were mobilised by the Personal Law Board proclaimed *Islami shariat humari Aizaaz* (Islamic shariat is our pride'), *Islam Zindabad, Islamic Shariat Zindabad, Muslim Personal Law Zindabad* (Hail Islam, Hail Islamic Shariat, Hail Muslim Personal Law).[61]

Sampling the Urdu press in Mumbai in the months when the Bill was proposed in Parliament conveys a sense of how Muslim Personal Law became a marker of a Muslim identity, a unified Muslim community and a Muslim family. The popular Urdu daily *Inquilab* termed the protest at Azad

Maidan a historic protest (*tareekhi ahtajaj*).[62] In a news report, the *Inquilab* described how women braved the scorching summer heat to gather in large numbers at Azad Maidan and register their protest against interference in the *shariat* and showed their awareness of the purity of the *shariat*. The article understood the *shariat* as *pakeezah* (pure, pristine, sacred) and government efforts at interference with the *shariat* as *napak* (impure, sacrilegious). Women became the bearers of this Muslim community's identity. It is ironic that this rhetoric revolved around the protection of Muslim personal law from state interference. There was little reflection on the fact that personal law itself was a creation of the state. In the posters and the protests, Muslim personal law, Muslimness and *shariat* were conflated into a unified Muslim identity.

The public sphere of debate on Muslim family law was constituted by a range of actors who conceptualised the public–private divide as well as state intervention in Muslim family law in multiple ways. While the BMMA framed violations in the family as a matter that needed to be debated and discussed in public, the AIMPLB conceptualised both religion and religion-based family law as a private space that needed to be shielded from the public and public interference. As Asad argues, the modern state produces the family as an instrument of regulation and governance in society.[63] He argued that in being identified with the family, the *sharia* became central to the 'political order and the total body that will be eventually represented as society'.[64] As is evinced by the public debate on legislation on Muslim law in India, there is no questioning in the debates on law reform of this politics of framing the family as a constitutive unit of society.

Remaking the private, reconstituting minority rights

In this chapter, I have drawn out how the public–private divide that forms the edifice of family law in religion-based personal laws is reconstituted by multiple actors – activists, female litigants and Muslim women – who engage in the question of Muslim personal law reform both normatively and in moments of political practice. As legal scholars and anthropologists of religion and secularism have observed, the public–private divide constitutes the edifice of family law, whereby the family is considered a private, gendered domain of nurturance and care different from the public sphere.[65] Through the processes of colonial codification and minoritisation of Muslims, religion has been relegated to the private sphere of the family and family law on marriage, divorce and maintenance. Even in contemporary public debates on Muslim law and minority rights, there is little reflection on the constructed nature of Muslim family law. There is rarely any discussion on how Muslim family law itself comes into being as a result of both the privatisation of religion as well as the creation of a public–private divide by the purported secular-liberal state. In this chapter, I have explored how the public–private divide, which ostensibly constitutes the edifice of Muslim family law, is reconstituted in multiple ways in both alternative dispute resolution forums and public debates on Muslim law reform. I have shown how the women's sharia court became a space where violations in the family could be publicised and staged in the language of rights and entitlements. The space of the *shariat* court can thus be defined as a semi-public space which is different from the home and also from fully public institutions such as courts. The women's *sharia adalat* created a space of comfort where women could articulate the grievances that they experienced in the family. To that extent, they served as a forum where wrongs in the family could be publicised. As these were spaces frequented by civil society activists, lawyers, researchers and other activists, they became spaces for discussion, deliberation and debate on putatively private matters of the family. Moreover, the sharia court witnessed the staging of a range of desires and subjectivities that are not captured by the legal categories of family law. This is evinced by women speaking about their sense of betrayal and forging alternative subjectivities as activists while navigating the *sharia* court. At the same time, this was a space where the notion of the family itself was conceptualised as a site of violence and a fragile entity that was susceptible to a breakdown. This chapter has also traced the public spheres of debates on Muslim law reform which revolve around the practice oral, unilateral divorce and the proposal by the right-wing government to criminalise the same. In these moments, the public–private divide is negotiated in different ways by the female activists and supporters of the BMMA and the AIMPLB. Activists of the BMMA conceptualise the issue of triple *talaq* as a matter that needs to be discussed and debated in public and eventually regulated through legislation by the state. The members of the AIMPLB, on the other hand, are opposed to any interference in Muslim personal law and the sharia. Members of the AIMPLB, hence, reinstate the public–private divide that forms the edifice of Muslim family law.

This chapter has drawn out the multiple publics and gendered logics that constitute Muslim family law. These are not reducible merely to the regulatory powers of the secular, liberal state. The gendered and spatial logics of Muslim law are constituted by a range of non-state actors in dialogue with both other non-state actors and the state. The division of spaces of family law into a public–private divide is threatened and challenged through acts of staging violations in the private sphere in both the public and semi-public spheres. An ethnographic exploration of the public–private divide prises open these aspects of Muslim family law. In doing so, I advance our knowledge on minority rights beyond abstract debates on liberal multiculturalism by focusing on the myriad negotiations with and reconstitution of the putative public–private divide in family law. Similarly, my contribution also nuances an anthropological understanding of family law that overdetermines the regulatory role of the state in conceptualising family law, religion and the public–private divide. As is evinced by this chapter, the public–private divide is tenuous, contested and constantly reworked by non-state actors in conversation with other non-state actors and through claims made against the state.

In staging these multiple iterations of the public life of Muslim family law, this chapter has advanced a spatial understanding of Muslim law and minority rights. It contributes to my larger project of decolonising knowledge on liberalism, minority rights and gender. It has been argued that the liberal nation state's project of defining and constituting the religious minority hinges on consolidating a regime of religion-based family law premised on a public–private divide. In this chapter, I have shown how this divide is tenuous and includes engagements with spaces that defy a clear categorisation into public–private.

Notes

1. Fieldnotes, Mumbai, 24 January 2018.
2. Fieldnotes, Mumbai, 7 November 2017.
3. *Shayara Bano v. Union of India.*
4. I must emphasize here how the public–private divide does not neatly map on to the demarcation between state and non-state law where the private might be presumed to belong in the domain of the non-state and the public to state law. The public sphere is constituted by Muslim women's organisations as well as organisations that claim to be custodians of Muslim family law such as the AIMPLB. On the other hand, there are forums like the *sharia* court which are not strictly speaking 'public' spaces as they are not accessible to

everyone. However, the actors in these spaces interact with, negotiate and sometimes transcend the categories set by debates on Muslim family law in the public sphere. It is this complex story that the chapter wants to shed light on. This story challenges our existing understanding of religious family law as confined to the private sphere within an imaginary of minority rights and family law. The conceptual ambition of this chapter, therefore, is different from frameworks that focus on 'shared' adjudication between the state and non-state actors in some important work such as Solanki's *Adjudication in Religious Family Laws* and Katherine Lemons's 'Sharia Courts and Muslim Personal Law in India: Intersecting Legal Regimes', *Law and Society Review* 52, no. 3 (2018): 603–629. Most importantly, unlike these works, this chapter moves beyond the question of 'adjudication' of marital disputes to focus on a range of affects and discourses that come into play in the gendered construction of Muslim family law.
5. Solanki has shown how the Muslim family and Muslim women's rights within the family are shaped by multiple ideas of Muslimness in multiple adjudicative spaces. For more details, see Solanki's *Adjudication in Religious Family Laws*. My work echoes her findings but draws out more carefully the nature of the public-private divide and how it is reconstituted by these multiple gendered logics of Muslim family law.
6. Mahmood, *Religious Difference in a Secular Age*.
7. Ibid., 117.
8. Janet Halley and Kerry Rittich, 'Critical Directions in Comparative Family Law: Genealogies and Contemporary Studies of Family Law Exceptionalism', *American Journal of Comparative Law*, no. 4 (2010): 753–776.
9. Ibid., 120.
10. Lemons, *Divorcing Traditions*.
11. Ibid., 6.
12. Ibid., 199.
13. Ibid., 199.
14. Fieldnotes, Mumbai, 27 November 2017.
15. Fieldnotes, Mumbai, 11 January 2018.
16. Fieldnotes, Mumbai, 11 January 2018.
17. Yuksel et al., *Qur'an*, 359.
18. Fieldnotes, Mumbai, 24 January 2017.
19. Fieldnotes, Mumbai, 24 January 2017.
20. Lemons, 'Paying for Kinship'.

21. Ibid.
22. Fieldnotes, Mumbai, 1 March 2018.
23. A *khula* is a divorce initiated by a woman, whereas a talaq is a divorce pronounced by men. The usual custom is for women to forego their dower (*mehar*) if they take a khula whereas in case of a divorce pronounced by men, the man owes her the dower promised at the time of marriage and post-divorce maintenance.
24. Veena Das, 'A Child Disappears: Law in the Courts, Law in the Interstices of Everyday Life', *Contributions to Indian Sociology* 53, no. 1 (2019): 97–132.
25. Ibid., 98.
26. Case No. 129, Case register, *Auraton ki Sharia Adalat*, BMMA.
27. Fieldnotes, Mumbai, 7 December 2017
28. Lemons, *Divorcing Traditions*, 29.
29. Fieldnotes, Mumbai, 30 November 2017
30. Case No. 151, Case Register, *Auraton Ki Shariat Adalat*.
31. Fieldnotes Mumbai, 24 November 2017.
32. Ibid.
33. Fieldnotes, Mumbai, 27 January 2018.
34. Fieldnotes, Mumbai, 27 January 2018.
35. Lemons, 'Paying for Kinship'.
36. Fieldnotes, Mumbai, 25 April 2018.
37. Fieldnotes, Mumbai, 25 April 2018.
38. Fieldnotes, Mumbai, 25 April 2018.
39. Fieldnotes, Mumbai, 19 December 2017.
40. Fieldnotes, Mumbai, 19 December 2017.
41. Fieldnotes, Mumbai, 19 December 2017.
42. Talaq-e-Mubarat papers, Reference No. – 20324/ 2018, Date: 27.01.2018
43. Writ Petition (Civil) 118/2016 (Supreme Court of India, 22 August 2017).
44. Vatuk, 'Islamic Feminism in India', 358.
45. Mandal, 'Out of Shah Bano's Shadow', 103.
46. Apoorva Mandhani, '#Triple Talaq: Personal Law Is Law within the Meaning of Art. 13, Narasu Appa Mali, Not Binding on SC: Jaising', LiveLaw, 13 May 2017, http://www.livelaw.in/tripletalaq-personal-law-law-within-meaningart-13-narasu-appa-mali-not-binding-sc-jaising-read-written-submissions (accessed 29 June 2018).
47. Submission by Zakia Soman.
48. *Shayara Bano v. Union of India* (2017) 9 SCC 1 (SC).
49. Vatuk, 'Islamic Feminism in India', 359.

50. Fieldnotes, 7 November 2017.
51. Fieldnotes, 7 November 2018.
52. BMMA, Muslim Family Law 2017 (Draft for the bill) (Belgaum: Omega Publications 2017), 2.
53. Justin Jones, 'Signs of Churning': Muslim Personal Law and Public Contestation in Twenty-first Century India', *Modern Asian Studies* 44, no. 1 (2010): 175–200.
54. Flavia Agnes, 'The Politics behind Criminalising Triple Talaq', *Economic and Political Weekly* 53, no. 1 (2018): 12–14.
55. Ibid., 12.
56. Ibid., 14.
57. Ibid., 14.
58. As my earlier ethnographic chapters have shown in great detail, this criticism itself is rather misplaced, if not totally erroneous. The BMMA and other Muslim women's organisations do play an important role in countering everyday sexism, gendered violence, and patriarchy in both state and non-state forums as well as make available cheap and effective ways for poor Muslim women to resolve marital disputes.
59. Ibid., 14.
60. Fieldnotes, Mumbai, 31 March 2017.
61. Fieldnotes, Mumbai, 31 March 2017.
62. Saeed Ahmad Khan, 'Muslim Khawateen kaa Misaali Majmua, Taarekhi Ahtajaj, Talaq Shalasha Bill na Manjur' (Muslim Women's Historic Protest, Not Happy with Triple Talaq Bill), *Inquilab*, 1 April 2018.
63. Asad, *Formations of the Secular*, 227.
64. Ibid.
65. Mahmood, *Religious Difference in a Secular Age*; Agrama, *Questioning Secularism*; Asad, *Formations of the Secular*.

Conclusion

At the time of writing this book, the Muslim minority identity itself seems to be under existential threat in India. With the passage of the Constitutional Amendment Act and the impending countrywide National Register of Citizenships, the Muslim minority stands to be shorn of whatever little rights it possessed in Indian democracy. This Act facilitates the naturalisation of migrants belonging to 'Hindu, Sikh, Buddhist, Jain, Parsi or Christian' communities and migrated to Indian from 'Afganisthan, Bangladesh, or Pakistan' who entered India on or before 31 December 2014.[1] This is yet another legislative move in a long history of marginalisation and otherisation of Muslim minorities by the purported secular, liberal Indian state. But it is more salient than earlier legislative interventions. Pratap Bhanu Mehta observes that this is the first time since India's Constitution was enacted in 1949 that the Parliament has 'explicitly linked religious identity to citizenship'.[2] Mehta observes that the act redefines Indian national identity 'emphatically in the direction of becoming an ethnocracy'.[3] He argues that this is the culmination of the long desired ideal of Hindu nationalists to remake India 'as a homeland for Hindus, embracing an idea of nationhood similar to the Israeli model'. This is an extension of the 'unfinished business of partition that Hindu nationalists' want to complete as they want to signal to 'Muslims inside India that they don't have an equal claim to belonging here'.[4] In addition to the implementation of the CAA, the expansive and arbitrary use of anti-terror laws in the recent past has led to widespread incarceration of Muslim youth.[5] There has been a concerted effort to police inter-faith marriages by several state governments using legislation that penalises such marriages by linking them to religious conversions.

Conclusion

Muslim youth in interfaith relationships have largely been the target of such legislation. The trope of love-jihad has been invoked by the Hindu right in India to demonise Muslim men marrying Hindu women; Muslim men are considered to be participating in a larger project of converting Hindu women to Islam.[6]

Along with the Constitutional Amendment Act, there is an impending proposal to initiate a nation-wide National Register of Citizens, a document which is meant to categorise the legal citizenship status of all individuals in India.[7] Scholars have pointed out that this could lead to a genuine humanitarian crisis in India, a country where poor people find it very hard to access identification documents.[8] Mehta argues that the Citizenship Amendment Act, along with the impending National Register of Citizenship, creates a 'legally sanctioned system of discrimination, one that is an affront to India's secular democracy'.[9]

Multiple sites of resistance emerged to this draconian legislation across the country. Several of these non-violent protests and occupations across the country, including the ones in Shaheen Bagh in Delhi and Mumbai Bagh in Mumbai were led by Muslim women. Many of my interlocutors in Mumbai were actively involved in these protests. Zakia Soman, one of the founder members of the BMMA, argued that this was a moment of assertion of a 'new Indian Muslim woman'.[10] In a perceptive piece written in the backdrop of the protest movements in Shaheen Bagh, Soman wrote:

> In recent years, we have seen the emergence of a new Muslim woman. She is bold and articulate. She is not willing to be confined to the four walls of her home and wants to participate in the democratic discourse taking place in the country. Importantly, she does not trust the orthodox clergy to represent her. She is aware of her rights as a citizen and as a Muslim with her religion. She does not tolerate violation of her rights by anyone.[11]

She goes on to argue in the piece that ordinary women led the democratic movement against triple *talaq*, and they are now 'protesting against a discriminatory and unjust law that makes religion the basis of citizenship'. The same women, she writes, who led the democratic movement against triple *talaq*, are yet again seeking to 'uphold the Constitution by protesting the religion-based Citizenship (Amendment) Act (CAA), which is seen in conjunction with a possible National Register of Citizens (NRC)'.[12]

The fieldwork for this project was carried out between October 2017 and September 2018. The Hindu right-wing BJP government was in power at that time. Numerous incidents of targeted violence against Muslim minorities, such as acts of lynching of Muslim youth, were in the news.[13] The legislation on the cultural practice of oral, unilateral divorce or triple *talaq*, which has been discussed at length in the Chapter 6, was read by many commentators as yet another assault on the minority community.[14] In the backdrop of this targeted violence against Muslim minorities, an account of Muslim women's agency might appear counterintuitive. My attempt in this book is not merely to recover agency in a place where one might presume its absence. My ethnographic exploration of the lifeworlds of Muslim women in India has brought to the fore modalities of agency that go beyond questions of mere absence or presence of agency.

While there is no denying that the right-wing onslaught on the minority community is palpable, an ethnographic exploration of Muslim women's everyday negotiations with authority shows that there is more to women's agency in these specific moments. A mere narrative of Muslim minority marginalisation does not capture these aspects of agency instantiated in moments of negotiation with and reconfiguration of authority. The ways in which agency is tied to a project of piety and negotiation with authority helps us move beyond formulations such as 'liberal Islam' and 'reformist Islam'. While normative theory debates are caught up in formulating a justification for religion, a conceptual reconstruction of Muslim women's navigation of rights shows how their conception of rights itself is closely tethered to a life of piety and transnational networks of activism.

My exploration of the everyday life of Muslim family law and minority rights comes close on the heels of the rising attacks on Muslim minorities and the disenfranchisement of Muslim citizens in India. As I have argued in the introduction, the inclusion of group-differentiated rights and minority rights was an important feature of the narrative of Indian liberalism in the twentieth century. The rise of Hindu nationalism and the concretisation of an authoritarian state that privileges an ethnic majority pose serious challenges to minority rights in India. When political theorists debate minority rights, we tend to reiterate liberal justifications for minority rights. The attacks on religious minorities in contemporary India is often couched in a language of liberal legalism. For example, liberal arguments are invoked by the Hindu right to attack separate family law codes as going against equality and hence the need for a uniform, legal code.¹⁵ In the enactment of love-jihad legislation, a kind of legal liberalism is invoked by the ruling state governments of the BJP. These legislations use the language of the freedom of religion and thereby emphasise the need to protect forcible religious conversions.¹⁶ Hence, political-theoretic interventions that merely invoke certain standard liberal guarantees for the protection of minority rights fall short of understanding the conundrums of liberalism and minority rights in India. These approaches run the risk of reifying the notion of the minority and merely reducing a range of engagements with minority rights and liberalism to standard liberal categories. This is especially troublesome when it comes to gender. Reducing the gendered negotiations of Muslim minorities with rights and the law merely to standard liberal debates on individual autonomy versus community rights or equality versus community limits our imaginaries of what ethical commitments and everyday practices and negotiations women bring to bear on their engagements with the practice of minority rights. We then run the risk of reinstating a troublesome neo-imperialist project of 'saving the Muslim woman'.¹⁷ Moreover, in an environment when the language of liberalism is also deployed to attack minorities, it is worth exploring the myriad ways in which minorities understand and constitute their relationship to the practice of minority rights and certain liberal categories within which these are nested, such as the right to freedom of religion, gender equality, the public–private divide and the state. Moreover, it is also helpful to challenge the hegemonic language and framework of liberal nationalism by drawing attention to transnational activist networks and ethical commitments that are not necessarily tied to the time and space of the liberal nation state.

In the face of persistent attacks against religious minorities and the strengthening of an authoritarian state that uses the law to target minorities, it is imperative to explore the meaning of minority rights in India from a grounded perspective. Such an exploration lays bare the modalities of power and the various iterations of liberalism and the liberal, secular, nationalist state that minority rights are tethered to. We can therefore avoid a myopic understanding of minority rights merely as claims that can be protected by a liberal, secular state. In this book, I embarked on an ethnographic exploration of minority rights, gender and liberalism based upon fieldwork with activists, adjudicators and litigants of alternative dispute resolution forums of the BMMA and activists and adjudicators of the MCMT. This book explored how these modes of power are being challenged and reconstituted in everyday negotiations with the law and the state in ethical and spatial ways. In doing so, I have presented a nuanced way of conceptualising minority rights, gender and liberalism in political theory by building upon the particularities of everyday negotiations with the law and rights in a non-Western context. My ethnographic exploration has shown a range of ethical ways of being, affective registers and spatial practices that are brought to bear on engagements with the legal domain of Muslim family law and its interaction with liberal freedoms, such as the right to freedom of religion and the right to gender equality in India by Muslim activists and adjudicators. The domain of minority rights is constituted through these registers and practices in moments of everyday interaction between Muslim citizens and a range of state and non-state actors.

My book is an important contribution to decolonising knowledge on minority rights, gender and liberalism. It has contributed to new ways of understanding minority rights and liberalism through an ethnographic exploration of Muslim family law. Paying attention to the lived life of the law as well as taking seriously a range of ethical, embodied and spatial ways in which Muslim family law is constituted helps us move beyond a reified and textual understanding of Muslim law. In doing so, I aim to dismantle colonial epistemologies of understanding the law and legality, especially in relation to religion-based family law, which has increasingly become a marker of a putatively homogeneous Muslim minority identity in postcolonial India.

Future scholarship in political theory and anthropology can further engage moments of popular engagements with liberal categories. Political theory can certainly benefit from an ethnographic exploration of these movements to conceptualise popular articulations of rights, liberalism and democracy. My own narrative has provided an assessment of how Muslim women's agency was already shaped by and also shaped modalities of power and governance of the postcolonial Indian nation state. If the widespread agitations and protests against the Citizenship Amendment Act and the proposed plan for the National Register of Citizens are anything to go by, Muslim women are still claiming a space for agency and resistance in the Indian republic. Legal historians and constitutional scholars writing in the popular press have celebrated this as a moment of triumph for constitutional values.[18] Yet the starting point of these conversations by legal and constitutional scholars is the Constitution and liberal constitutional guarantees. My book takes an alternative route by reconstructing liberal notions from ground up to delineate a range of lifeworlds that animate moments of engagement with liberal categories.

Notes

1. The Citizenship (Amendment) Act, 2019.
2. Pratap Bhanu Mehta, 'Modi Pushes India into Revolt: A New Law Upends What It Means to Be Indian', *Foreign Affairs*, 20 December 2019, https://www.foreignaffairs.com/articles/india/2019-12-20/modi-pushes-india-revolt (accessed 8 March 2020).
3. Ibid.
4. Ibid.
5. According to the government's own records collated by the National Crime Records Bureau, the number of people arrested under the anti-terror laws has gone up by 37 per cent in 2019. See Al Jazeera, '"Misused, Abused": India's Harsh Terror Law under Rare Scrutiny', https://www.aljazeera.com/news/2021/8/16/india-uapa-terror-law-scrutiny (accessed 9 December 2022). For a detailed theoretical discussion on this, see Alice Finden and Sagnik Dutta, 'Counterterrorism, Political Anxiety and Legitimacy in Postcolonial India and Egypt', *Critical Studies on Terrorism* 17, no. 2 (2024): 176–200.
6. Kenneth Bo Nielsen and Alf Gunvald Nilsen, 'Love Jihad and the Governance of Gender and Intimacy in Hindu Nationalist Statecraft', *Religions* 12, no. 12 (2021): 1–18.
7. Ibid.
8. Ibid.; Shruti Rajagopalan, 'The Inevitability of Errors in Determining Citizenship', *The Mint*, https://www.livemint.com/opinion/columns/the-inevitability-of-errors-in-determining-citizenship-11575909663129.htm (accessed 8 March 2020).
9. Mehta, 'Modi Pushes India into Revolt'.
10. Zakia Soman, 'The Rise of the New Indian Muslim Woman', *Hindustan Times*, 23 January 2020, https://www.hindustantimes.com/analysis/the-rise-of-the-new-indian-muslim-woman-analysis/story-NA2GeOguvZn9ETT1NtsDaJ.html (accessed 8 March 2020).
11. Ibid.
12. Ibid.
13. Aatish Taseer, 'Anatomy of a Lynching', *New York Times*, 16 April 2017.
14. Agnes, 'Triple Talaq', 427.

15. Nielsen and Nilsen, 'Love Jihad and the Governance of Gender and Intimacy'.
16. Ibid.
17. Abu-Lughod, *Do Muslim Women Need Saving?*
18. Rohit De and Surabhi Ranganathan, 'We Are Witnessing a Rediscovery of India's Republic', *New York Times*, 27 December 2019, https://www.nytimes.com/2019/12/27/opinion/india-constitution-protests.html (accessed 8 March 2020).

Bibliography

Statutes

Citizenship Amendment Act, 2019.
Constitution of India, 1950.
Criminal Code of Procedure, 1973.
Dissolution of Muslim Marriages Act, 1939.
Muslim Women's Protection of Rights of Marriage Act, 2019.
Muslim Women (Protection of Rights on Divorce) Act, 1986.
Shariat Application Act, 1937.

Cases

A Yousuf Rawether v. Sowramma AIR 1971 Ker 261.
Abul Fatha v. Russomoy Dhar Chaudhuri (1891) ILR 18 Cal 399.
Mohd. Ahmed Khan v. Shah Bano Begum, 1985 AIR 945.
Shamim Ara v. State of U.P. AIR 2002 SCW 4162.
Shayara Bano v. Union of India (2017) 9 SCC 1.
Shamim Ara v. State of UP and Anr (2002) 7 SCC 518.
Jaiuddin Ahmed v. Anwara Begum (1981) 1 Gau LR 358.
Rukia Khatun v. Abdul Khalique Laskar (1981) 1 Gau LR 375.
Vishwa Lochan Madan v. Union of India, 2014 SCCOnline SC 542.

Official Records

Oriental and India Office Collections

Public and Judicial Department Proceedings (L/PJ).

University of Cambridge Library

Legislative Assembly Debates (1937 onwards).

Nehru Memorial Museum and Library, New Delhi

Constituent Assembly Debates
Lok Sabha Debates

Books and Articles

Abu-Lughod, Lila. *Do Muslim Women Need Saving?* Cambridge, MA: Harvard University Press, 2013.
———. 'Orientalism and Middle East Feminist Studies'. *Feminist Studies* 27, no. 1 (2001): 101–113.
Ackerly, Brooke, and Rochana Bajpai. 'Comparative Political Thought'. In *Methods in Analytical Political Theory*, edited by Adrian Blau, 270–296. New York, NY: Cambridge University Press, 2017.
Afzal, M. R. (ed.). *Selected Speeches and Statements of the Qaid-e-Azam: Mohammad Ali Jinnah (1911–1934 and 1947–1948)*. Lahore: Research Society of Pakistan, 1966.
Agnes, Flavia. *Family Laws and Constitutional Claims*. New Delhi: Oxford University Press, 2011.
———. 'Redefining the Agenda of the Women's Movement within a Secular Framework'. In *Women and Right-Wing Movement: Indian Experiences*, edited by Tanika Sarkar and Urvashi Butalia, 136–157. New Delhi: Kali for Women, 1995.
———. 'The Politics behind Criminalising Triple Talaq'. *Economic and Political Weekly* 53, no. 1 (2018): 12–14.

———. 'Triple Talaq: Gender Concerns and Minority Safeguards within a Communalised Polity: Can Conditional Nikahnama Offer a Solution'. *National University of Juridical Sciences Law Review* 10 (2017): 427–450.

———. 'Two Riots and After: A Fact-finding Report on Bandra (East)'. *Economic and Political Weekly* 28, no. 7 (1993): 265–268.

Agrama, Hussein Ali. *Questioning Secularism: Islam, Sovereignty, and the Rule of Law in Modern Egypt*. Chicago, IL: University of Chicago Press, 2012.

Ahmad, W. (ed.). *The Nation's Voice: Towards Consolidation: Speeches and Statement of Quaid-e-Azam–March 1935–March 1940*. Karachi: Quaid-e-Azam Academy, 1992.

Ambedkar, B. R. *Dr Babasaheb Ambedkar Writings and Speeches*. 16 vols. Edited by Vasant Moon. Bombay: Government of Maharashtra, 1979.

———. *Pakistan or Partition of India*. 2nd ed. Bombay: Thacker and Company, 1945.

Anzaldua, Gloria. *La Frontera/La Frontera: The New Mestiza*. San Francisco, CA: Aunt Lute Books, 1987.

Asad, Talal. *Formations of the Secular: Christianity, Islam, Modernity*. Redwood City, CA: Stanford University Press, 2003.

Asani, Ali Sultaan, Kamal Abdel-Malek and Annemarie Schimmel. *Celebrating Muḥammad: Images of the Prophet in Popular Muslim Poetry* (Columbia, SC: University of South Carolina Press, 1995).

Bayly, Christopher. *Recovering Liberties: Indian Thought in the Age of Liberalism and Empire*. Cambridge: Cambridge University Press, 2011.

Basu, Srimati. 'Separate and Unequal: Muslim Women and Un-Uniform Family Law in India'. *International Feminist Journal of Politics* 10, no. 4 (2008): 495–517.

———. *The Trouble with Marriage: Feminists Confront Law and Violence in India*, vol. 1 (Oakland, CA: University of California Press, 2015),

Bajpai, Rochana. 'Liberalisms in India: A Sketch'. In *Liberalism as Ideology: Essays in Honour of Michael Freeden*, edited by Ben Jackson and Marc Stears, 53–76. Oxford: Oxford University Press, 2012.

Bargu, Banu. *Starve and Immolate: The Politics of Human Weapons*. New York: Columbia University Press, 2014.

Benhabib, Seyla. *The Claims of Culture: Equality and Diversity in the Global Era*. Princeton, N.J.: Princeton University Press, 2002.

Bhatia, Gautam. 'Horizontal Discrimination and Article 15 (2) of the Indian Constitution: A Transformative Approach'. *Asian Journal of Comparative Law* 11, no. 1 (2016): 87–109.

———. *The Transformative Constitution: A Radical Biography in Nine Acts*. New Delhi: Harper Collins, 2019.
Bharatiya Muslim Mahila Andolan. *Muslim Family Law, 2017: Draft for the Bill*. Belgaum: Omega Publications, 2017.
———. *The Legal Rights of Muslim Women: Protected and Promoted by the Quran*. N.p., n.d.
Butler, Judith. *Undoing Gender*. New York; London: Routledge, 2004.
Chambers, Clare. *Sex, Culture, and Justice: The Limits of Choice*. University Park, PA: Pennsylvania State University Press, 2008.
Chatterji, Joya. 'South Asian Histories of Citizenship, 1946–1970'. *Historical Journal* 55, no. 4 (2012): 1049–1071.
Chetan, Achyut. *Founding Mothers of the Indian Republic: Gender Politics of the Framing of the Constitution*. New Delhi: Cambridge University Press, 2021.
Colley, Linda. 'Britishness and Otherness: An Argument'. *Journal of British Studies* 31, no. 4 (1992): 309–329.
Commonwealth Human Rights Initiative. *Batein Jo Aap Police Ke Baare mei Jan na Chahtey Hai, Lekin Puchne Se Ghabraate Hai* (Things That You Might Want to Ask the Police). New Delhi: Commonwealth Human Rights Initiative, 2014.
Contractor, Qudsiya, '"Unwanted in My City" – The Making of a "Muslim Slum" in Mumbai'. In *Muslims in Indian Cities: Trajectories of Marginalisation*, edited by Laurent Gayer and Christophe Jafferlot, 23–42. London: Hurst and Company, 2012.
Dalvi, Mustansir. 'Mumbai Two Decades After: Landscapes of Exclusion, Mindscapes of Denial'. *Economic and Political Weekly* 48, no. 7 (2013): 24–26.
Das, Veena. 'A Child Disappears: Law in the Courts, Law in the Interstices of Everyday Life'. *Contributions to Indian Sociology* 53, no. 1 (2019): 97–132.
———. *Life and Words: Violence and the Descent into the Ordinary*. Berkeley, CA; London: University of California Press, 2007.
Deeb, Lara. 'Piety Politics and the Role of a Transnational Feminist Analysis'. *Journal of the Royal Anthropological Institute* 15, no. S1 (2009): 110–126.
De, Rohit. *A People's Constitution: The Everyday Life of Law in the Indian Republic*. Princeton, NJ: Princeton University Press, 2018.
De, Rohit, and Surabhi Ranganathan. 'We Are Witnessing a Rediscovery of India's Republic', *New York Times*, 27 December 2019. https://www.nytimes.com/2019/12/27/opinion/india-constitution-protests.html. Accessed 8 March 2020.

Desai, Manali. 'A History of Violence: Gender, Power, and the Making of the 2002 Pogrom in Gujarat'. In *States of Trauma: Gender and Violence in South Asia*, edited by Piya Chatterjee, Manali Desai, and Parama Roy, 293–313. New Delhi: Zubaan, 2009.

Devji, Faisal. *Muslim Zion: Pakistan as a Political Idea*. Cambridge, MA: Harvard University Press, 2013.

Dixon, Deborah P., and Sallie A. Marston. 'Introduction: Feminist Engagements with Geopolitics'. *Gender, Place and Culture* 18, no. 4 (2011): 445–453.

Dutta, Sagnik. 'Becoming Equals: The Meaning and Practice of Gender Equality in an Islamic Feminist Movement in India'. *Feminist Theory* 23, no. 4 (2022): 423–443.

———. 'Competing Allies: Legal Pluralism, and Gendered Agency in Mumbai's Sharia Courts'. *Law and Social Inquiry* 47, no. 2 (2022): 514–534.

———. 'Divorce, Kinship, and Errant Wives: Islamic Feminism in India, and the Everyday Life of Divorce and Maintenance'. *Ethnicities* 21, no. 3 (2021): 454–476.

———. 'From Accommodation to Substantive Equality: Muslim Personal Law, Secular Law, and the Indian Constitution 1985–2015'. *Asian Journal of Law and Society* 4, no. 1 (2017): 191–227.

Engineer, Asghar Ali. *Quran ko Samajhne ki Paddhati*. In *21wi Sadi Ki Chunotiya aur Islam* (The Correct Method of Understanding the Quran). Mumbai: Centre for Islamic Studies, 2004.

Finden, Alice, and Sagnik Dutta. 'Counterterrorism, Political Anxiety and Legitimacy in Postcolonial India and Egypt'. *Critical Studies on Terrorism* 17, no. 2 (2024): 176–200.

Foucault, Michel. 'The Ethics of the Concern of the Self as a Practice of Freedom. In *Ethics: Subjectivity and Truth*, vol. 1: *Essential Works of Foucault, 1954–1984*, edited by P. Rabinow, translated by Roberty Hurley, 281–301. New York: New Press, 1997.

———. 'The Moral and Social Experience of Poles Can No Longer Be Obliterated'. In *Essential Works of Michel Foucault 1954–1984*, vol. 3, edited by James D. Faubion, 474–475. London: Allen Lane, The Penguin Press, 1994.

Galanter, Marc. 'Hinduism, Secularism, and the Indian Judiciary'. In *Secularism and Its Critics*, edited by Rajeev Bhargava, 268–296. Oxford: Oxford University Press, 1998.

———. 'Justice in Many Rooms: Courts, Private Ordering, and Indigenous Law'. *Journal of Legal Pluralism and Unofficial Law* 13, no. 19 (1981): 1–47.

Gandhi, Leela. *Postcolonial Theory: A Critical Introduction*. New York: Columbia University Press, 2019.

Gayer, Laurent, and Christophe Jaffrelot. *Muslims in Indian Cities: Trajectories of Marginalisation*. Comparative Politics and International Studies Series. London: Hurst, 2012.

Golder, Ben. *Foucault and the Politics of Rights*. Redwood City, CA: Stanford University Press, 2015.

Gupta, Pallavi, Banu Gökarıksel and Sara Smith. 'The Politics of Saving Muslim Women in India: Gendered Geolegality, Security, and Territorialization'. *Political Geography* 83 (2020): 1–10.

Gupta, Radhika. 'There Must Be Some Way Out of Here: Beyond a Spatial Conception of Muslim Ghettoization in Mumbai?' *Ethnography* 16, no. 3 (2015): 352–370.

Halley, Janet, and Kerry Rittich. 'Critical Directions in Comparative Family Law: Genealogies and Contemporary Studies of Family Law Exceptionalism'. *American Journal of Comparative Law*, no. 4 (2010): 753–776.

Hansen, Thomas Blom. *The Saffron Wave: Democracy and Hindu Nationalism in Modern India*. Princeton, NJ: Princeton University Press, 1999.

———. *Wages of Violence: Naming and Identity in Postcolonial Bombay*. Princeton, NJ: Princeton University Press, 2001.

Hasan, Zoya. 'Gender Politics, Legal Reform, and the Muslim Community'. In Appropriating Gender: Women's Activism and Politicized Religion in South Asia, edited by P. Jeffery and A. Basu, 71–88. New York: Routledge, 1998.

———. *Forging Identities: Gender, Communities and the State in India*. Boulder: Westview, 1994.

Herzog, Lisa and Bernardo Zacka. 'Fieldwork in Political Theory: Five Arguments for an Ethnographic Sensibility'. *British Journal of Political Science* 49, no. 2 (2019): 763–784.

hooks, bell. *Feminist Theory: From Margin to Center*. Boston, MA: South End Press, 1981.

Iqbal, Muhammad. *The Reconstruction of Religious Thought in Islam*. Lahore: Ashraf Press, 1960.

Iqtidar, Humeira. 'Jizya against Nationalism: Abul A'la Maududi's Attempt at Decolonizing Political Theory'. *Journal of Politics* 83, no. 3 (2021): 1145–1157.

———. *Secularizing Islamists? Jama'at-e-Islami and Jama'at-ud-Da'wa in Urban Pakistan*. Chicago, IL: University of Chicago Press, 2011.

———. 'Theorizing Popular Sovereignty in the Colony: Abul A'la Maududi's "Theodemocracy"'. *Review of Politics* 82, no. 4 (2020): 595–617.

Jones, Justin. '"Signs of Churning": Muslim Personal Law and Public Contestation in Twenty-first Century India'. *Modern Asian Studies* 44, no. 1 (2010): 175–200.

———. '"Where Only Women May Judge"': Developing Gender-Just Islamic Laws in India's All-Female "Sharī'ah Courts"'. *Islamic Law and Society* 2019, no. 4 (2019): 437–466.

Kapila, Shruti. 'Ambedkar's Agonism: Sovereign Violence and Pakistan as Peace'. *Comparative Studies of South Asia, Africa and the Middle East* 39, no. 1 (2019): 184–195.

Kapur, Ratna. 'In the Aftermath of Critique We Are Not in Epistemic Free Fall: Human Rights, the Subaltern Subject, and Non-liberal Search for Freedom and Happiness'. *Law and Critique* 25, no. 1 (2014): 25–45.

———. 'Precarious Desires and Ungrievable Lives: Human Rights and Postcolonial Critiques of Legal Justice'. *London Review of International Law* 3, no. 2 (2015): 267–294.

Kelly, Duncan. *The Propriety of Liberty: Persons, Passions, and Judgement in Modern Political Thought*. Princeton, NJ: Princeton University Press, 2010.

Kelly, Paul. 'Liberalism and Nationalism'. In *The Cambridge Companion to Liberalism*, edited by Steven Wall, 329–352. Cambridge: Cambridge University Press, 2015.

Khader, Serene J. *Decolonizing Universalism: A Transnational Feminist Ethic*. Oxford: Oxford University Press, 2019.

Khan, Aga. *India in Transition: A Study in Political Evolution*. London: The Medici Society, 1918.

Khan, Saeed Ahmed. 'Muslim Khawateen kaa Misaali Majmua, Taarekhi Ahtajaj, Talaq Shalasha Bill na Manjur' (Muslim Women's Historic Protest, Not Happy with Triple Talaq Bill). *Inquilab*, 1 April 2018.

Khan, Sameera. 'Negotiating the Mohalla: Exclusion, Identity and Muslim Women in Mumbai'. *Economic and Political Weekly* (2007): 1527–1533.

Kirmani, Nida. 'Beyond the Impasse: "Muslim Feminism(s)" and the Indian Women's Movement'. *Contributions to Indian Sociology* 45, no. 1 (2011): 1–26.

Krause, Sharon R. *Freedom Beyond Sovereignty: Reconstructing Liberal Individualism*. Chicago, IL: University of Chicago Press, 2015.

Kukathas, Chandran. 'Are There Any Cultural Rights?' *Political Theory*, no. 20 (1992): 107–139.

Kymlicka, Will. *Liberalism, Community, and Culture.* Oxford: Oxford University Press, 1989.

Laborde, Cecil. *Critical Republicanism: The Hijab Controversy and Political Philosophy*, Oxford: Oxford University Press, 2008.

———. *Liberalism's Religion.* Cambridge, MA: Harvard University Press, 2017.

Larouche, Catherine, and Katherine Lemons. 'The Narrowness of Muslim Personal Law: Practices of Legal Harmonization in a Delhi Family Court'. *Journal of Legal Pluralism and Unofficial Law* 52, no. 3 (2020): 308–329.

Lemons, Katherine. *Divorcing Traditions: Islamic Marriage Law and the Making of Indian Secularism.* Ithaca, NY: Cornell University Press, 2019.

———. 'Paying for Kinship: Muslim Divorce and the Privatization of Insecurity'. *History of the Present* 7, no. 2 (2017): 197–218.

———. 'Sharia Courts and Muslim Personal Law in India: Intersecting Legal Regimes'. *Law and Society Review* 52, no. 3 (2018): 603–629.

Lewis, Alexandra, and Marie Lall. 'From Decolonisation to Authoritarianism: The Co-option of the Decolonial Agenda in Higher Education by Right-wing Nationalist Elites in Russia and India'. *Higher Education* (2023): 1–18.

Madhok, Sumi. *Vernacular Rights Cultures: The Politics of Origins, Human Rights, and Gendered Struggles for Justice.* New York: Cambridge University Press, 2022.

Madhok, Sumi, Anne Phillips and Kalpana Wilson. *Gender, Agency, and Coercion: Thinking Gender in Transnational Times.* Basingstoke: Palgrave Macmillan, 2013.

Mahmood, Saba. *Politics of Piety: The Islamic Revival and the Feminist Subject.* Princeton, N.J.: Princeton University Press, 2005.

———. *Religious Difference in a Secular Age: A Minority Report.* Princeton: Princeton University Press, 2015.

———. 'Religious Reason and Secular Affect: An Incommensurable Divide?' *Critical Inquiry* 35, no. 4 (2009): 836–862.

———. 'Secularism, Hermeneutics, and Empire: The Politics of Islamic Reformation'. *Public Culture* 18, no. 2 (2006): 323–347.

Mamdani, Mahmood. *Neither Settler Nor Native: The Making and Unmaking of Permanent Minorities.* Cambridge, MA: Harvard University Press, 2020.

Mandal, Saptarshi. 'Out of Shah Bano's Shadow: Muslim Women's Rights and the Supreme Court's Triple Talaq Verdict'. *Indian Law Review* 2, no. 1 (2018): 89–107.

Mandhani, Apoorva. '#Triple Talaq: Personal Law Is Law within the Meaning of Art. 13, Narasu Appa Mali, Not Binding on SC: Jaising'. LiveLaw, 13 May

2017. http://www.livelaw.in/tripletalaq-personal-law-law-within-meaningart-13-narasu-appa-mali-not-binding-sc-jaising-read-written-submissions. Accessed 29 June 2018.

Mantena, Karuna. *Alibis of Empire: Henry Maine and the Ends of Liberal Imperialism*. Princeton, NJ; Oxford: Princeton University Press, 2010.

March, Andrew F. *Islam and Liberal Citizenship: The Search for an Overlapping Consensus*. Oxford: Oxford University Press, 2009.

———. 'Rethinking Religious Reasons in Public Justification'. *American Political Science Review* 107, no. 3 (2013): 523–539.

Masud, Muhammad Khalid. 'Apostasy and Judicial Separation in British India'. In *Islamic Legal Interpretation: Muftis and Their Fatwás*, edited by Muhammad Khalid Masud, Brinkley Messick and David Powers, 193–203. Cambridge, MA: Harvard University Press, 1996.

Mehta, Pratap Bhanu. 'Modi Pushes India into Revolt: A New Law Upends What It Means to be Indian'. *Foreign Affairs*, 20 December 2019. https://www.foreignaffairs.com/articles/india/2019-12-20/modi-pushes-india-revolt. Accessed 8 March 2020.

Menon, Nivedita. 'A Uniform Civil Code in India: The State of the Debate in 2014'. *Feminist Studies* 40, no. 2 (2014): 480–486.

———. *Recovering Subversion: Feminist Politics beyond the Law*. Urbana, IL: Permanent Black/University of Illinois Press, 2004.

———. *Secularism as Misdirection: Critical Thought from the Global South*. Durham and London: Duke University Press, 2024.

Menski, Werner. 'The Uniform Civil Code Debate in Indian Law: New Developments and Changing Agenda'. In *The Many Faces of India: Law and Politics of the Subcontinent*, edited by M. McLauren, 136–182. New Delhi: Samskriti, 2012.

Mernissi, Fatima. *Women and Islam: An Historical and Theological Enquiry*. Oxford: Blackwell, 1991.

Mian, Ali Altaf. 'Invoking Islamic Rights in British India: Mawlana Ashraf "Ali Thanawi's Ḥuqūq Al-Islam"'. *Muslim World* 99, no. 2 (2009): 312–334.

Miller, Daniel. *Capitalism: An Ethnographic Approach – Explanations in Anthropology*. University College London Series. Oxford: Berg, 1997.

Mir-Hosseini, Ziba. 'Feminist Voices in Islam: Promise and Potential'. *Open Democracy*, 19 November 2012. https://www.opendemocracy.net/5050/ziba-mir-hosseini/feminist-voices-in-islam-promise-and-potential.

———. 'Muslim Legal Tradition and the Challenge of Gender Equality'. In *Men in Charge: Rethinking Authority in Muslim Legal Tradition*, edited by Ziba

Mir Hosseini, Mulki Al-Sharmani and Jana Rumminger, 13–43. London: Oneworld, 2015.

Mohanty, Chandra Talpade. 'Transnational Feminist Crossings: On Neoliberalism and Radical Critique'. *Signs* 38 no. 4 (2013): 967–991.

Mohanty, Chandra Talpade, Ann Russo and Lourdes Torres (eds.). *Third World Women and the Politics of Feminism*, vol. 632. Bloomington, IN: Indiana University Press, 1991.

Moore, Erin P. 'Gender, Power, and Legal Pluralism: Rajasthan, India'. *American Ethnologist* 20, no. 3 (1993): 522–542.

Narain, Vrinda, *Reclaiming the Nation: Muslim Women and the Law in India*. Toronto; London: University of Toronto Press, 2008.

Narayan, Uma. *Dislocating Cultures: Identities, Traditions, and Third World Feminism*. New York: Routledge, 2013.

———. 'Essence of Culture and a Sense of History: A Feminist Critique of Cultural Essentialism'. *Hypatia* 13, no. 2 (1998): 86–106.

Niaz, Noorjehan Safia. *Women's Shariah Court: Muslim Women's Quest for Justice*. Chennai: Notion Press, 2016.

Niaz, Noorjehan Safia and Zakia Soman. *Seeking Justice within Family: A National Study on Muslim Women's Views on Reforms in Muslim Personal Law*. Belgaum: Omega Publications, 2015.

Nielsen, Kenneth Bo, and Alf Gunvald Nilsen. 'Love Jihad and the Governance of Gender and Intimacy in Hindu Nationalist Statecraft'. *Religions* 12, no. 12 (2021): 1–18.

Nussbaum, Martha. *The Clash Within: Democracy, Religious Violence, and India's Future*. Cambridge, MA; London: Belknap Press of Harvard University Press, 2007.

Okin, Susan Moller. 'Is Multiculturalism Bad for Women?' In *Is Multiculturalism Bad for Women?* edited by Joshua Cohen, Howard Matthew and Martha Nussbaum, 7–24. Princeton, NJ: Princeton University Press, 1999.

Parekh, Bhikhu. *Rethinking Multiculturalism: Cultural Diversity and Political Theory*. Basingstoke: Macmillan, 2000.

Pathak, Zakia and Rajeswari Sunder Rajan. 'Shahbano'. *Signs: Journal of Women in Culture and Society* 14, no. 3 (1989): 558–582.

Phadke, Shilpa. 'Dangerous Liaisons: Women and Men – Risk and Reputation in Mumbai'. *Economic and Political Weekly* 42, no. 17 (2007): 1510–1518.

Phillips, Anne. *Gender and Culture*. Cambridge: Polity, 2010.

———. *Multiculturalism without Culture*, vol. 8. Princeton, NJ: Princeton University Press, 2007.

———. 'Religion: Ally, Threat or Just Religion'. In *Religion, Secularism and Constitutional Democracy*, edited by Jean L. Cohen and Cecile Laborde. Columbia University Press, New York, 2016.

———. 'Why Don't Gender Theorists Talk More About Equality?' *Debate Feminista* 57 (2019): 17–30.

Prakash, Gyan. *Mumbai Fables*. Princeton, NJ: Princeton University Press, 2010.

Punwani, Jyoti. 'Muslim Women: Historic Demand for Change'. *Economic and Political Weekly* 51, no. 42 (2016): 12–15.

———. 'Triple Talaq Judgment and After'. *Economic and Political Weekly* 53, no. 17 (2018): 12–16.

Qureshi, Saleem M. M. 'Iqbal and Jinnah: Personalities, Perceptions and Politics'. In *Iqbal, Jinnah, and Pakistan: The Vision and the Reality*, edited by C.M. Naim, 11–40. Syracuse: Maxwell School of Citizenship and Public Affairs, 1979.

Rahman, Fazlur. *Islam and Modernity: Transformation of an Intellectual Tradition*. Publications of the Center for Middle Eastern Studies, No. 15. Chicago: University of Chicago Press, 1982.

Rajagopalan, Shruti. 'The Inevitability of Errors in Determining Citizenship'. *The Mint*, 9 December 2019. https://www.livemint.com/opinion/columns/the-inevitability-of-errors-in-determining-citizenship-11575909663129.html. Accessed 8 March 2020.

Randeria, Shalini. 'Entangled Histories: Civil Society, Caste Solidarities and Legal Pluralism in Post-Colonial India'. In *Civil Society: Berlin Perspectives*, edited by John Keane, 213–242. New York: Berghen Books.

Rao, Anupama. *The Caste Question: Dalits and the Politics of Modern India*. Berkeley and Los Angeles: University of California Press, 2009.

Raz, Joseph. *Ethics in the Public Domain: Essays in the Morality of Law and Politics*. Oxford: Oxford University Press, 1994.

Redding, Jeffrey A. *A Secular Need: Islamic Law and State Governance in Contemporary India*. Washington, DC: University of Washington Press, 2020.

Sachar Committee. *Social, Economic and Educational Status of the Muslim Community of India: A Report*. 2006. http://www.minorityaffairs.gov.in/sites/default/files/sachar_comm.pdf. Accessed 20 December 2024.

Saxena, Saumya. *Divorce and Democracy: A History of Personal Law in Post-Independence India*. New Delhi: Cambridge University Press, 2022.

Shachar, Ayelet. *Multicultural Jurisdictions Cultural Differences and Women's Rights*. Cambridge: Cambridge University Press, 2001.

Sharafi, Mitra. *Law and Identity in Colonial South Asia: Parsi Legal Culture, 1772–1947*. Cambridge: Cambridge University Press, 2014.

Solanki, Gopika. *Adjudication in Religious Family Laws: Cultural Accommodation, Legal Pluralism, and Gender Equality in India* (Cambridge Studies in Law and Society). Cambridge: Cambridge University Press, 2011.

Soman, Zakia. 'The Rise of the New Indian Muslim Woman'. *Hindustan Times*, 23 January 2020. https://www.hindustantimes.com/analysis/the-rise-of-the-new-indian-muslim-woman-analysis/story-NA2GeOguvZn9ETT1NtsDaJ.html. Accessed 8 March 2020.

Stephens, Julia. *Governing Islam: Law, Empire, and Secularism in Modern South Asia*. Cambridge: Cambridge University Press, 2018.

Subramaniam, Banu. 'Recolonizing India: Troubling the Anticolonial, Decolonial, Postcolonial'. *Catalyst: Feminism, Theory, Technoscience* no. 1 (2017): 1–47.

Taseer, Aatish. 'Anatomy of a Lynching'. *New York Times*, 16 April 2017.

Taylor, Charles. 'The Politics of Recognition'. In *Multiculturalism and the Politics of Recognition*, edited by Arny Gutmann, 25–73. Princeton, NJ: Princeton University Press.

Tejani, Shabnum. *Indian Secularism: An Intellectual History 1890–1950*, Bloomington: Chesham: Indiana University Press, 2008.

Thanavi, Ashraf Ali. *Hilyah-yi Najizah, ya ni Auraton ka Haq-I Tansikh e nikah*. Karachi: Dār al-Isha'āt, 1987.

The Mohalla Committee Movement Trust. *Towards Gender Justice and Peace: Ten Years of Women's Grievance Redressal Cell*. Mumbai: Ujjval Press, 2008.

Travers, Robert. *Ideology and Empire in Eighteenth-Century India: The British in Bengal*, vol. 14. Cambridge: Cambridge University Press, 2007.

Tschalaer, Mengia Hong. *Muslim Women's Quest for Justice: Gender, Law and Activism in India*. Cambridge: Cambridge University Press, 2017.

Uthmani, Mufti Muhammad Taqi. *Asan Tarjuma-e-Quran*. New Delhi: Islamic Book Private Limited, 2009.

van der Veer, P. T. *Imperial Encounters: Religion, Nation, and Empire*. Princeton, NJ: Princeton University Press, 2001.

Vatuk, Sylvia. 'Islamic Feminism in India: Indian Muslim Women Activists and the Reform of Muslim Personal Law'. In *Islamic Reform in South Asia*, edited by F. Osella and C. Osella, 346–382. Cambridge: Cambridge University Press, 2013.

———. 'The "Women's Court" in India: An Alternative Dispute Resolution Body for Women in Distress'. *Journal of Legal Pluralism and Unofficial Law* 45, no. 1 (2013): 76–103.

Wacquant, Lois. *Urban Outcasts: A Comparative Sociology of Advanced Marginality*, Cambridge: Polity Press, 2008.

Wadud, Amina. *Qur'an and Woman Rereading the Sacred Text from a Woman's Perspective*. New York; Oxford: Oxford University Press, 1999.

———. 'The Ethics of Tawhid over the Ethics of Qiwamah'. In *Men in Charge? Rethinking Authority in Muslim Legal Tradition*, edited by Ziba Mir-Hosseini, Mulki Al-Sharmani and Jana Rumminger, 256–274. London: Oneworld, 2015.

Waldron, Jeremy. 'Locke: Toleration and the Rationality of Persecution'. In *Justifying Toleration: Conceptual and Historical Perspectives*, edited by Susan Mendus, 61–86. Cambridge: Cambridge University Press, 1988.

Wedeen, Lisa. 'Conceptualizing Culture: Possibilities for Political Science'. *American Political Science Review* 96, no. 4 (2002): 713–728.

———. 'Ethnography as Interpretive Enterprise'. In *Political Ethnography: What Immersion Contributes to the Study of Power*, edited by Edward Schatz, 75–94. Chicago, IL: University of Chicago Press.

———. 'Reflections on Ethnographic Work in Political Science'. *Annual Review of Political Science* 13 (2010): 255–272.

Williams, Jill and Vanessa Massaro. 'Feminist Geopolitics: Unpacking (in)Security, Animating Social Change'. *Geopolitics* 18, no. 4 (2013): 751–758.

Yuksel, Edip, Layth Saleh al-Shaiban and Martha Schulte-Nafeh. *Qur'an: A Reformist Translation*. United States: Brainbow Press, 2007.

Zamindar, Vazira Fazila-Yacoobali. *The Long Partition and the Making of Modern South Asia: Refugees, Boundaries, Histories*. New York: Columbia University Press, 2007.

Zayd, Nasr Hamid Abu. *Naqd al-khitab al-dini* (Critique of Religious Discourse). Cairo: Maktabat Madbuli, 1995.

Zia, Afiya Shehrbano. 'The Reinvention of Feminism in Pakistan'. *Feminist Review* 91, no. 1 (2009): 29–46.

Zivi, Karen. *Making Rights Claims: A Practice of Democratic Citizenship*. New York; Oxford: Oxford University Press, 2012.

Index

akhlaqiyat, 54
alim, 52
All India Muslim League, 16–17
All India Muslim Personal Law Board (AIMPLB), 24–25, 54, 103, 107, 136, 148
    rallies at Azad Maidan, 153–154
All India Muslim Women's Rights Network (MWRN), 14, 26
All India Tablighi Seerat, 103
All India Women's Personal Law Board, 14, 26
alternative dispute resolution forums, 115–117, 133, 137, 142. *See also sharia adalat* (shariah court)
    and feminist geopolitics, 126–128
    role of activists to cultivate relationship, 121–126
    state shadow over, 117–119
Ambedkar, B. R., 8, 22
    depressed classes representation, 20–21
    minority representation of Dalits from Muslims, 20
    minority's relationship with majority, 21
    political conception of minorities, 65, 82
    role in notion of minority rights, 20
Anjuman-e-Islam, 99
Anwar-ul-Azim, Muhammad, 17–18
apa, 106
aql, 51
Awaaz-e-Niswaan (Women's Voice [AeN]), 14, 26, 149
awliya, 95

Babri Masjid demolition (1992), 91
Bahadur, Mahboob Ali Baig Sahib, 23
Bajpai, Rochana, 8
barabari, 51
    aspects of, 74
Bazme Khawateen, 14, 26
Benhabib, Seyla
    individual freedom, 5
    model of accommodation of cultures, 5
Bharatiya Janata Party (BJP) government (Hindu right-wing government), 33, 117–118, 131, 150, 152, 162–163
Bharatiya Muslim Mahila Andolan (BMMA, or Indian Muslim Women's Movement), 1–3, 12, 29–30, 32, 49, 59, 67, 92, 95, 97, 99,

115, 117, 120–122, 135, 142, 148, 154, 163
activism of, 50
activists, 27, 113–114
adjudication of marital disputes in women's *shariat adalat*, 75–80
aim of, 12, 27–28, 53
demands of, 13–14
emergence of, 12
emphasis on marginalised social location of Indian Muslim women, 13
gender-just framework, 12–13
members, 27
minority rights, 62–66
organisational structure of, 70–71
practice equality, 71–75
press conferences and public meetings, 150–153
right to religious freedom, 51–57
role in spreading Quran message, 57
shariat adalat (*see sharia adalat* [shariah court])
survey in 2015, 13
women's sharia courts of, 114
workshops and training sessions on Muslim women rights, 50–51, 61

Centre for the Study of Society and Secularism, 149
chutkara, 141–142
Citizenship (Amendment) Act (CAA), 160–161, 164
colonial codification, 24
colonial production, 24
communal solidarity, 16
communal violence in India, 26, 93, 122–123
Constituent Assembly, 8, 22
Constitutional Amendment Act, 160–161

Dalit, 8, 20
dar-ul-qaza, 75, 103–105, 107, 134
Dar-ul-uloom e Niswan, 52
Das, Veena, 138
decolonial feminist theory, 12
decolonising political theory, 9–12
Dissolution of Muslim Marriages Act, 17–18, 75
divorce rights of Muslim women, 57–62
Domestic Violence Act, 51, 71
Dowry Prohibition Act, 51

Egypt, social life of Muslim women's rights, 9
ethical self-fashioning of women, 68–69

*fatwa*s, 18
female *qazi*s, 1, 14, 32, 51–52, 54, 67, 70, 113, 117–118, 135, 139, 147
feminist authorial voice, 8

Gandhi, Indira, 104
gendered family relations, domain of, 69
gendered reconceptualisations of public–private divide, 132
gender equality, 3, 5–6, 12, 31–32, 59, 62, 67–68, 78–83
ghetto
  characteristics of, 93
  defined, 93
Global South, 9
global war on terror, 96

Hastings, Warren, 15
Hindu law reform in public sphere, 22
Hindu nationalism, 162
huq of Muslim women, 49, 52, 61, 79, 99

ibadat karna, 60
iddat period, 73–75, 80
ilm, 61

Indian Law Commission
  1833, 15
  1864, 15–16
Indian National Congress/Congress party, 16, 20–23, 92, 101
Indian Union Muslim League (IUML), 24
insaf, 51
Iqbal, Muhammad
  on Muslim nationalism, 19
  Protestant reformation of Europe, 19
Iqtidar, Humeira, 28
Islamic feminism, 12, 27, 77
Islamic feminist movement in India, 14
Islamophobia, 78

Jamat-e-Islami, 28
Jamat-e-Ulema-e-Hind, 24
Jinnah, Mohammad Ali, 16–17
journals/magazines
  Communalism Combat, 96
  Islam and Modern Age, 95

*khalifa*s, 51, 54–55
Khan, Aga
  India in Transition, 19
Khan, Muhammad Yamin, 17
khula, 62, 136, 138
khula nama, 147

Lemons, Katherine, 134
liberal feminists, 51, 68–70
liberal Islam, 162
liberalism, 3–4, 10–11, 15, 28, 63–65, 81, 109, 128, 156
  legal, 16–17
liberalism in India, 8, 65, 162
liberal multiculturalism, 10–11
liberal nationalism, 10
love-jihad, 161, 163

Madhok, Sumi, 9
*mahila mandal*s, 91
Mahila Shakti Mandal, 71, 98–99, 101
Mamdani, Mahmood
  national majorities and minorities, relationship between, 10
  notion of tolerance, 10
  on postcolonial nationalists' struggle, 10
Mahmood, Saba
  double movement of political secularism, 7
  Islamic discursive tradition, 68–69
  on minority rights, 7
*maulana*s, 54, 118
*maulvi*s, 52, 60
mehr, 146
Mehta, Hansa, 22
Mehta, Pratap Bhanu, 160–161
minority politics, 22–23
minority rights in India, 69, 163–164
  complex domain of interaction, 82
  decolonial theory of, 4–9
  framework of liberal multiculturalism and nationalism, 10
  history of, 14–16
  legal domain of, 109
  lived life of, 11
  minorities creation under colonial rule, 10
  politics and practice of, 31
  politics of, 3
  reconstituting, 154–156
  religion-based personal laws, 11
  standard liberal approaches to, 11
Mir-Hosseini, Ziba, 51
misogyny, 78
mobilisation of Muslim women against gendered domination, 26–27
Mohalla Committee Movement Trust (MCMT), Mumbai, 3, 12, 29–30,

77, 92, 97, 103–104, 113–115, 123, 163
  aim of, 2
Mohanty, Chandra Talpade, 6
Morley Minto reforms in 1909, 16
*mufti*s, 118
*mullah*s, 52
multiculturalism, 4–5, 10, 68–69
Mumbai communal riots (1992–1993), 2, 76, 91–94, 98, 102–103
Muslim community/family
  as a juridical and legal entity, 17
  political representation of, 16, 20
Muslim family law in India, 69
  framework of, 2–3
  Hindu majoritarian engagements with, 25
  history of, 23
  postcolonial, 22–28
Muslim fundamentalists, 97
Muslim ghetto in Indian cities, 33, 93–97
  in Behrampada (Mumbai), 97–102
  reframing minority rights, 108–109
  and women's grievance redressal cell, 102–107
Muslim minorities, 2–3, 12–13, 16, 22–23, 27, 32–33, 55, 58, 63, 75, 82, 104, 106–107, 160
  communal violence against, 26, 91–92, 162
  desire for political power, 21
  entanglement between religion-based Muslim personal law and, 15
  and Hindu majority, relationship between, 21
  identity, 17
  premised upon geopolitical instrumentalisation, 116
  tied to liberal nationalism, 19

Muslim Personal Law (Shariat) Application Act, 17, 149
Muslim personal laws in India, 32, 54
  adjudication, categories of, 24
  history of, 14–16, 19
  intra-Muslim differences about, 24
  staged in police stations and local communities, 108
Muslim politics, 19
Muslim Satyasodhak Samaj, 25
Muslim Women's (Protection of Rights) to Divorce Act, 23, 75, 153
Mussalman Wakf Validating Act, 17

Narayan, Uma, 6
nationalism, 10
National Register of Citizens (NRC), 160–161, 164
Niaz, Noorjehan Safia, 27, 134
nikah halala, 148, 151

Okin, Susan Moller, 4
  crude characterisation of cultures, 68
  on gender equality and cultural accommodation, 5

Phillips, Anne, 6, 68
political ethnography, 28–29
polygamy, 13, 62, 78, 105–106, 144, 148–149, 151
protest in Shaheen Bagh and Mumbai Bagh, 161
public rallies, 56
purdah, 94

qadi, 29, 30, 95
qadi courts, 29, 30
Quran, 1–2, 19, 26–27, 29, 32, 50, 52, 56–57, 72–73, 95, 97
  empiricist notion of history, 96
  huq of Muslim women rights, 57–62

raham, 1, 51, 58, 62
Rao, Anupama, 8
reformist Islam, 162
religion-based personal laws, 11
religious authority, 49
religious freedom, 51–57

Sachar Committee report, 13, 93,
secularisation, 28
secular women's movements in India, 25
Shachar, Ayelet
   concept of citizenship, 5
   mulitcultural state, 5
Shaikh, Khatun, 1, 76–81, 95, 125, 134–135, 137–138, 145–146
Shaikh, Mumtaz, 49, 53
sharia adalat (shariah court), 1, 17, 21, 67, 77–78, 113–114, 117, 125–127, 131–132, 136
   booklets and leaflets, 120–121
   challenge to gendered ideology of family, 134
   change in women claims, 139
   Dar-ul-uloom e Niswan initiative, 29
   demands of maintenance, 140
   fragility of gendered roles, 140–141
   gendered performances of female litigants, 138
   involvement in everyday running of forum, 141
   panoply of desires petitions and pleas by women in, 142–145
   predominated by women, 30
   space of self-making, 2
   women domestic labour, 137
*sharia jamaat*s, 94
Shiv Sena, 91, 102
Singh, Manmohan, 13
Soman, Zakia, 27

South Asia, emergence of personal law in, 15
Southborough and Simon commissions, 20
subject populations, 16
Supreme Court judgments
   Shah Bano, 23, 25
   Shamim Ara, 25–26
   on triple *talaq*, 56, 131, 149–150

Tablighi-e-Jamaat, 103
tafsir, 79
talaq, 25
   talaq-dilani waali auratei, 77
   talaq-e-bain, 141, 146–147
   talaq-e-ehsaan, 146
   triple *talaq*, 26, 55–57, 60, 106, 118–119, 126–127, 145–150, 161
taqwa, 51
tawhid, 51, 54–55
terror attack on 9/11, 96
Thanawi, Maulana Ashraf Ali
   Bihisht Zewar, 18
   Heelat ul Najeeza, 18–19
transnational feminist, 12

*ulema*s, 18

vernacularisation of rights, 9
violent nationalisms, 10

Wadud, Amina, 51, 75
White House National Security Council (NSC)
   Muslim World Outreach program, 96
women *qazi*s, 52
Women's Research and Action Group (WRAG), 72

zimmedari, 51